Acts

A LIFE APPLICATION™ BIBLE STUDY

Part 1:
Complete text of Acts with study notes from the
Life Application Bible

Part 2:
Thirteen lessons for individual or group study

Study questions written and edited by
REV. DAVID R. VEERMAN
DR. JAMES C. GALVIN
DR. BRUCE B. BARTON

Tyndale House Publishers, Inc.
Wheaton, Illinois

Have you ever opened your Bible and asked the following:

- What does this passage really mean?
- How does it apply to my life?
- Why does some of the Bible seem irrelevant?
- What do these ancient cultures have to do with today?
- I love God; why can't I understand what he is saying to me through his Word?
- What's going on in the lives of these Bible people?

Many Christians do not read the Bible regularly. Why? Because in the pressures of daily living they cannot find a connection between the timeless principles of Scripture and the ever-present problems of day-by-day living.

God urges us to apply his Word (Isaiah 42:23; 1 Corinthians 10:11; 2 Thessalonians 3:4), but too often we stop at accumulating Bible knowledge. This is why the *Life Application Bible* was developed—to show how to put into practice what we have learned.

Applying God's Word is a vital part of one's relationship with God; it is the evidence that we are obeying him. The difficulty in applying the Bible is not with the Bible itself, but with the reader's inability to bridge the gap between the past and present, the conceptual and practical. When we don't or can't do this, spiritual dryness, shallowness, and indifference are the results.

The words of Scripture itself cry out to us, "Do not merely listen to the word, and so deceive yourselves. Do what it says" (James 1:22). The *Life Application Bible* does just that. Developed by an interdenominational team of pastors, scholars, family counselors, and a national organization dedicated to promoting God's Word and spreading the Gospel, the *Life Application Bible* took many years to complete, and all the work was reviewed by several renowned theologians under the directorship of Dr. Kenneth Kantzer.

The *Life Application Bible* does what a good resource Bible should—it helps you understand the context of a passage, gives important background and historical information, explains difficult words and phrases, and helps you see the interrelationship of Scripture. But it does much more. The *Life Application Bible* goes deeper into God's Word, helping you discover the timeless truth being communicated, see the relevance for your life, and make a personal application. While some study Bibles attempt application, over 75% of this Bible is application-oriented. The notes answer the questions, "So what?" and "What does this passage mean to me, my family, my friends, my job, my neighborhood, my church, my country?"

Imagine reading a familiar passage of Scripture and gaining fresh insight, as if it were the first time you had ever read it. How much richer your life would be if you left each Bible reading with a new perspective and a small change for the better. A small change every day adds up to a changed life—and that is the very purpose of Scripture.

NOTES

In addition to providing the reader with many application notes, the *Life Application Bible* offers several explanatory notes that help the reader understand culture, history, context, difficult-to-understand passages, background, places, theological concepts, and the relationship of various passages in Scripture to other passages.

BOOK INTRODUCTION

The Book Introduction is divided into several easy-to-find parts:

Timeline. A guide that puts the Bible book into its historical setting. It lists the key events and the dates when they occurred.

Vital Statistics. A list of straight facts about the book—those pieces of information you need to know at a glance.

Overview. A summary of the book with general lessons and applications that can be learned from the book as a whole.

Blueprint. The outline of the book. It is printed in easy-to-understand language and is designed for easy memorization. To the right of each main heading is a key lesson that is taught in that particular section.

Megathemes. A section that gives the main themes of the Bible book, explains their significance, and then tells why they are still important for us today.

Map. If included, this shows the key places found in that book and retells the story of the book from a geographical perspective.

OUTLINE

The *Life Application Bible* has a new, custom-made outline that was designed specifically from an application point of view. Several unique features should be noted:

1. To avoid confusion and to aid memory work, the book outline has only three levels for headings. Main outline heads are marked with a capital letter. Subheads are marked by a number. Minor explanatory heads have no letter or number.

2. Each main outline head marked by a letter also has a brief paragraph below it summarizing the Bible text and offering a general application.

3. Parallel passages are listed where they apply.

PERSONALITY PROFILES
Another unique feature of this Bible is the profiles of key Bible people, including their strengths and weaknesses, greatest accomplishments and mistakes, and key lessons from their lives.

MAPS
The *Life Application Bible* has a thorough and comprehensive Bible atlas built right into the book. There are two kinds of maps: A book introduction map, telling the story of the book, and thumbnail maps in the notes, plotting most geographic movements.

CHARTS AND DIAGRAMS
Many charts and diagrams are included to help the reader better visualize difficult concepts or relationships. Most charts not only present the needed information, but show the significance of the information as well.

CROSS-REFERENCES
An updated, exhaustive cross-reference system in the margins of the Bible text helps the reader find related passages quickly.

TEXTUAL NOTES
Directly related to *The Living Bible* text, the textual notes provide explanations on certain wording in the translation, alternate translations, and information about readings in the ancient manuscripts.

HIGHLIGHTED NOTES
In each Bible study lesson you will be asked to read specific notes as part of your preparation. These notes have been highlighted by a bullet (●) so that you can find them easily.

ACTS

ACTS

VITAL STATISTICS

PURPOSE:
To give an accurate account of the birth and growth of the Christian church

AUTHOR:
Luke

TO WHOM WRITTEN:
Theophilus

DATE WRITTEN:
Between A.D. 63 and 70

SETTING:
Acts is the connecting link between Christ's life and the life of the church, between the Gospels and the Epistles

KEY VERSE:
"But when the Holy Spirit has come upon you, you will receive power to testify about me with great effect, to the people in Jerusalem, throughout Judea, in Samaria, and to the ends of the earth . . . " (1:8).

KEY PEOPLE:
Peter, John, James, Stephen, Philip, Paul, Barnabas, Cornelius, James (Jesus' brother), Timothy, Lydia, Silas, Titus, Apollos, Agabus, Ananias, Felix, Festus, Agrippa, Luke

KEY PLACES:
Jerusalem, Samaria, Lydda, Joppa, Antioch, Cyprus, Antioch in Pisidia, Iconium, Lystra, Derbe, Philippi, Thessalonica, Beroea, Athens, Corinth, Ephesus, Caesarea, Malta, Rome

SPECIAL FEATURES:
Acts is a sequel to the Gospel of Luke. Because it ends so abruptly, Luke may have planned to write a third book, continuing the story.

WITH a flick of the fingers, friction occurs and a spark leaps from match to tinder. A small flame burns the edges and grows, fueled by wood and air. Heat builds, and soon the kindling is licked by orange-red tongues. Higher and wider it spreads, consuming the wood. The flame has become a fire.

Nearly 2,000 years ago, a match was struck in Palestine. At first, just a few in that corner of the world were touched and warmed; but the fire spread beyond Jerusalem and Judea out to the world and to all people. Acts provides an eyewitness account of the flame and fire—the birth and spread of the church. Beginning in Jerusalem with a small group of disciples, the message traveled across the Roman empire. Empowered by the Holy Spirit, this courageous band preached, taught, healed, and demonstrated love in synagogues, schools, homes, markets, and courtrooms; on streets, hills, ships, and desert roads—wherever God sent them, lives and history were changed.

Written by Luke as a sequel to his Gospel, Acts is an accurate historical record of the early church. But Acts is also a theological book, with lessons and living examples of the work of the Holy Spirit, church relationships and organization, the implications of grace, and the law of love. And Acts is an apologetic work, building a strong case for the validity of Christ's claims and promises.

The book of Acts begins with the outpouring of the promised Holy Spirit and the commencement of the proclamation of the gospel of Jesus Christ. This Spirit-inspired evangelism begins in Jerusalem and eventually speads to Rome, covering most of the Roman empire. The gospel first goes to the Jews; but they, as a nation, continually reject it. A remnant of Jews, of course, gladly received the Good News. But the continual rejection of the gospel by the vast majority of the Jews led to the ever-increasing proclamation of the gospel to the Gentiles. Now this was according to Jesus' plan: the gospel was to go from Jerusalem, to Judea, to Samaria, and to the ends of the earth (1:8). This, in fact, is the pattern that the Acts narrative follows. The glorious proclamation begins in Jerusalem (chapters 1—7), goes to Judea and Samaria (chapter 8 and following), and to the countries beyond Judea (11:19; 13:4 and on to the end of Acts). The second half of Acts is focused primarily on Paul's missionary journeys to many countries north of the Mediterranean Sea. He, with his companions, takes the gospel first to the Jews and then to the Gentiles. Some of the Jews believe, and many of the Gentiles receive the Good News with joy. New churches are started, and new believers begin to grow in the Christian life.

As you read Acts, put yourself in the place of the disciples—feel with them as they are filled with the Holy Spirit, and thrill with them as they see thousands respond to the gospel message. Sense their commitment as they give every ounce of talent and treasure to Christ. And as you read, watch the Spirit-led boldness of these first-century believers, who through suffering and in the face of death take every opportunity to tell of their crucified and risen Lord. Then decide to be a 20th-century version of those men and women of God.

THE BLUEPRINT

A. PETER'S MINISTRY (1:1—12:25)
  1. Establishment of the church
  2. Expansion of the church

After the resurrection of Jesus Christ, Peter preached boldly and performed many miracles. This demonstrates vividly the source and effects of Christian power. Because of the Holy Spirit, God's people were empowered so they could accomplish their tasks. The Holy Spirit is still available to empower believers today. We should turn to the Holy Spirit to give us the strength, courage, and insight to accomplish our work for God.

B. PAUL'S MINISTRY (13:1—28:31)
  1. First missionary journey
  2. Meeting of the church council
  3. Second missionary journey
  4. Third missionary journey
  5. Paul on trial

Paul's missionary adventures show us the progress of Christianity. The gospel could not be confined to one corner of the world. This was a faith that offered hope to all mankind. We too should venture forth and share in this heroic task to witness for Christ in all the world.

MEGATHEMES

THEME	EXPLANATION	IMPORTANCE
Church beginnings	Acts is the history of how Christianity was founded and organized and solved its problems. The community of believers began by faith in the risen Christ and in the power of the Holy Spirit, who enabled them to witness, to love, and to serve.	New churches are continually being founded. By faith in Jesus Christ and in the power of the Holy Spirit, the church can be a vibrant agent for change. As we face new problems, Acts gives important remedies for solving them.
Holy Spirit	The church did not start or grow by its own power or enthusiasm. The disciples were empowered by God's Holy Spirit. He was the promised Comforter and Guide sent when Jesus went to heaven.	The Holy Spirit's work demonstrated that Christianity was supernatural. Thus the church became more Holy Spirit-conscious than problem-conscious. By faith, any believer can claim the Holy Spirit's power to do Christ's work.
Church growth	Acts presents the history of a dynamic, growing community of believers from Jerusalem to Syria, Africa, Asia, and Europe. In the first century it spread from believing Jews to non-Jews in 39 cities and 30 countries, islands, or provinces.	When the Holy Spirit works, there is movement, excitement, and growth. He gives us the motivation, energy, and ability to get the gospel to the whole world. How are you fitting into God's plan for expanding Christianity? What is your place in this movement?
Witnessing	Peter, John, Philip, Paul, Barnabas, and thousands more witnessed to their new faith in Christ. By personal testimony, preaching, or defense before authorities, they told the story with boldness and courage to groups of all sizes.	We are God's people, chosen to be part of his plan to reach the world. In love and by faith, we can have the Holy Spirit's help as we witness or preach. Witnessing is also beneficial to us because it strengthens our faith as we confront those who challenge it.
Opposition	Through imprisonment, beatings, plots, and riots, Christians were persecuted by both Jews and Gentiles. But the opposition became a catalyst for the spread of Christianity. This showed that Christianity was not the work of man, but of God.	God can work through any opposition. When severe treatment from hostile unbelievers comes, realize that it has come because you have been a faithful witness and look for the opportunity to present the Good News about Christ. Seize the opportunities that opposition brings.

Modern names and boundaries are shown in gray.

The apostle Paul, whose missionary journeys fill much of this book, traveled tremendous distances as he tirelessly spread the gospel across much of the Roman empire. His combined trips, by land and ship, equal more than 13,000 airline miles, to say nothing of the circuitous land routes he walked and climbed.

1 **Judea** Jesus ascended to heaven from the Mount of Olives outside Jerusalem, and his followers returned to the city to await the infilling of the Holy Spirit, which occurred at Pentecost. Peter gave a powerful sermon that was heard by Jews from across the empire. The Jerusalem church grew, but Stephen was martyred for his faith by Jewish leaders who did not believe in Jesus (1:1—7:59).

2 **Samaria** After Stephen's death, persecution of Christians intensified, but it caused the believers to leave Jerusalem and spread the gospel to other cities in the empire. Philip took the gospel into Samaria, and even to a man from Ethiopia (8:1—40).

3 **Syria** Paul began his story as a persecutor of Christians, only to be met by Jesus himself on the road to Damascus. He became a believer, but his new faith caused opposition, so he returned to Tarsus, his home, for safety. Barnabas sought out Paul in Tarsus and brought him to the church in Antioch in Syria, where they worked together. Meanwhile, Peter had received a vision that led him to Caesarea, where he presented the gospel to a Gentile family, who became believers (9:1—12:25).

4 **Cyprus and Galatia** Paul and Barnabas were dedicated by the church in Antioch in Syria for God's work of spreading the gospel to other cities. They set off on their first missionary journey through Cyprus and Galatia (13:1—14:28).

5 **Jerusalem** Controversy between Jewish Christians and Gentile Christians over the matter of keeping the law led to a special council, with delegates from the churches in Antioch and Jerusalem meeting in Jerusalem. Together, they resolved the conflict and the news was taken back to Antioch (15:1—35).

6 **Macedonia** Barnabas traveled to Cyprus while Paul took a second missionary journey. He revisited the churches in Galatia and headed toward Ephesus, but the Holy Spirit said no. He then turned north toward Bithynia and Pontus, but again was told not to go. He then received the "Macedonian call," and followed the Spirit's direction into the cities of Macedonia (15:36—17:14).

7 **Achaia** Paul traveled from Macedonia to Athens and Corinth in Achaia, then traveled by ship to Ephesus before returning to Caesarea, Jerusalem, and finally back to Antioch (17:15—18:22).

8 **Ephesus** Paul's third missionary journey took him back through Cilicia and Galatia, this time straight to Ephesus in Asia. He visited other cities in Asia before going back to Macedonia and Achaia. He returned to Jerusalem by ship, despite his knowledge that arrest awaited him there (18:23—23:30).

9 **Caesarea** Paul was arrested in Jerusalem and taken to Antipatris, then on to Caesarea under Roman guard. Paul always took advantage of any opportunity to share the gospel, and he did so before many Gentile leaders. But because Paul appealed to Caesar, he began the long journey to Rome (23:31—26:32).

10 **Rome** After storms, layovers in Crete, and shipwreck on the island of Malta, Paul arrived in Sicily, and finally in Italy, where he traveled by land, under guard, to his long-awaited destination, Rome, the capital of the empire.

A. PETER'S MINISTRY (1:1—12:25)

The book of Acts begins where the Gospels leave off, reporting on the actions of the apostles and the work of the Holy Spirit. Beginning in Jerusalem, the church is established and grows rapidly, then faces intense persecution, which drives the believers out into the surrounding areas. Through this dispersion, Samaritans and Gentiles hear the Good News and believe.

1. Establishment of the church

Jesus ascends to heaven

1:1
Lk 1:3
1:2
Mt 28:19,20
Lk 24:49-51
Jn 20:22,23
1:3
Mk 16:12,14
Lk 24:33-36
Jn 20:19,26
21:1,14
1:4
Jn 14:16,17,26
Lk 24:49
Acts 2:33
1:5
Acts 2:4; 11:16

1 Dear friend who loves God:

In my first letter I told you about Jesus' life and teachings and how he returned to heaven after giving his chosen apostles further instructions from the Holy Spirit. ³During the forty days after his crucifixion he appeared to the apostles from time to time, actually alive, and proved to them in many ways that it was really he himself they were seeing. And on these occasions he talked to them about the Kingdom of God.

⁴In one of these meetings he told them not to leave Jerusalem until the Holy Spirit came upon them in fulfillment of the Father's promise, a matter he had previously discussed with them.

⁵"John baptized you with water," he reminded them, "but you shall be baptized with the Holy Spirit in just a few days."

1:5 *with water,* or, "in water." *with the Holy Spirit,* or "in the Holy Spirit."

●**1:1** The book of Acts continues the story Luke began in his Gospel, covering the 30 years after Jesus' ascension. In that short time the church was established and the gospel of salvation was taken throughout the world, even to the capital of the Roman Empire. Those preaching the gospel, though ordinary people with human frailties and limitations, were empowered by the Holy Spirit to turn the world "upside down" (17:6). Throughout the book of Acts we learn about the nature of the church and how we today are also to go about turning our world upside down.

1:1 Luke's first writing was the Gospel of Luke; it was also addressed to Theophilus, whose name means "dear friend who loves God." (See note on Luke 1:1.)

1:1–3 Luke says that the disciples were eyewitnesses to all that had happened to Jesus Christ. It is important to know this so we can have confidence in their testimony. Twenty centuries later we can still be confident that our faith is based on fact, not mere enthusiasm.

●**1:3** Verses 1–8 are the bridge between the events recorded in the Gospels and the life of the early church. Jesus spent 40 days teaching his disciples, and they were changed drastically. Before, they had argued with each other, deserted their Lord, even lied about knowing Jesus. Now, in a series of meetings with the living, resurrected Christ, the disciples had many questions answered. They became convinced about the resurrection, learned about the Kingdom of God, and learned about their power source—the Holy Spirit. By reading the Bible, we can sit with the resurrected Christ in his school of discipleship. By believing in him, we can receive his power by the Holy Spirit to be new people. By joining with other Christians in his church, we can take part in doing his work.

1:3 Jesus explained that with his coming, the Kingdom of God was inaugurated. When he ascended into heaven, God's Kingdom would remain in the hearts of all believers through the presence of the Holy Spirit. But the Kingdom of God will not be fully realized until Jesus Christ comes again to judge all people and remove all evil from the world. Before that time, believers are to work to spread God's Kingdom across the world. The book of Acts records how this was begun. We must continue the work the early church started.

●**1:3** Today there are still people who doubt Jesus' resurrection. But Jesus appeared to the apostles on many occasions after his resurrection, proving he was alive. Look at the change the resurrection made in the disciples' lives. At Jesus' death, they

scattered. They were disillusioned and feared for their lives. After seeing the resurrected Christ, they were fearless and risked everything to spread the Good News about him around the world. They faced imprisonment, beatings, rejection, and martyrdom yet never compromised their mission. These men would not have risked their lives for something they knew was a fraud. They knew Jesus was raised from the dead, and the early church was fired with their enthusiasm to tell others.

●**1:4** The *Trinity* is a description of the unique relationship of God the Father, the Son, and the Holy Spirit. If Jesus had stayed on earth, his physical presence would have limited the spread of the gospel, for physically he could be in only one place at a time. After his ascension, he would be spiritually present everywhere through the Holy Spirit. The Holy Spirit was sent so God would be with and within his followers after Jesus returned to heaven. His Spirit would comfort them, guide them to know his truth, remind them of Jesus' words, give them the right words to say, and fill them with power (John 14—16).

●**1:4** Jesus instructed his disciples to witness to people of all nations about him. But they were told to wait first for the Holy Spirit. God has important work for you to do for him, but you must do it by the power of the Holy Spirit. We often like to get on with the job, even if it means running ahead of God. But waiting is sometimes part of God's plan. Are you waiting and listening for God's complete instructions, or are you running ahead of his plans? We need God's timing and power to be truly effective.

●**1:5** At Pentecost (Acts 2:4) the Holy Spirit was made available to all who believe in Jesus. We receive the Holy Spirit (are baptized by him) when we receive Jesus Christ. The baptism of the Holy Spirit must be understood in the light of his total work in Christians.

(1) The Spirit marks the beginning of the Christian experience. We cannot belong to Christ without his Spirit (Romans 8:9); we cannot be united to Christ without his Spirit (1 Corinthians 6:17); we cannot be adopted as his children without his Spirit (Romans 8:14–17; Galatians 4:6, 7); we cannot be in the body of Christ except by baptism in the Spirit (1 Corinthians 12:13).(2) The Spirit is the power of our new lives. He begins a lifelong process of change as we become more like Christ (1 John 3:2; Philippians 1:6). When we receive Christ by faith, we begin an immediate personal relationship with God. The Holy Spirit works in us to help us become like Christ.(3) The Spirit unites the Christian community in Christ (Ephesians 2:22). The Holy Spirit can be experienced by all and works through all (1 Corinthians 12:11; Ephesians 4:4).

6And another time when he appeared to them, they asked him, "Lord, are you going to free Israel [from Rome] now and restore us as an independent nation?"

7"The Father sets those dates," he replied, "and they are not for you to know. 8But when the Holy Spirit has come upon you, you will receive power to testify about me with great effect, to the people in Jerusalem, throughout Judea, in Samaria, and to the ends of the earth, about my death and resurrection."

9It was not long afterwards that he rose into the sky and disappeared into a cloud, leaving them staring after him. 10As they were straining their eyes for another glimpse, suddenly two white-robed men were standing there among them, 11and said, "Men of Galilee, why are you standing here staring at the sky? Jesus has gone away to heaven, and some day, just as he went, he will return!"

Matthias is chosen to replace Judas

12They were at the Mount of Olives when this happened, so now they walked the half mile back to Jerusalem 13and held a prayer meeting in an upstairs room of the house where they were staying.

14Here is the list of those who were present at the meeting: Peter, John, James, Andrew, Philip, Thomas, Bartholomew, Matthew, James (son of Alphaeus), Simon (also called "The Zealot"), Judas (son of James), And the brothers of Jesus. Several women, including Jesus' mother, were also there.

15This prayer meeting went on for several days. During this time, on a day when about 120 people were present, Peter stood up and addressed them as follows:

16"Brothers, it was necessary for the Scriptures to come true concerning Judas,

1:6 *from Rome,* implied.

1:6
Dan 7:27
Amos 9:11
1 Cor 15:7

1:7
Mt 24:36
1 Thess 5:1,2

1:8
Mt 28:19
Lk 24:48,49
Jn 15:27
Acts 2:4; 8:1
Rom 10:18

1:11
Zech 14:4
Rev 1:7

1:12
Lk 24:50

1:13
Lk 22:12
Acts 12:12; 20:8

1:14
Mt 10:2-4
Mk 3:16-19
Lk 6:14-16

1:16
Ps 41:9
Jn 18:3

●**1:6** During the years of Jesus' ministry on earth, the disciples continually wondered about his kingdom. When would it come? What would be their role? In the traditional view, the Messiah would be an earthly conqueror who would free Israel from Rome. But the kingdom Jesus spoke about was first a *spiritual* kingdom established in the hearts and lives of believers. God's presence and power dwell in believers in the person of the Holy Spirit.

1:6, 7 Like other Jews, the disciples chafed under their Roman rulers. They wanted Jesus to free Israel from Roman power and then become their king. Jesus replied that God the Father sets the timetable for all events—worldwide, national, and personal. If you want changes that God isn't making immediately, don't become impatient. It is not God, but you who should adjust your timetable.

1:8 This verse describes a series of ever-widening circles. The gospel was to spread, geographically, from Jerusalem, into Judea and Samaria, and finally to the whole world. It would begin with the devout Jews in Jerusalem and Samaria, spread to the mixed race in Samaria, and finally be offered to the Gentiles in the uttermost parts of the earth. God's gospel has not reached its final destination if someone in your family, your workplace, your school, or your community hasn't heard about Jesus Christ. Make sure that you are contributing in some way to the ever-widening circle of God's loving message.

●**1:8** Power from the Holy Spirit is not limited to strength beyond the ordinary—it involves courage, boldness, confidence, insight, ability, and authority. The disciples would need all these to fulfill their mission. If you believe in Jesus Christ, you can experience the power of the Holy Spirit in your life.

●**1:8** Jesus promised the apostles that they would receive power to witness after they received the Holy Spirit. Notice the progression: (1) they received the Holy Spirit, (2) he gave them power, and (3) they witnessed with extraordinary results. We often try to reverse the order and witness by our own power and authority. Witnessing is not showing what we can do for God, but showing and telling what God has done for us.

1:9 It was important for the disciples to see Jesus ascend. Then they knew without a doubt that he was God and that his home is in heaven.

1:9–11 After 40 days with his disciples, Jesus ascended into heaven. Two angels proclaimed to the disciples that one day Jesus would return in the same way he went—bodily and visibly. History is not haphazard; it is moving toward a specific point—the return of Jesus to judge and rule over the earth. We should be ready for his sudden return (1 Thessalonians 5:2), not by standing around "gazing into the sky," but by working hard to share the gospel so others will be able to share in God's great blessings.

●**1:12, 13** After Christ ascended into heaven, the apostles immediately returned to Jerusalem and had a prayer meeting. Jesus had said they would be baptized with the Holy Spirit in a few days, so they waited and prayed. When you face a difficult task, an important decision, or a baffling dilemma, your first step should be to pray for the Holy Spirit's power and guidance. Don't rush into the work and hope it happens the way it should.

1:14 Jesus' brothers are now with the disciples. During Jesus' lifetime they did not believe he was the Messiah, but his resurrection must have convinced them. Jesus' special appearance to James, one of his brothers, may have been an especially significant event in their conversion (see 1 Corinthians 15:7).

1:15–26 This was the first church business meeting. The small group of 11 had already grown to more than 120. The main order of business was to appoint a new disciple, or apostle, as the 12 were now called. While the apostles waited, they were doing what they could—praying, seeking God's guidance, and getting organized. Waiting for God to work does not mean sitting around doing nothing. We must do what we can, while we can, as long as we don't run ahead of God.

1:16 How could someone who had been with Jesus daily betray him? Judas received the same calling and teaching as everyone else. But he chose to reject Christ's warning as well as his offers of mercy. He hardened his heart and joined in the plot with Jesus' enemies to betray him. He remained unrepentant to the end, and he finally committed suicide. Although Jesus predicted this would happen, it was Judas' choice. Those privileged to be *close* to the truth are not necessarily *committed* to the truth. See Judas' Profile in Mark 14 for more information on his life.

who betrayed Jesus by guiding the mob to him, for this was predicted long ago by the Holy Spirit, speaking through King David. [17]Judas was one of us, chosen to be an apostle just as we were. [18]He bought a field with the money he received for his treachery and falling headlong there, he burst open, spilling out his bowels. [19]The news of his death spread rapidly among all the people of Jerusalem, and they named the place 'The Field of Blood.' [20]King David's prediction of this appears in the Book of Psalms, where he says, 'Let his home become desolate with no one living in it.' And again, 'Let his work be given to someone else to do.'

[21, 22]"So now we must choose someone else to take Judas' place and to join us as witnesses of Jesus' resurrection. Let us select someone who has been with us constantly from our first association with the Lord—from the time he was baptized by John until the day he was taken from us into heaven."

[23]The assembly nominated two men: Joseph Justus (also called Barsabbas) and Matthias. [24, 25]Then they all prayed for the right man to be chosen. "O Lord," they said, "you know every heart; show us which of these men you have chosen as an apostle to replace Judas the traitor, who has gone on to his proper place."

[26]Then they drew straws, and in this manner Matthias was chosen and became an apostle with the other eleven.

The Holy Spirit comes at Pentecost

2 Seven weeks had gone by since Jesus' death and resurrection, and the Day of Pentecost had now arrived. As the believers met together that day, [2]suddenly there was a sound like the roaring of a mighty windstorm in the skies above them and it filled the house where they were meeting. [3]Then, what looked like flames or tongues of fire appeared and settled on their heads. [4]And everyone present was filled with the Holy Spirit and began speaking in languages they didn't know, for the Holy Spirit gave them this ability.

[5]Many godly Jews were in Jerusalem that day for the religious celebrations, having arrived from many nations. [6]And when they heard the roaring in the sky

1:17
Jn 6:70,71
Acts 1:24,25
20:24; 21:19

1:18
Mt 26:14,15
27:3-10

1:20
Ps 69:25; 109:8

1:21,22
Mk 1:1-4
Acts 1:2; 2:32

1:24
1 Sam 16:7
Acts 6:6; 15:8

1:25
Acts 1:17
Rom 1:5

1:26
Lev 16:8
Josh 14:1,2
1 Sam 14:41
Prov 16:33

2:1
Lev 23:15,16
Deut 16:9,10
Acts 1:14,15
20:16

2:2
Acts 4:31

2:4
Mk 16:7
Acts 4:8,31 10:46;
13:9,19:6
1 Cor 12:10; 13:1
Eph 5:18

1:26 *they drew straws,* literally, "cast lots," or "threw dice."   **2:4** *in languages they didn't know,* literally, "in other tongues."

1:18 Matthew says Judas hanged himself (Matthew 27:5); Acts says he fell. The traditional explanation is that when Judas hanged himself, the rope or branch broke, Judas fell, and his body burst open.

1:21, 22 The disciples became *apostles*. *Disciple* means follower or learner, and *apostle* means messenger or missionary. These men now had the special assignment of spreading the Good News of Jesus' death and resurrection.

1:21, 22 There were many who consistently followed Jesus throughout his ministry on earth. The 12 apostles were his inner circle, but others shared their level of love and commitment.

1:21, 22 The apostles had to choose a replacement for Judas Iscariot. They outlined specific criteria for making the choice. When the "finalists" had been chosen, the apostles prayed, asking God to guide the selection process. This gives us a good example of how to proceed when we are making important decisions. Set up criteria consistent with the Bible, examine the alternatives, and pray for wisdom and guidance to reach a wise decision.

2:1 Held 50 days after Passover, Pentecost was also called the Feast of Weeks and Feast of Harvests. It was one of three major feasts of the year (Leviticus 23:16), a festival of thanksgiving for the harvested crops. Jesus was crucified at Passover, and he ascended 40 days later. The Holy Spirit came 50 days after the crucifixion, 10 days after the ascension. Jews of many nations gathered in Jerusalem for this festival. Thus Peter's speech was given to an international audience. It resulted in a worldwide harvest of new believers—the first converts to Christianity.

2:3 This was a fulfillment of John the Baptist's words (Luke 3:16)

about the Holy Spirit's baptizing with fire. Verses 3 and 4 are also a fulfillment of Joel 2:28, 29 about the outpouring of the Holy Spirit.

Why tongues of fire? Tongues symbolize speech and the communication of the gospel. Fire symbolizes God's purifying presence, burning away the undesirable elements of our lives and setting our hearts aflame to ignite the lives of others. On Mount Sinai, God confirmed the validity of the Old Testament law with fire from heaven (Exodus 19:16–18). At Pentecost, God confirmed the validity of the Holy Spirit's ministry by sending fire. At Mount Sinai, fire came down on one place; at Pentecost, fire came down on many believers, symbolizing that God's presence is now available to all who believe in him.

●**2:3, 4** God made his presence known to this group of believers in a spectacular way—roaring wind, fire, and his Holy Spirit. Would you like God to reveal himself to you in such recognizable ways? He may, but be wary of forcing your expectations on God. In 1 Kings 19:11, 12, Elijah also needed a message from God. There was a mighty wind, then an earthquake, and finally a fire. But God's message came in a gentle whisper. God may use dramatic methods to work in your life—or he may speak in gentle whispers. Wait patiently and always listen.

●**2:4** These people literally spoke in other languages—a miraculous attention-getter for the crowds gathered in town for the feast. All the nationalities represented recognized their own languages being spoken. But more than miraculous speaking drew people's attention; they saw the presence and power of the Holy Spirit. The apostles continued to minister in the power of the Holy Spirit wherever they went.

above the house, crowds came running to see what it was all about, and were stunned to hear their own languages being spoken by the disciples.

7"How can this be?" they exclaimed. "For these men are all from Galilee, 8and yet we hear them speaking all the native languages of the lands where we were born! 9Here we are—Parthians, Medes, Elamites, men from Mesopotamia, Judea,

2:7
Mt 26:73
Acts 1:11

2:9
Acts 6:9; 19:10
1 Pet 1:1

A JOURNEY THROUGH THE BOOK OF ACTS

Beginning with a brief summary of Jesus' last days on earth with his disciples, his ascension, and the replacement for Judas Iscariot, Luke moves quickly to his subject— the spread of the gospel and the growth of the church. Pentecost, celebrated by the filling of the Holy Spirit (2:1–13) and Peter's powerful sermon (2:14–42), was the beginning. Then the Jerusalem church grew daily through the bold witness of Peter and John and the love of the believers (2:43—4:37). The infant church was not without problems, however, with external opposition (resulting in imprisonment, beatings, and death) and internal deceit and complaining. Greek-speaking Jewish believers were appointed to help with the administration of the church to free the apostles to preach. Stephen and Philip were among the first deacons, and Stephen became the church's first martyr (5:1—8:3).

Instead of stopping Christianity, opposition and persecution served as catalysts for its spread, for the believers took the message with them wherever they fled (8:4). Soon there were converts throughout Samaria and even in Ethiopia (8:5–40).

At this point, Luke introduces us to a bright young Jew, zealous for the law and intent on ridding Judaism of the Jesus heresy. But on the way to Damascus to capture believers, Saul was converted, confronted in person by the risen Christ (9:1–9). Through the ministry of Ananias and the sponsorship of Barnabas, Saul (Paul) was welcomed into the fellowship and then sent to Tarsus for safety (9:10–30).

Meanwhile, the church continued to thrive throughout Judea, Galilee, and Samaria. Luke recounts Peter's preaching and how he healed Aeneas in Lydda and Dorcas in Joppa (9:31–43). While in Joppa, Peter learned through a vision that he could take the gospel to the "unclean" Gentiles. Peter understood and he faithfully shared the truth with Cornelius, whose entire household became believers (chapter 10). This was startling news to the Jerusalem church; but when Peter told his story, they praised God for his plan for *all* people to hear the Good News (11:1–18). This pushed the church into even wider circles as the message was preached to Greeks in Antioch, where Barnabas went to encourage the believers and find Paul (11:20–26).

To please the Jewish leaders, Herod joined in the persecution of the Jerusalem church, killing James (John's brother) and imprisoning Peter. But God freed Peter, and he walked from prison to a prayer meeting on his behalf at John Mark's house (chapter 12).

Here Luke shifts the focus to Paul's ministry. Commissioned by the Antioch church for a missionary tour (13:1–3), Paul and Barnabas took the gospel to Cyprus and south Galatia with great success (13:4—14:28). But the Jewish-Gentile controversy still smoldered, and with so many Gentiles responding to Christ, it threatened to divide the church. So a council met in Jerusalem to rule on the relationship of Gentile Christians to the Old Testament laws. After hearing both sides, James (Jesus' brother and the leader of the Jerusalem church) resolved the issue and sent messengers to the churches with the decision (15:1–31).

After the council, Paul and Silas preached in Antioch. Then they left for Syria and Cilicia as Barnabas and Mark sailed for Cyprus (15:36–41). On this second missionary journey, Paul and Silas traveled throughout Macedonia and Achaia, establishing churches in Philippi, Thessalonica, Beroea, Corinth, and Ephesus before returning to Antioch (16:1—18:21). Luke also tells of the ministry of Apollos (18:24–28).

On Paul's third missionary trip he traveled through Galatia, Phrygia, Macedonia, and Achaia, encouraging and teaching the believers (19:1—21:9). During this time, he felt compelled to go to Jerusalem; and although he was warned by Agabus and others of impending imprisonment (21:10–12), he continued his journey in that direction.

While in Jerusalem, Paul was accosted in the Temple by an angry mob and taken into protective custody by the Roman commander (21:17—22:30). Now we see Paul as a prisoner and on trial before the Jewish Council (23:1–9), Governor Felix (23:22—24:27), and Festus and Agrippa (25:1—26:32). In each case, Paul gave a strong and clear witness for his Lord.

Because he appealed to Caesar, however, they sent him to Rome for the final hearing of his case. But on the way the ship was destroyed in a storm, and the sailors and prisoners had to swim ashore. Even in this circumstance Paul shared his faith (27:1—28:11). Eventually the journey continued, and Paul arrived in Rome where he was held under house arrest while awaiting trial (28:12–31).

Luke ends Acts abruptly, with the encouraging word that Paul had freedom in his captivity to tell visitors and guards with boldness "about the Kingdom of God and about the Lord Jesus Christ; and no one tried to stop him" (28:31).

2:10
Ex 12:48
Mt 23:15; 27:32
Acts 13:13; 16:6

Cappadocia, Pontus, Asia minor, 10Phrygia, Pamphylia, Egypt, the Cyrene language areas of Libya, visitors from Rome—both Jews and Jewish converts—11Cretans, and Arabians. And we all hear these men telling in our own languages about the mighty miracles of God!"

12They stood there amazed and perplexed. "What can this mean?" they asked each other.

2:13
1 Cor 2:14; 14:23
Eph 5:18

13But others in the crowd were mocking. "They're drunk, that's all!" they said.

Peter preaches to the crowd

2:16
Joel 2:28-32

2:17
Isa 44:3
Ezek 11:10
36:27
Zech 12:10
Acts 10:45

2:18
1 Cor 12:10

2:20
Mt 24:29

2:21
Ps 55:16;
88:9 116:2,4,13,
17; 145:18
Acts 9:14,21 22:16
Rom 10:13

2:22
Jn 17:4
Acts 10:38
Heb 2:4

2:23
Acts 3:17,18
1 Pet 1:11,20
Rev 13:8

2:24
Acts 3:15;
10:40; 17:31

2:25-27
Ps 16:8-11
Acts 13:30-35

14Then Peter stepped forward with the eleven apostles, and shouted to the crowd, "Listen, all of you, visitors and residents of Jerusalem alike! 15Some of you are saying these men are drunk! It isn't true! It's much too early for that! People don't get drunk by 9 A.M.! 16No! What you see this morning was predicted centuries ago by the prophet Joel— 17'In the last days,' God said, 'I will pour out my Holy Spirit upon all mankind, and your sons and daughters shall prophesy, and your young men shall see visions, and your old men dream dreams. 18Yes, the Holy Spirit shall come upon all my servants, men and women alike, and they shall prophesy. 19And I will cause strange demonstrations in the heavens and on the earth—blood and fire and clouds of smoke; 20the sun shall turn black and the moon blood-red before that awesome Day of the Lord arrives. 21But anyone who asks for mercy from the Lord shall have it and shall be saved.'

22"O men of Israel, listen! God publicly endorsed Jesus of Nazareth by doing tremendous miracles through him, as you well know. 23But God, following his prearranged plan, let you use the Roman government to nail him to the cross and murder him. 24Then God released him from the horrors of death and brought him back to life again, for death could not keep this man within its grip.

25"King David quoted Jesus as saying:

'I know the Lord is always with me. He is helping me. God's mighty power supports me.

26'No wonder my heart is filled with joy and my tongue shouts his praises! For I know all will be well with me in death—

2:23 the Roman government, literally, "men without the Law." See Rom 2:12.

2:7, 8 Christianity is not limited to any race or group of people. Christ offers salvation to all people without regard to nationality. Visitors in Jerusalem were surprised to hear the apostles speaking in their native languages, but they need not have been. God works all kinds of miracles to spread the gospel, using many languages as he calls all people to become his followers. No matter what your race, color, nationality, or language, God speaks to you. Are you listening?

2:9–11 Why are all these places mentioned? This is a list of many lands from which Jews came to the festivals in Jerusalem. These Jews were not living in Palestine, because through captivities and persecutions they had been widely dispersed throughout the world. The Jews who responded to Peter's message returned to their homelands with God's Good News of salvation. Thus God prepared the way for the spread of the gospel. As you read Acts, you will see how the way was often prepared for Paul and others through people who became believers at Pentecost. The church at Rome, for example, was begun by such Jewish believers—not by Peter, Paul, or any of the other apostles.

2:14ff Peter tells the people why they should listen to the believers: because the Old Testament prophecies had been entirely fulfilled in Jesus (2:14–21), because Jesus is the Messiah (2:25–36), and because the risen Christ could change their lives (2:37–40).

●**2:14** Peter had been an unstable leader during Jesus' ministry, letting his bravado be his downfall, even denying that he knew Jesus (John 18:15–18, 25–27). But Christ forgave and restored him after his denial. This is a new Peter, humble but bold. His

confidence comes from the Holy Spirit, who makes him a powerful and dynamic speaker. Have you ever felt as if you've made such bad mistakes that God could never forgive and use you? No matter what sins you have committed, God promises to forgive them and make you useful for his kingdom. Allow him to forgive you and use you effectively to serve him.

2:16–21 Not everything mentioned in Joel 2:28, 29 was happening that particular morning. The "last days" include all the days between Christ's first and second comings, another way of saying "from now on." "The Day of the Lord" denotes the whole Christian age. Even Moses yearned for the Lord to pour his Spirit on everyone (Numbers 11:29). At Pentecost the Holy Spirit was released throughout the entire world—to men, women, sons, daughters, Jews, Gentiles. Now everyone can receive the Spirit. This was a revolutionary thought for first-century Jews.

2:24 Peter began with a public proclamation of the resurrection, at a time when it could be verified by many witnesses. This was a powerful statement because many of the people listening to Peter's words were in Jerusalem 50 days earlier at Passover and may have seen or heard about the crucifixion of this "great teacher." Jesus' resurrection was the ultimate sign that what he said about himself was true. Without the resurrection, we would have no reason to believe in Jesus.

2:25–32 Hell (2:27) is literally Hades, and the audience understood this as the grave, not the place of final punishment. The emphasis here is that Jesus' body was not left to decay, but was resurrected and glorified.

27 'You will not leave my soul in hell or let the body of your Holy Son decay.
28 'You will give me back my life, and give me wonderful joy in your presence.'

29 "Dear brothers, think! David wasn't referring to himself when he spoke these words I have quoted, for he died and was buried, and his tomb is still here among us. 30 But he was a prophet, and knew God had promised with an unbreakable oath that one of David's own descendants would [be the Messiah and] sit on David's throne. 31 David was looking far into the future and predicting the Messiah's resurrection, and saying that the Messiah's soul would not be left in hell and his body would not decay. 32 He was speaking of Jesus, and we all are witnesses that Jesus rose from the dead.

33 "And now he sits on the throne of highest honor in heaven, next to God. And just as promised, the Father gave him the authority to send the Holy Spirit—with the results you are seeing and hearing today.

34 "[No, David was not speaking of himself in these words of his I have quoted], for he never ascended into the skies. Moreover, he further stated, ''God spoke to my Lord, the Messiah, and said to him, Sit here in honor beside me 35 until I bring your enemies into complete subjection.'

36 "Therefore I clearly state to everyone in Israel that God has made this Jesus you crucified to be the Lord, the Messiah!"

37 These words of Peter's moved them deeply, and they said to him and to the other apostles, "Brothers, what should we do?"

38 And Peter replied, "Each one of you must turn from sin, return to God, and be baptized in the name of Jesus Christ for the forgiveness of your sins; then you also shall receive this gift, the Holy Spirit. 39 For Christ promised him to each one of you who has been called by the Lord our God, and to your children and even to those in distant lands!"

40 Then Peter preached a long sermon, telling about Jesus and strongly urging all his listeners to save themselves from the evils of their nation. 41 And those who believed Peter were baptized—about 3,000 in all!

The believers become the first church

42 They joined with the other believers in regular attendance at the apostles' teaching sessions and at the Communion services and prayer meetings. 43 A deep sense of awe was on them all, and the apostles did many miracles.

44 And all the believers met together constantly and shared everything with each other, 45 selling their possessions and dividing with those in need. 46 They wor-

2:30 *be the Messiah and,* implied in vs 31.   **2:34** *No, David was not speaking of himself in these words of his I have quoted,* implied in vs 31.   **2:42** *at the Communion services,* literally, "the breaking of bread," i.e., "The Lord's Supper."

2:29
1 Kings 2:10
Neh 3:16
Acts 13:35,36
2:30
2 Sam 7:12-14
Ps 89:3,4
Lk 1:32
2 Tim 2:8
2:31
Acts 13:35,36
2:33
Lk 24:49
Jn 14:26
Acts 1:4,8
Eph 4:8
Phil 2:9
Heb 10:12
2:34
Ps 110:1
2:35
1 Cor 15:25
2:36
Lk 2:11
Acts 5:31
2:37
Zech 12:10
Acts 16:30
2:38
Mk 16:16
Lk 24:47
Acts 3:19;
5:31 8:12; 22:16
2:39
Isa 44:3
Joel 2:32
Rom 9:8
Eph 2:13,17
2:40
Phil 2:15
2:42
Acts 20:7
2:44
Acts 4:32-37
2:45
Isa 58:7

2:37 After Peter's powerful, Spirit-filled message, the people were deeply moved and asked, "What should we do?" This is the basic question we must ask. It is not enough to be sorry for our sins—we must let God forgive them, and then we must live like forgiven people. Has God spoken to you through his Word or through the words of another believer? Like Peter's audience, ask him what you should do, and then obey.

2:38, 39 If you want to receive salvation, you must turn from sin, changing the direction of your life from selfishness and rebellion against God's laws. At the same time, you must turn to Christ, depending on him for forgiveness, mercy, guidance, and purpose. We cannot save ourselves—only God can save us. Baptism shows identification with Christ and with the community of believers.

2:40–43 About 3,000 people became new believers when Peter preached the Good News about Christ. These new Christians were "joined with the other believers," taught by the apostles, and included in the prayer meetings and fellowship. New believers in Christ need to be in a group where they can learn God's Word, pray, and mature in the faith. If you have just begun a relationship

with Christ, seek out other believers for fellowship, prayer, and teaching. This is the way to grow.

2:42 These communion services were celebrated in remembrance of Jesus and were patterned after the last supper that Jesus had with his disciples before his death (Matthew 26:26–29).

2:44 Recognizing the other believers as brothers and sisters in the family of God, the Christians in Jerusalem shared all they had so that all could benefit from God's blessings. It is tempting—especially if we have material wealth—to cut ourselves off from one another, each taking care of his own, each providing for and enjoying his own little piece of the world. But as part of God's spiritual family, we have a responsibility to help one another in every way possible. God's family works best when its members work together.

2:46 A common misconception about the first Christians (who were Jews) was that they rejected the Jewish religion. But these believers saw Jesus' message and resurrection as the fulfillment of everything they knew and believed from the Old Testament. The

shiped together regularly at the Temple each day, met in small groups in homes for Communion, and shared their meals with great joy and thankfulness, 47praising God. The whole city was favorable to them, and each day God added to them all who were being saved.

Peter heals a crippled beggar

3 Peter and John went to the Temple one afternoon to take part in the three o'clock daily prayer meeting. 2As they approached the Temple, they saw a man lame from birth carried along the street and laid beside the Temple gate—the one called The Beautiful Gate—as was his custom every day. 3As Peter and John were passing by, he asked them for some money.

4They looked at him intently, and then Peter said, "Look here!"

5The lame man looked at them eagerly, expecting a gift.

6But Peter said, "We don't have any money for you! But I'll give you something else! I command you in the name of Jesus Christ of Nazareth, *walk!*"

7, 8Then Peter took the lame man by the hand and pulled him to his feet. And as he did, the man's feet and ankle-bones were healed and strengthened so that he came up with a leap, stood there a moment and began walking! Then, walking, leaping, and praising God, he went into the Temple with them.

9When the people inside saw him walking and heard him praising God, 10and realized he was the lame beggar they had seen so often at The Beautiful Gate, they were inexpressibly surprised! 11They all rushed out to Solomon's Hall, where he was holding tightly to Peter and John! Everyone stood there awed by the wonderful thing that had happened.

Peter preaches in the Temple

12Peter saw his opportunity and addressed the crowd. "Men of Israel," he said, "what is so surprising about this? And why look at us as though we by our own power and godliness had made this man walk? 13For it is the God of Abraham, Isaac, Jacob and of all our ancestors who has brought glory to his servant Jesus by doing this. I refer to the Jesus whom you rejected before Pilate, despite Pilate's determination to release him. 14You didn't want him freed—this holy, righteous

2:47
Acts 4:4; 6:7
Rom 14:18,19

3:6
Acts 4:10
1 Pet 4:10

3:8
Isa 35:6
3:9
Acts 4:16,21
3:10
Jn 9:8
3:11
Jn 10:22,23
Acts 5:12

3:12
2 Cor 3:5

3:13
Mt 22:32; 27:2
Lk 23:4
Jn 17:1
Acts 5:30,31
Phil 2:9-11

Jewish believers at first did not separate from the rest of the Jewish community. They still went to the Temple and synagogues for worship and instruction in God's Word. But their belief in Jesus created great friction with Jews who didn't believe Jesus was the Messiah. Thus believing Jews were forced to meet in private homes for communion, prayer, and teaching about Jesus. By the end of the first century, many of these Jewish believers were excommunicated from their synagogues altogether.

2:46, 47 A healthy Christian community attracts people to Christ. The Jerusalem church's zeal for worship and brotherly love was contagious. A healthy, loving church will grow. What are you doing to make your church the kind of place that will attract others to Christ?

3:1 The Jews observed three times of prayer—morning (9:00 a.m.), afternoon (3:00 p.m.), and evening (sunset). At these times devout Jews and God-fearing Gentiles often went to the Temple to pray.

3:2 The Beautiful Gate was an entrance to the Temple, not to the city. It was one of the favored entrances, and many people passed through it on their way to worship. The lame man was begging where he would be seen by the most people.

●**3:6** The lame beggar asked for money, but Peter gave him something much better—the use of his legs. We often ask God to solve a small problem, but he wants to give us a new life and help for *all* our problems. When we ask God for help, he may say, "I've got something even better for you." Ask God for what you want, but don't be surprised when he gives you what you really *need*.

●**3:6** "In the name of Jesus" means "by the authority of Jesus." The

apostles were doing this healing through the Holy Spirit's power, not their own.

3:7–10 In his excitement the formerly lame man began to jump and run around. He also praised God! And then others too were awed by God's power. Don't forget to thank people who help you, but also remember to praise God for his blessings.

●**3:12** Peter had an audience, and he capitalized on the opportunity to share Jesus Christ. He clearly presented his message by telling (1) who Jesus is, (2) how they had rejected him, (3) why their rejection was fatal, and (4) what they needed to do to change the situation. He told them that they still had a choice: God still offered them the opportunity to believe and receive Jesus as their Messiah and as their Lord. Displays of God's mercy and grace such as the healing of this lame man often create teachable moments. Pray to have courage like Peter to see these opportunities and speak up for Christ.

3:13 The word *servant* is the same word used in Isaiah 52:13. By choosing this word, Peter indicated that the servant in Isaiah's prophecy is Jesus Christ. Jesus came to serve God and people by dying on the cross for our sin and by giving us an example of perfect service (Mark 10:44, 45).

●**3:13** Pilate had decided to release Jesus, but the people had clamored to have Barabbas released instead (see Luke 23:13-25). When Peter said "You," he meant it literally. Jesus' trial and death had occurred right there in Jerusalem only weeks earlier. It wasn't an event of the distant past—most of these people had heard about it, and some had probably taken part in condemning him.

one. Instead you demanded the release of a murderer. [15]And you killed the Author of Life; but God brought him back to life again. And John and I are witnesses of this fact, for after you killed him we saw him alive!

[16]"Jesus' name has healed this man —and you know how lame he was before. Faith in Jesus' name—faith given us from God—has caused this perfect healing.

[17]"Dear brothers, I realize that what you did to Jesus was done in ignorance; and the same can be said of your leaders. [18]But God was fulfilling the prophecies that the Messiah must suffer all these things. [19]Now change your mind and attitude to God and turn to him so he can cleanse away your sins and send you wonderful times of refreshment from the presence of the Lord [20]and send Jesus your Messiah back to you again. [21], [22]For he must remain in heaven until the final recovery of all things from sin, as prophesied from ancient times. Moses, for instance, said long ago, 'The Lord God will raise up a Prophet among you, who will resemble me! Listen carefully to everything he tells you. [23]Anyone who will not listen to him shall be utterly destroyed.'

[24]"Samuel and every prophet since have all spoken about what is going on today. [25]You are the children of those prophets; and you are included in God's promise to your ancestors to bless the entire world through the Jewish race—that is the promise God gave to Abraham. [26]And as soon as God had brought his servant to life again, he sent him first of all to you men of Israel, to bless you by turning you back from your sins."

3:15	Acts 2:24; 5:31,32; Heb 2:10; 5:9
3:17	Lk 23:34; Acts 13:27; 1 Cor 2:8; 1 Tim 1:13
3:18	Ps 22: 41:9; 69:4,21; Isa 50:6; 53:4-11; Zech 12:10; 13:7; 1 Pet 1:10
3:19	Acts 2:38; 26:20
3:21	Rom 8:21
3:22	Deut 18:15,18; Jn 1:20,21; 7:40,41,52
3:23	Deut 18:19
3:25	Gen 12:3; 22:18; Rom 9:4-8
3:26	Acts 13:46

Peter and John face the Sanhedrin

4 While they were talking to the people, the chief priests, the captain of the Temple police, and some of the Sadducees came over to them, [2]very disturbed

4:1 Lk 22:4

3:21, 22 *who will resemble me,* literally, "like unto me." **3:23** *be utterly destroyed,* literally, "destroyed from among the people." **4:1** *the Sadducees,* who were members of a Jewish religious sect that denied the resurrection of the dead.

3:15 The religious leaders thought they had put an end to Jesus when they crucified him. But their confidence was shaken when Peter told them that Jesus was alive again and that this time they could not harm him. Peter's message emphasized that (1) the religious leaders killed Jesus, (2) God brought him back to life, and (3) the apostles were witnesses to this fact. After pointing out the sin and injustice of these leaders, Peter showed the significance of the resurrection, God's triumph and power over death.

3:16 Jesus, not the apostles, received the glory for the healing. In those days a man's name represented his character; it stood for his authority and power. By using Jesus' name, Peter showed who gave him the authority and power to heal. The apostles did not emphasize what they could do, but what God could do through them. Jesus' name is not to be used as magic—it must be used by faith. When we pray in Jesus' name, we must remember that it is Jesus himself, not merely the sound of his name, that gives our prayers their power.

3:18 These prophecies are found in Psalm 22 and Isaiah 50:6 and 53:5. Peter was explaining the kind of Messiah God sent to earth. The Jews expected a great governor, not a suffering servant.

3:19 John the Baptist prepared the way for Jesus by preaching repentance. The apostles' call to salvation also included repentance—acknowledging personal sin and turning away from it. Many people want the benefits of being identified with Christ without turning from sin and acknowledging their own disobedience. The first step to being forgiven is to confess your sin and turn from it (see 2:38).

3:19 When we repent, God promises not only to wipe away our sin, but to bring spiritual refreshment. Repentance may at first seem painful because it is hard to give up certain sins. But God will give you a better way. As Hosea promised, "Let us press on to know him, and he will respond to us as surely as the coming of dawn or the rain of early spring" (Hosea 6:3). Do you feel a need to be refreshed?

3:21 The "recovery of all things from sin" points to the Second Coming, the last judgment, and the removal of sin from the universe.

3:21, 22 Most Jews thought that Joshua was this Prophet predicted by Moses (Deuteronomy 18:15). Peter was saying that he was Jesus Christ. Peter wanted to show them that their long-awaited Messiah had come! He and all the apostles were calling the Jewish nation to realize what they had done to their Messiah, to repent, and to believe. From this point on in Acts, we see many Jews rejecting the gospel. So the message went also to the Gentiles, many of whom had hearts open to receive Jesus.

3:24 The prophet Samuel lived during the transition between the judges and the kings of Israel, and he was seen as the first in a succession of prophets. He anointed David king, founding David's royal line, from which the Messiah eventually came. All the prophets point forward to a future Messiah. For more on Samuel, see his Profile in 1 Samuel 8.

3:25 God promised Abraham that he would bless the world through his descendants, the Jewish race (Genesis 12:3), from which the Messiah would come. God intended the Jewish nation to be a separate and holy nation that would teach the world about God, introduce the Messiah, and then carry on his work in the world. After the days of Solomon, the nation gave up its mission to tell the world about God, and now, in apostolic times, it also rejected its Messiah.

4:1 The chief priests were prominent priests, often close relatives of the high priests, as well as priests of special ability or influence. The Temple police were guards set around the Temple to insure order. The Sadducees were members of a Jewish religious sect who did not believe in the resurrection of the dead. Most of those who engineered and carried out Jesus' arrest and crucifixion were from these three groups.

● **4:2** Peter and John spoke to the people during the afternoon prayer time. The Sadducees moved in quickly to investigate.

4:3
Acts 5:18
4:4
Acts 4:21

that Peter and John were claiming that Jesus had risen from the dead. 3They arrested them and since it was already evening, jailed them overnight. 4But many of the people who heard their message believed it, so that the number of believers now reached a new high of about 5,000 men!

5The next day it happened that the Council of all the Jewish leaders was in session in Jerusalem— 6Annas the High Priest was there, and Caiaphas, John, Alexander, and others of the High Priest's relatives. 7So the two disciples were brought in before them.

4:6
Mt 26:3
Lk 3:1,2
Jn 11:49; 18:13
4:7
Mt 21:23

"By what power, or by whose authority have you done this?" the Council demanded.

4:8
Lk 12:1

8Then Peter, filled with the Holy Spirit, said to them, "Honorable leaders and elders of our nation, 9if you mean the good deed done to the cripple, and how he was healed, 10let me clearly state to you and to all the people of Israel that it was done in the name and power of Jesus from Nazareth, the Messiah, the man you crucified—but God raised back to life again. It is by his authority that this man stands here healed! 11For Jesus the Messiah is (the one referred to in the Scriptures when they speak of) a 'stone discarded by the builders which became the capstone of the arch.' 12There is salvation in no one else! Under all heaven there is no other name for men to call upon to save them."

4:10
Acts 2:22,24; 3:6

4:11
Ps 118:22
Isa 28:16
Mt 21:42
Rom 9:33

4:12
Mt 1:21
Acts 10:43
Rom 3:24
1 Tim 2:5

13When the Council saw the boldness of Peter and John, and could see that they were obviously uneducated non-professionals, they were amazed and realized what being with Jesus had done for them! 14And the Council could hardly discredit the healing when the man they had healed was standing right there beside them! 15So they sent them out of the Council chamber and conferred among themselves.

4:13
Mt 11:25
1 Cor 1:27

4:16
Jn 11:47
Acts 3:7-10
4:17
Jn 15:20,21

16"What shall we do with these men?" they asked each other. "We can't deny that they have done a tremendous miracle, and everybody in Jerusalem knows about it. 17But perhaps we can stop them from spreading their propaganda. We'll

4:11 *became the capstone of the arch,* implied. Literally, "became the head of the corner."

Because they did not believe in the resurrection, they were disturbed with what the apostles were saying. Peter and John were refuting one of their fundamental beliefs and thus threatening their authority as religious teachers. Even under Roman rule, the Sadducees had almost unlimited power over the Temple grounds. Thus they were able to arrest Peter and John for no other reason than teaching something that contradicted their beliefs.

●**4:3** Not often will our witnessing send us to prison as it did Peter and John. Still, we run risks in trying to win others to Christ. We might be willing to face a night in prison if it would bring 2,000 people to Christ, but shouldn't we also be willing to suffer for even one? What do you risk in witnessing—vulnerability, rejection, persecution? Whatever the risks, realize that nothing done for God is ever wasted.

4:5 This Council of Jewish leaders was the Sanhedrin or Jewish Supreme Court—the same Council that had condemned Jesus to death. It had 70 members plus the current High Priest, who presided. The Sadducees held a majority in this ruling group. These were the wealthy, intellectual, and powerful men of Jerusalem. Jesus' followers stood before this Council just as he had.

4:6 Annas had been deposed as High Priest by the Romans, who then appointed Caiaphas, Annas' son-in-law, in his place. But since the Jews considered the office of High Priest a lifetime position, they still called Annas by that title and gave him respect and authority within the Council. Annas and Caiaphas had played significant roles in Jesus' trial (John 18:24, 28). It did not please Annas or Caiaphas that the man they thought they had sacrificed for the good of the nation (John 11:50, 51) had followers who were just as persistent and promised to be just as troublesome as he was.

●**4:7** The Council asked Peter and John by whose power they had

healed the man (3:6) and by what authority they preached (3:12–26). The actions and words of Peter and John threatened these religious leaders who, for the most part, were more interested in their reputations and positions than in God. Through the help of the Holy Spirit (Mark 13:11), Peter spoke boldly before the Council, actually putting the Council on trial by showing them that the one they had crucified had risen again. Instead of being defensive, the apostles were going on the offensive, boldly speaking out for God and presenting the gospel to these leaders.

4:11 A capstone is the center stone of an arch, and it holds the arch in place. The cornerstone unites two walls at the corner of a building and holds the building together. Peter said the Jews rejected Jesus, but now he has become the cornerstone of the church (or the capstone of the arch—Psalm 118:22; Mark 12:10; 1 Peter 2:7). Without him there would be no church, because it could not stand.

4:12 Many people react negatively to the fact that there is no other name than that of Jesus to call upon for salvation. Yet this is not something the Church decided; it is the specific teaching of Jesus himself (John 14:6). Christians are to be open-minded on many issues, but not on how we are saved from sin. No other religious teacher could die for the sins of the whole human race; no other religious teacher came to earth as God's only Son; no other religious teacher rose from the dead. Our focus should be on Jesus, whom God offered as a way to have an eternal relationship with himself.

●**4:13** The Council knew Peter and John were uneducated, and they were amazed at what being with Jesus had done for them. A changed life convinces people of Jesus' power. One of your greatest testimonies is the difference others see in your life and attitudes since you have believed in Jesus.

tell them that if they do it again we'll really throw the book at them." 18So they
called them back in, and told them never again to speak about Jesus.

19But Peter and John replied, "You decide whether God wants you to obey you
instead of him! 20We cannot stop telling about the wonderful things we saw Jesus
do and heard him say."

21The Council then threatened them further, and finally let them go because they
didn't know how to punish them without starting a riot. For everyone was praising
God for this wonderful miracle— 22the healing of a man who had been lame for
forty years.

The believers pray for boldness

23As soon as they were freed, Peter and John found the other disciples and told
them what the Council had said.

24Then all the believers united in this prayer:

"O Lord, Creator of heaven and earth and of the sea and everything in them—
25, 26you spoke long ago by the Holy Spirit through our ancestor King David, your
servant, saying, 'Why do the heathen rage against the Lord, and the foolish nations
plan their little plots against Almighty God? The kings of the earth unite to fight
against him, and against the anointed Son of God!'

27"That is what is happening here in this city today! For Herod the king, and
Pontius Pilate the governor, and all the Romans—as well as the people of Israel—are united against Jesus, your anointed Son, your holy servant. 28They won't
stop at anything that you in your wise power will let them do. 29And now, O Lord,
hear their threats, and grant to your servants great boldness in their preaching,
30and send your healing power, and may miracles and wonders be done by the
name of your holy servant Jesus."

31After this prayer, the building where they were meeting shook and they were
all filled with the Holy Spirit and boldly preached God's message.

The believers share their possessions

32All the believers were of one heart and mind, and no one felt that what he
owned was his own; everyone was sharing. 33And the apostles preached powerful
sermons about the resurrection of the Lord Jesus, and there was warm fellowship
among all the believers, 34, 35and no poverty—for all who owned land or houses

4:33 *there was warm fellowship among all the believers,* literally, "great grace was upon them all."

4:18
Act 5:28
4:19
Acts 5:29
4:20
Acts 1:8
1 Cor 9:16
1 Jn 1:1
4:21
Mt 21:26
Lk 20:6; 22:2
Acts 3:7,8

4:24
Ex 20:11
Ps 103:1;
107:1; 146:6
4:25,26
Ps 2:1,2
4:27
Isa 61:1
Lk 23:12
Acts 3:13
4:28
Acts 2:23
4:29
Eph 6:19
2 Thess 3:1
4:30
Acts 3:6,16
5:12
4:31
Acts 2:2,4
16:26
Phil 1:14

4:32
Acts 2:44
Phil 2:2
4:33
Lk 24:48

●**4:20** We are sometimes afraid to share our faith in God because
people might feel uncomfortable and disapprove. But Peter and
John's zeal for the Lord was so strong that they could not keep
quiet, even when threatened. If your courage to witness for God
has weakened, pray that your boldness may increase. Remember
Jesus' promise, "If anyone publicly acknowledges me as his friend,
I will openly ackowledge him as my friend before my Father in
heaven" (Matthew 10:32).

4:24–30 Notice how the believers prayed. First they praised God;
then they told God their specific problem and asked for his help.
They did not ask God to remove the problem, but to help them
deal with it. This is a model for us to follow when we pray. We may
ask God to remove our problems, and he may choose to do so, but
we must recognize that often he will leave the problem in place
and give us the grace to deal with it.

4:27 This was Herod Antipas, appointed by the Romans to rule
over the territory of Galilee. For more information on Herod, see his
Profile in Mark 6. Pontius Pilate was the Roman governor over
Judea. He bent to pressure from the crowd and sentenced Jesus
to death. For more information on Pilate, see his Profile in Mark 15.

●**4:29–31** Boldness is not reckless impulsiveness. Boldness
requires courage to press through our fears and do what we know
is right. How can we be more bold? Like the disciples, we need to
pray with others for that courage. To gain boldness, you can (1)
pray for the power of the Holy Spirit to give you courage, (2) look

for opportunities in your family and neighborhood to talk about
Christ, (3) realize that rejection, social discomfort, and
embarrassment are not persecution, and (4) start where you are by
being bolder in small ways.

4:32 Differences of opinion are inevitable among human
personalities and can actually be helpful if handled well. But
spiritual unity is essential—loyalty, commitment, and love for God
and his Word. Without spiritual unity, the church could not survive.
Paul wrote the letter of 1 Corinthians to urge the church in Corinth
toward greater unity.

4:32 None of these Christians felt what they had was their own,
and so they were able to give and share, eliminating poverty
among them. They would not let a brother or sister suffer when
others had plenty. How do you feel about your possessions? We
should adopt the attitude, "Everything we have comes from God,
and we are only sharing what is already his."

4:32–35 The early church was able to share possessions and
property as a result of the unity brought by the Holy Spirit working
in and through the believers' lives. This is different from
communism because (1) it was voluntary sharing; (2) it didn't
involve *all* private property, but only as much as was needed; (3) it
was not a membership requirement in order to be a part of the
church. The spiritual unity and generosity of these early believers
attracted others to them. This organizational structure is not a
biblical command, but it offers vital principles for us to follow.

4:36
Acts 9:27
11:19-30
12:25; 13:1-4
15:39
4:37
Prov 11:24,25

sold them and brought the money to the apostles to give to others in need.

36For instance, there was Joseph (the one the apostles nicknamed "Barnabas, the encourager"! He was of the tribe of Levi, from the island of Cyprus). 37He was one of those who sold a field he owned and brought the money to the apostles for distribution to those in need.

The judgment of Ananias and Sapphira

5:2
Acts 4:37
1 Tim 6:10
5:3
Num 30:1,2
Deut 23:21
Eccles 5:4
Isa 29:15

5:5
Ezek 11:13

5 But there was a man named Ananias (with his wife Sapphira) who sold some property, 2and brought only part of the money, claiming it was the full price. (His wife had agreed to this deception.)

3But Peter said, "Ananias, Satan has filled your heart. When you claimed this was the full price, you were lying to the Holy Spirit. 4The property was yours to sell or not, as you wished. And after selling it, it was yours to decide how much to give. How could you do a thing like this? You weren't lying to us, but to God."

5As soon as Ananias heard these words, he fell to the floor, dead! Everyone was terrified, 6and the younger men covered him with a sheet and took him out and buried him.

7About three hours later his wife came in, not knowing what had happened. 8Peter asked her, "Did you people sell your land for such and such a price?"

"Yes," she replied, "we did."

5:9
Deut 6:16
Mt 4:7
Lk 4:12
1 Cor 10:9

9And Peter said, "How could you and your husband even think of doing a thing like this—conspiring together to test the Spirit of God's ability to know what is going on? Just outside that door are the young men who buried your husband, and they will carry you out too."

10Instantly she fell to the floor, dead, and the young men came in and, seeing that she was dead, carried her out and buried her beside her husband. 11Terror gripped the entire church and all others who heard what had happened.

The apostles heal many people

5:12
Mk 16:15-20
Jn 10:23
Acts 3:10
Heb 2:4
5:13
Jn 9:22,23
12:42
Acts 2:47

12Meanwhile, the apostles were meeting regularly at the Temple in the area known as Solomon's Hall, and they did many remarkable miracles among the people. 13The other believers didn't dare join them, though, but all had the highest regard for them. 14And more and more believers were added to the Lord, crowds both of men and women. 15Sick people were brought out into the streets on beds and mats so that at least Peter's shadow would fall across some of them as he went

5:9 to test the Spirit of God's ability to know what is going on, literally, "to try the Spirit of the Lord."

4:36 Barnabas (which means "son of encouragement" or "son of consolation") was a respected leader of the church. He traveled with Paul on his first missionary journey (13:1–4). For more information on Barnabas, see his Profile in chapter 13.

5:1ff In Acts 5:1—8:3 we see both internal and external problems facing the church. Inside, there was dishonesty (5:1–11) and adminstrative headaches (6:1–7); outside, the church was being pressured by persecution. While church leaders were careful and sensitive in dealing with the internal problems, there was not much they could do to prevent the external pressures. Through it all, the leaders kept their focus on what was most important—spreading the gospel about Jesus Christ.

5:3 Although Satan was defeated by Christ at the cross, he was still actively trying to make the believers stumble—as he does today (Ephesians 6:12; 1 Peter 5:8). Satan's overthrow is inevitable, but it will not occur until the last days, when Christ returns to judge the world (Revelation 20:10).

5:5 The sin Ananias and Sapphira committed was not stinginess or holding back part of the money—they could choose whether or not to sell the land and how much to give. Their sin was lying to God and God's people—saying they gave the whole amount but holding back some for themselves, trying to make themselves appear more generous than they really were. This act was judged harshly because dishonesty and covetousness are destructive in a

church, preventing the Holy Spirit from working effectively. All lying is bad, but when we lie to try to deceive God and his people about our relationship with him, we destroy our testimony for Christ.

5:11 God's judgment on Ananias and Sapphira produced shock and fear among the believers, making them realize how seriously God regards sin in the church.

5:12, 13 Solomon's Hall was part of the Temple complex built by King Herod the Great in an attempt to strengthen his relationship with the Jews. Jesus taught and performed miracles in the Temple many times. When the apostles went to the Temple, they were near the same religious leaders who had conspired to kill Jesus.

5:13 Believers did not dare join the apostles or work beside them because they were afraid to face the same kind of persecution the apostles had just faced (4:17).

5:14 What makes Christianity attractive? It is easy to be drawn to churches because of programs, good speakers, size, beautiful facilities, or fellowship. Believers were attracted to the early church by God's power and miracles, the generosity, sincerity, honesty, and unity of the members, and the character of the leaders. Have our standards slipped? God wants to add to his *church,* not just to programs or congregations.

5:15 These people were not healed by Peter's shadow, but by God's power working through Peter.

by! 16And crowds came in from the Jerusalem suburbs, bringing their sick folk and those possessed by demons; and every one of them was healed.

The apostles meet furious opposition

17The High Priest and his relatives and friends among the Sadducees reacted with violent jealousy 18and arrested the apostles, and put them in the public jail.

19But an angel of the Lord came at night, opened the gates of the jail and brought them out. Then he told them, 20"Go over to the Temple and preach about this Life!"

21They arrived at the Temple about daybreak, and immediately began preaching! Later that morning the High Priest and his courtiers arrived at the Temple, and, convening the Jewish Council and the entire Senate, they sent for the apostles to be brought for trial. 22But when the police arrived at the jail, the men weren't there, so they returned to the Council and reported, 23"The jail doors were locked, and the guards were standing outside, but when we opened the gates, no one was there!"

24When the police captain and the chief priests heard this, they were frantic, wondering what would happen next and where all this would end! 25Then someone arrived with the news that the men they had jailed were out in the Temple, preaching to the people!

26, 27The police captain went with his officers and arrested them (without violence, for they were afraid the people would kill them if they roughed up the disciples) and brought them in before the Council.

28"Didn't we tell you never again to preach about this Jesus?" the High Priest demanded. "And instead you have filled all Jerusalem with your teaching and intend to bring the blame for this man's death on us!"

29But Peter and the apostles replied, "We must obey God rather than men. 30The God of our ancestors brought Jesus back to life again after you had killed him by hanging him on a cross. 31Then, with mighty power, God exalted him to be a Prince and Savior, so that the people of Israel would have an opportunity for repentance, and for their sins to be forgiven. 32And we are witnesses of these things, and so is the Holy Spirit, who is given by God to all who obey him."

33At this, the Council was furious, and decided to kill them. 34But one of their

5:17 Acts 4:1,2

5:18 Lk 21:12

5:19 Ps 34:7 Acts 12:7; 16:26 Heb 1:14

5:20 Jn 6:63,68; 17:3 1 Jn 5:11

5:21 Acts 4:5,6

5:26 Mt 14:5; 21:26

5:28 Mt 23:35; 27:25 Acts 2:23; 3:15 4:18; 7:52

5:29 Acts 4:19

5:30 Acts 10:39-41 1 Pet 2:24

5:31 Isa 9:6 Mt 1:21 Acts 2:33 Phil 2:9 Heb 2:10; 12:2 Rev 1:5

5:32 Lk 24:28 Jn 15:26 Rom 8:16 Heb 2:4

5:33 Acts 2:37; 7:54

5:21 *Later that morning,* implied.   **5:24** *the police captain,* literally, "the captain of the Temple."

5:16 What did these miraculous healings do for the early church? (1) They attracted believers. (2) They confirmed the truth of the apostles' teaching. (3) They demonstrated that the power of the Messiah who had been crucified and risen was now with his followers.

5:17 The religious leaders were jealous—Peter and the apostles were already commanding more respect than they had ever received. The difference, however, was that the religious leaders demanded respect and reverence for themselves; the apostles' goal was to bring respect and reverence to God. The apostles were respected not because they demanded it, but because they deserved it.

●**5:17, 18** The apostles had power to do miracles, great boldness in preaching, and God's presence in their lives; yet they were not free from hatred and persecution. They were arrested and put in jail, beaten with rods and whips, and slandered by community leaders. Faith in God does not make troubles disappear; it makes troubles appear less fearsome because it puts them in the right perspective. You cannot expect everyone to react favorably when you share something as dynamic as your faith in Christ. Some will be jealous of you, frightened, or threatened. Expect some negative reactions. But remember that you must be more concerned about God's reactions than peoples'.

●**5:21** The Jewish Council and Senate are not two different groups—this phrase simply means they convened the entire group, the 70 men of the Jewish Council (also called the Supreme Court or Sanhedrin). This was going to be no small trial. The religious leaders would do anything to stop these apostles from

challenging their authority, threatening their secure position, and exposing their hypocritical motives to the people.

●**5:21** Suppose someone threatened to kill you if you didn't stop talking about God. You might be tempted to keep quiet. But the apostles, after being threatened by powerful leaders, arrested, beaten, jailed, and finally released, went back to preaching. This was nothing less than God's power working through this group of men (4:13). When we are convinced of the power of Christ's resurrection and have experienced the presence of his Holy Spirit, we can have the confidence to speak out for Christ.

5:21 The Temple at daybreak was a busy place. Many people stopped at the Temple to pray and worship at sunrise, and the apostles were already there, ready to tell them the Good News.

●**5:29** The apostles knew their priorities. While we should try to keep peace with everyone (Romans 12:18), conflict with the world and its authorities is sometimes inevitable for a Christian (John 15:18). There will be situations where you cannot obey both God and man. Then you must obey God and trust his Word. Let Jesus' words encourage you: "What happiness it is when others hate you and exclude you and insult you and smear your name because you are mine! When that happens, rejoice! Yes, leap for joy! For you will have a great reward awaiting you in heaven" (Luke 6:22, 23).

5:34 The Pharisees were the other major party in the Jewish Council with the Sadducees (5:17). They were the strict keepers of the law—not only God's law, but hundreds of other rules they had added to God's law. They were careful about outward purity, but many had hearts full of impure motives. Jesus confronted the

members, a Pharisee named Gamaliel (an expert on religious law and very popular with the people), stood up and requested that the apostles be sent outside the Council chamber while he talked.

35Then he addressed his colleagues as follows:

"Men of Israel, take care what you are planning to do to these men! 36Some time ago there was that fellow Theudas, who pretended to be someone great. About 400 others joined him, but he was killed, and his followers were harmlessly dispersed. 37"After him, at the time of the taxation, there was Judas of Galilee. He drew away some people as disciples, but he also died, and his followers scattered. 38"And so my advice is, leave these men alone. If what they teach and do is merely on their own, it will soon be overthrown. 39But if it is of God, you will not be able to stop them, lest you find yourselves fighting even against God."

40The Council accepted his advice, called in the apostles, had them beaten, and then told them never again to speak in the name of Jesus, and finally let them go. 41They left the Council chamber rejoicing that God had counted them worthy to suffer dishonor for his name. 42And every day, in the Temple and in their home Bible classes, they continued to teach and preach that Jesus is the Messiah.

The church appoints seven deacons

6 But with the believers multiplying rapidly, there were rumblings of discontent. Those who spoke only Greek complained that their widows were being discriminated against, that they were not being given as much food, in the daily distribution, as the widows who spoke Hebrew. 2So the Twelve called a meeting of all the believers.

5:36
Acts 8:9
5:37
Lk 2:1
5:38
Ps 127:1
5:39
Prov 21:30
Isa 46:9,10
Mt 16:18
Acts 9:5
1 Cor 1:25
5:40
Mt 10:17
Mk 13:9
5:41
Mt 5:11,12
Jn 15:20,21
Rom 5:3
Phil 1:29
Heb 10:34
1 Pet 4:13,14,16

6:1
Ex 18:17
Acts 2:47; 4:35
1 Tim 5:3

Pharisees often during his ministry on earth.

5:34 Gamaliel was an unexpected ally for the apostles, although he probably did not support their teachings. He was a distinguished member of the Jewish Council and a teacher. While he may have saved their lives, his real intentions were to keep the Council from being divided over them and to avoid arousing the Romans. The apostles were popular with the people and killing them would probably start a riot. But Gamaliel's advice to the Council gave the apostles some breathing room to continue their work. The Council waited and hoped that this would all fade away harmlessly. They couldn't have been more wrong. Ironically, Paul, who would become one of the greatest apostles, was tutored by Gamaliel (22:3).

5:39 Gamaliel presented some sound advice about reacting to religious movements. Unless they endorse obviously dangerous doctrine or practices, it is often wiser to be tolerant rather than repressive. Sometimes only time will tell if they are merely the work of men or if God is trying to say something through them. Next time a group promotes differing religious ideas, consider Gamaliel's advice, "lest you find yourselves fighting even against God."

5:40 Peter and John were warned repeatedly not to preach, but they continued in spite of the threats. We, too, should live as Christ has asked, sharing our faith no matter what the cost. We may not be beaten or thrown in jail, but we may be ridiculed, ostracized, or slandered. To what extent are you willing to suffer for the sake of sharing the gospel with others?

● **5:41** Have you ever thought of persecution as a blessing? This beating suffered by Peter and John was the first time any of the apostles had been physically abused for their faith. These men knew how Jesus had suffered, and they praised God that he allowed them to be persecuted like their Lord. If you are mocked or persecuted for your faith, it isn't because you're doing something wrong, but that God has counted you "worthy to suffer dishonor for his name."

5:42 Home Bible studies are not new. The apostles had to teach in homes because the synagogues and the Temple were not open to their teaching. Home Bible studies met the needs of believers and also introduced new people to the Christian faith. During later times of persecution, this became the primary method of passing on Bible knowledge. Christians throughout the world still use home Bible study both as a strategy under persecution and as a way to build up believers.

6:1ff Another internal problem developed in the early church. The native Jewish Christians spoke Aramaic, a semitic language. The Greek-speaking Christians were probably Jews from other lands who were converted at Pentecost. The Greek-speaking Christians complained that their widows were being unfairly treated. This favoritism may not have been intentional, but was caused by a language barrier. To correct the problem, the apostles put seven respected Greek-speaking men in charge of the food distribution program. This put an end to the problem and allowed the apostles to keep their focus on their ministry of teaching and preaching the Good News about Jesus.

6:1 When we read the descriptions of the early church—the miracles, the sharing and generosity—we may wish we could have been a part of this "perfect" church. But in reality, they had problems just as we do today. No church has ever been or will ever be perfect until Christ and his church are united at his Second Coming. All churches have problems. If your church's shortcomings distress you, ask yourself: "Would a perfect church let me be a member?" Then do what you can to make your church better. A church does not have to be perfect to be faithful.

6:2 The Twelve are the 11 original disciples and Matthias, who was chosen to replace Judas Iscariot (1:26).

6:2–4 As the early church increased in size, their needs also increased. One need was to organize the distribution of food to the needy. The apostles needed to focus on preaching, so they chose others to administer the food program. Each person has a necessary part to play in the life of the church (see 1 Corinthians 12:27, 28). If you are in a position of leadership and find yourself bogged down, determine your God-given abilities and priorities and then find others to help. If you are not in leadership, you have gifts that can be used by God in various areas of the church's ministry. Offer these gifts in service to him.

"We should spend our time preaching, not administering a feeding program," they said. ³"Now look around among yourselves, dear brothers, and select seven men, wise and full of the Holy Spirit, who are well thought of by everyone; and we will put them in charge of this business. ⁴Then we can spend our time in prayer, preaching, and teaching."

⁵This sounded reasonable to the whole assembly, and they elected the following: Stephen (a man unusually full of faith and the Holy Spirit), Philip, Prochorus, Nicanor, Timon, Parmenas, Nicolaus of Antioch (a Gentile convert to the Jewish faith, who had become a Christian). ⁶These seven were presented to the apostles, who prayed for them and laid their hands on them in blessing.

⁷God's message was preached in ever-widening circles, and the number of disciples increased vastly in Jerusalem; and many of the Jewish priests were converted too.

Stephen is arrested

⁸Stephen, the man so full of faith and the Holy Spirit's power, did spectacular miracles among the people.

⁹But one day some of the men from the Jewish cult of "The Freedmen" started an argument with him, and they were soon joined by Jews from Cyrene, Alexandria in Egypt, and the Turkish provinces of Cilicia, and Asia Minor. ¹⁰But none of them was able to stand against Stephen's wisdom and spirit.

¹¹So they brought in some men to lie about him, claiming they had heard Stephen curse Moses, and even God.

¹²This accusation roused the crowds to fury against Stephen, and the Jewish leaders arrested him and brought him before the Council. ¹³The lying witnesses testified again that Stephen was constantly speaking against the Temple and against the laws of Moses.

¹⁴They declared, "We have heard him say that this fellow Jesus of Nazareth will destroy the Temple, and throw out all of Moses' laws." ¹⁵At this point everyone in the Council chamber saw Stephen's face become as radiant as an angel's!

6:8 *full of faith and the Holy Spirit's power,* literally, "full of grace and truth." See vs 5.   **6:12** *the Jewish leaders,* literally, "the elders and the scribes."

6:3
Acts 2:4
Eph 5:18
1 Tim 3:7,8
6:4
Acts 1:14; 2:42
6:5
Acts 8:5; 21:8
6:6
Num 8:10
Acts 1:24; 13:3
1 Tim 4:14
2 Tim 1:6
6:7
Jn 12:42
Acts 12:24; 19:20
21:20
Col 1:6

6:8
Jn 14:12
6:9
Mt 27:32
Acts 2:10;
18:24 21:39; 24:18
6:10
Ex 4:12
Lk 21:15
6:11
Mt 26:59
6:12
Lk 20:1
Acts 4:1
6:13
Mt 26:59
Acts 7:58; 21:28
6:14
Jn 2:19-21
Heb 9; 10
6:15
Mt 28:3

6:3 This administrative task was not taken lightly. Notice the requirements for the men who were to handle the feeding program: (1) wise, (2) full of the Holy Spirit, and (3) well thought of by everyone. Jobs that require responsibility and dealing with people need leaders with these qualities. We must look for those who are wise, spiritually mature, and with good reputations to lead our churches today.

6:4 The apostles' priorities were correct. The ministry of the Word should never be neglected because of administrative burdens. Pastors should never try, or be expected, to do everything. The work of the church should be spread out among its members.

6:6 Spiritual leadership is serious business and must not be taken lightly by the church or the leaders. In the early church, the chosen men were commissioned (set apart by prayer and laying on of hands) by the apostles. Laying hands on someone, an ancient Jewish practice, was a way to set a person apart for special service (see Numbers 27:23; Deuteronomy 34:9).

6:7 Jesus had told the apostles that they were to witness first in Jerusalem (1:8). In a short time, their message had infiltrated the entire city and all levels of society. Even some priests were being converted, going against the directives of the Jewish Council and endangering their position.

6:7 The gospel spread in "ever-widening circles" like ripples on a pond where, from a single center, each wave touches the next, spreading wider and farther. The gospel still spreads this way today. You don't have to change the world single-handedly—it is enough just to be part of the wave, touching those around you, who in turn will touch others until all have felt the movement. Don't ever feel that your part is insignificant or unimportant.

6:8–10 The most important prerequisite for any kind of Christian service is to be filled with the Holy Spirit. By the Spirit's power, Stephen was a good administrator, miracle worker (6:8), and evangelist (6:10). By the Spirit's power, you can exercise the gifts God has given you.

6:9 The Freedmen were a group of Jewish slaves who had been freed by Rome and had formed their own synagogue in Jerusalem.

6:11 The Sadducees were the dominant party in the Jewish Council. They accepted and studied only the writings of Moses (Genesis through Deuteronomy). In their view, to curse Moses was a crime. But from Stephen's speech (chapter 7), we learn that this accusation was false. Stephen based his review of Israel's history on Moses' writings.

●**6:14** When Stephen was brought before the Council of religious leaders, the Freedmen used the same false accusation that the religious leaders had used against Jesus (Matthew 26:61). They falsely accused Stephen of wanting to do away with Moses' laws because they knew that the Sadducees, who controlled the Council, believed *only* in Moses' laws.

Stephen addresses the Sanhedrin

7:2
Gen 15:7

7:3
Gen 12:1

7:4
Gen 11:31; 12:4
Heb 11:8

7 Then the High Priest asked him, "Are these accusations true?"
²This was Stephen's lengthy reply: "The glorious God appeared to our ancestor Abraham in Iraq before he moved to Syria, ³and told him to leave his native land, to say good-bye to his relatives and to start out for a country that God would direct him to. ⁴So he left the land of the Chaldeans and lived in Haran, in Syria, until his

7:2 *Iraq,* literally, "Mesopotamia." *Syria,* literally, "Haran," a city in the area we now know as Syria.

STEPHEN

Around the world, the gospel has most often taken root in places prepared by the blood of martyrs. Before a person can *give* his life for the gospel, however, he must first *live* his life for the gospel. One way God trains his servants is to place them in insignificant positions. Their desire to serve Christ is translated into the reality of serving others. Stephen was an effective administrator and messenger before becoming a martyr.

Stephen was named among the managers of food distribution in the early church. Long before violent persecution broke out against Christians, there was already social ostracism. Jews who accepted Jesus as Messiah were usually cut off from their families. As a result, the believers depended on each other for support. The sharing of homes, food, and resources was both a practical and necessary mark of the early church. Eventually, the number of believers made it necessary to organize the sharing. People were being overlooked. There were complaints. Those chosen to help manage were chosen for their integrity and sensitivity to God.

Stephen, besides being a good administrator, was also a powerful speaker. When confronted in the Temple by various antagonistic groups, Stephen's logic in responding was convincing. This is clear from the defense he made before the Court. He presented a summary of the Jews' own history and made powerful applications that stung his listeners. During his defense Stephen must have known he was speaking his own death sentence. Members of the Court could not stand to have their evil motives exposed. They stoned him to death while he prayed for their forgiveness. His final words show how much like Jesus he had become in a short time. His death had a lasting impact on young Saul (Paul) of Tarsus, who would move from being a violent persecutor of Christians to being one of the greatest champions of the gospel the church has known.

Stephen's life is a continual challenge to all Christians. Because he was the first to die for the faith, his sacrifice raises questions: How many risks do we take in being Jesus' followers? Would we be willing to die for him? Are we really willing to live for him?

Strengths and accomplishments:
● One of seven leaders chosen to supervise food distribution to the needy in the early church
● Known for his spiritual qualities of faith, wisdom, grace, and power, and for the Spirit's presence in his life
● Outstanding leader, teacher, and debater
● First to give his life for the gospel

Lessons from his life:
● Striving for excellence in small assignments prepares one for greater responsibilities
● Real understanding of God always leads to practical and compassionate actions toward people

Vital statistics:
● Church responsibilities: Deacon—distributing food to the needy
● Contemporaries: Paul, Caiaphas, Gamaliel, the apostles

Key verses:
"And as the murderous stones came hurtling at him, Stephen prayed, 'Lord Jesus, receive my spirit.' And he fell to his knees, shouting, 'Lord, don't charge them with this sin!' and with that, he died" (Acts 7:59, 60).

Stephen's story is told in Acts 6:3—8:2. He is also mentioned in Acts 11:19; 22:20.

7:1 This High Priest was Caiaphas, the same High Priest who had earlier questioned and condemned Jesus (John 18:24).

●**7:2ff** Stephen launched into a long speech about Israel's relationship with God. From Old Testament history he showed that the Jews had constantly rejected God's message and his prophets, and that this Council had rejected the Messiah, God's Son. He made three main points: (1) Israel's history is the history of God's acts in the world; (2) men worshiped God long before there was a temple, for God does not live in a temple; (3) Jesus' death

was just one more example of Israel's rebellion and rejection of God.

●**7:2ff** Stephen wasn't really defending himself. Instead he took the offensive, seizing the opportunity to summarize his teaching about Jesus. Stephen was accusing these religious leaders of failing to obey God's laws—the laws they prided themselves in following so meticulously. This was the same accusation Jesus leveled against them. When we witness for Jesus, we don't need to be on the defensive, but instead simply share our faith.

father died. Then God brought him here to the land of Israel, 5but gave him no property of his own, not one little tract of land.

"However, God promised that eventually the whole country would belong to him and his descendants—though as yet he had no children! 6But God also told him that these descendants of his would leave the land and live in a foreign country and there become slaves for 400 years. 7'But I will punish the nation that enslaves them,' God told him, 'and afterwards my people will return to this land of Israel and worship me here.'

8"God also gave Abraham the ceremony of circumcision at that time, as evidence of the covenant between God and the people of Abraham. And so Isaac, Abraham's son, was circumcised when he was eight days old. Isaac became the father of Jacob, and Jacob was the father of the twelve patriarchs of the Jewish nation. 9These men were very jealous of Joseph and sold him to be a slave in Egypt. But God was with him, 10and delivered him out of all of his anguish, and gave him favor before Pharaoh, king of Egypt. God also gave Joseph unusual wisdom, so that Pharaoh appointed him governor over all Egypt, as well as putting him in charge of all the affairs of the palace.

11"But a famine developed in Egypt and Canaan and there was great misery for our ancestors. When their food was gone, 12Jacob heard that there was still grain in Egypt, so he sent his sons to buy some. 13The second time they went, Joseph revealed his identity to his brothers, and they were introduced to Pharaoh. 14Then Joseph sent for his father Jacob and all his brothers' families to come to Egypt, seventy-five persons in all. 15So Jacob came to Egypt, where he died, and all his sons. 16All of them were taken to Shechem and buried in the tomb Abraham bought from the sons of Hamor, Shechem's father.

17, 18"As the time drew near when God would fulfill his promise to Abraham to free his descendants from slavery, the Jewish people greatly multiplied in Egypt; but then a king was crowned who had no respect for Joseph's memory. 19This king plotted against our race, forcing parents to abandon their children in the fields.

20"About that time Moses was born—a child of divine beauty. His parents hid him at home for three months, 21and when at last they could no longer keep him hidden, and had to abandon him, Pharaoh's daughter found him and adopted him as her own son, 22and taught him all the wisdom of the Egyptians, and he became a mighty prince and orator.

23"One day as he was nearing his fortieth birthday, it came into his mind to visit his brothers, the people of Israel. 24During this visit he saw an Egyptian mistreating a man of Israel. So Moses killed the Egyptian. 25Moses supposed his brothers would realize that God had sent him to help them, but they didn't.

26"The next day he visited them again and saw two men of Israel fighting. He tried to be a peacemaker. 'Gentlemen,' he said, 'you are brothers and shouldn't be fighting like this! It is wrong!'

27"But the man in the wrong told Moses to mind his own business. 'Who made

7:12 *his sons,* literally, "our fathers."

7:5 Gen 12:7 13:15,16 17:7,8; 26:3
7:6 Gen 15:13 Ex 12:40 Gal 3:17 1 Pet 2:11
7:7 Ex 3:12
7:8 Gen 17:9,10 21:1,2; 25:26 35:23-26 1 Chron 1:34 Mt 1:2
7:9 Gen 37:4,11,28 39:2 Ps 105:17
7:10 Gen 42:6 Ps 37:23; 105:21
7:11 Gen 41:54
7:12 Gen 42:2
7:13 Gen 45:1-4
7:14 Gen 45:9; 46:27 Deut 10:22
7:15 Gen 49:33 Ex 1:6
7:16 Gen 23:16
7:17,18 Gen 15:13 Ex 1:7,8
7:19 Ex 1:10,15,16
7:20 Ex 2:1,2 Heb 11:23
7:22 1 Kgs 4:30
7:23 Ex 2:11
7:24 Ex 2:12
7:27,28 Ex 2:14

Stephen's death was not in vain. Below are some of the events that were by-products (either directly or indirectly) of the persecution that began with Stephen's martyrdom.

THE EFFECTS OF STEPHEN'S DEATH

1. Philip's evangelistic tour (Acts 8:4–40)
2. Paul's conversion (Acts 9:1–30)
3. Peter's missionary tour (Acts 9:32—11:18)
4. The church in Antioch in Syria founded (Acts 11:1ff)

● **7:8** Circumcision was a sign of the promise made between God, Abraham, and the entire nation of Israel (Genesis 17:9–13). Stephen's speech was a summary of Israel's history, thus a summary of how this covenant fared over time. Stephen pointed out that God always kept his side of the promise, but Israel failed again and again to uphold its end. Although the Jews in Stephen's day still adhered to the ceremony of circumcision, they neglected to obey. The people's hearts were far from God, and so they had gone back on their side of the promise.

you a ruler and judge over us?' he asked. 28'Are you going to kill me as you killed that Egyptian yesterday?'

29"At this, Moses fled the country, and lived in the land of Midian, where his two sons were born.

30"Forty years later, in the desert near Mount Sinai, an Angel appeared to him in a flame of fire in a bush. 31Moses saw it and wondered what it was, and as he ran to see, the voice of the Lord called out to him, 32'I am the God of your ancestors—of Abraham, Isaac and Jacob.' Moses shook with terror and dared not look.

33"And the Lord said to him, 'Take off your shoes, for you are standing on holy ground. 34I have seen the anguish of my people in Egypt and have heard their cries. I have come down to deliver them. Come, I will send you to Egypt.' 35And so God sent back the same man his people had previously rejected by demanding, 'Who made *you* a ruler and judge over us?' Moses was sent to be their ruler and savior. 36And by means of many remarkable miracles he led them out of Egypt and through the Red Sea, and back and forth through the wilderness for forty years.

37"Moses himself told the people of Israel, 'God will raise up a Prophet much like me from among your brothers.' 38How true this proved to be, for in the wilderness, Moses was the go-between—the mediator between the people of Israel and the Angel who gave them the Law of God—the Living Word—on Mount Sinai.

39"But our fathers rejected Moses and wanted to return to Egypt. 40They told Aaron, 'Make idols for us, so that we will have gods to lead us back; for we don't know what has become of this Moses, who brought us out of Egypt.' 41So they made a calf-idol and sacrificed to it, and rejoiced in this thing they had made.

42"Then God turned away from them and gave them up, and let them serve the sun, moon and stars as their gods! In the book of Amos' prophecies the Lord God asks, 'Was it to me you were sacrificing during those forty years in the desert, Israel? 43No, your real interest was in your heathen gods—Sakkuth, and the star god Kaiway, and in all the images you made. So I will send you into captivity far away beyond Babylon.'

44"Our ancestors carried along with them a portable Temple, or Tabernacle, through the wilderness. In it they kept the stone tablets with the Ten Commandments written on them. This building was constructed in exact accordance with the plan shown to Moses by the Angel. 45Years later, when Joshua led the battles against the Gentile nations, this Tabernacle was taken with them into their new territory, and used until the time of King David.

46"God blessed David greatly, and David asked for the privilege of building a permanent Temple for the God of Jacob. 47But it was Solomon who actually built it. 48, 49However, God doesn't live in temples made by human hands. 'The heaven is my throne,' says the Lord through his prophets, 'and earth is my footstool. What kind of home could you build?' asks the Lord. 'Would I stay in it? 50Didn't I make both heaven and earth?'

51"You stiff-necked heathen! Must you forever resist the Holy Spirit? But your fathers did, and so do you! 52Name one prophet your ancestors didn't persecute! They even killed the ones who predicted the coming of the Righteous One—the

7:37 *much like me,* literally, "like unto me."

7:29
Ex 2:15
7:30
Ex 3:2
Deut 33:16
7:32
Ex 3:6
7:33
Josh 5:15
7:34
Ex 3:7,10
7:35
Ex 14:19
Num 20:16
7:36
Ex 7:3; 12:40,41
7:37
Deut 18:15
Mt 17:5
Acts 3:22
7:38
Ex 19:2,3,17
Deut 32:47
Rom 3:2
7:39
Num 14:3
7:40
Ex 32:1,23
7:42
Deut 17:2,3
Josh 24:20
2 Kgs 17:16
Amos 5:25-27
7:44
Ex 25.8,40
Heb 8:5
7:45
Josh 3:13,14
18:1; 22:19
2 Sam 7:6
1 Chron 17:5 21:29
2 Chron 1:3
7:46
2 Sam 7:1-14
1 Kgs 8:17
Ps 132:1-5
7:47
2 Sam 7:12,13
1 Kgs 8:20
7:48
2 Chron 2:6
Isa 57:15
Eph 2:22
1 Pet 2:5
7:49,50
Isa 66:1-2
7:51
Ex 32:9
Isa 48:4
Ezek 44:9
7:52
2 Chron 36:16
Mt 23:30-34

7:37 The Jews originally thought this "Prophet" was Joshua. But Moses was prophesying of the coming Messiah (Deuteronomy 18:15). Peter also quotes this verse in referring to the Messiah (Acts 3:22).

7:38 From Galatians 3:19 and Hebrews 2:2, it appears that God gave the law to Moses through angels. Exodus 31:18 says God wrote the Ten Commandments himself ("written with the finger of God"). Apparently God used angelic messengers to deliver his law to Moses.

7:44–50 Stephen had been accused of speaking against the Temple (6:13). Although he recognized the importance of the

Temple, he knew that it was not more important than God. God is not limited; he doesn't live only in a sanctuary, but wherever hearts of faith are open to receive him. Solomon knew this when he prayed at the dedication of the Temple (2 Chronicles 6:18; Isaiah 66:1, 2.)

7:52 Many prophets indeed were persecuted: Jeremiah (Jeremiah 38:1–6); Isaiah (tradition says he was killed by King Manasseh; see 2 Kings 21:16); Amos (Amos 7:10–13); Zechariah (2 Chronicles 24:20–22); Elijah (1 Kings 19:2). Jesus also told a parable about how the Jews had constantly rejected God's messages and persecuted his messengers (Luke 20:9–15).

Messiah whom you betrayed and murdered. 53Yes, and you deliberately destroyed God's Laws, though you received them from the hands of angels."

7:53
Ex 20:1
Gal 3:19

Stephen is martyred by stoning

54The Jewish leaders were stung to fury by Stephen's accusation, and ground their teeth in rage. 55But Stephen, full of the Holy Spirit, gazed steadily upward into heaven and saw the glory of God and Jesus standing at God's right hand. 56And he told them, "Look, I see the heavens opened and Jesus the Messiah standing beside God, at his right hand!"

7:55
Mt 26:64
Heb 1:3,13

7:56
Mt 3:16
Heb 9:24

57Then they mobbed him, putting their hands over their ears, and drowning out his voice with their shouts, 58and dragged him out of the city to stone him. The official witnesses—the executioners—took off their coats and laid them at the feet of a young man named Paul.

7:58
Lev 24:14-16
Deut 17:7

59And as the murderous stones came hurtling at him, Stephen prayed, "Lord Jesus, receive my spirit." 60And he fell to his knees, shouting, "Lord, don't charge them with this sin!" and with that, he died.

7:59
Ps 31:5
Lk 23:46

7:60
Mt 5:44
Lk 6:28; 23:34

2. Expansion of the church

Widespread persecution scatters the believers

8 Paul was in complete agreement with the killing of Stephen. And a great wave of persecution of the believers began that day, sweeping over the church in Jerusalem, and everyone except the apostles fled into Judea and Samaria. 2(But some godly Jews came and with great sorrow buried Stephen.) 3Paul was like a wild man, going everywhere to devastate the believers, even entering private homes and dragging out men and women alike and jailing them.

8:1
Acts 7:58

8:3
Acts 9:1; 22:4
26:10
1 Cor 15:9
Gal 1:13

4But the believers who had fled Jerusalem went everywhere preaching the Good News about Jesus! 5Philip, for instance, went to the city of Samaria and told the people there about Christ. 6Crowds listened intently to what he had to say because of the miracles he did. 7Many evil spirits were cast out, screaming as they left their victims, and many who were paralyzed or lame were healed, 8so there was much joy in that city!

8:4
Acts 11:19

8:5
Acts 6:5

8:7
Mt 10:1

7:53 *God's Laws, though you received them from the hands of angels,* literally, "the Law as it was ordained by angels." **7:56** *the Messiah,* literally, "the Son of Man." **7:58** *Paul,* also known as Saul. **8:2** *godly Jews,* literally, "devout men." It is not clear whether these were Christians who braved the persecution, or whether they were godly and sympathetic Jews. **8:4** *the believers,* literally, "the church."

●**7:55** Stephen saw the glory of God and Jesus the Messiah standing at God's right hand. Stephen's words are similar to Jesus' words spoken before the Council (Matthew 26:64; Mark 14:62; Luke 22:69). Stephen's vision supported Jesus' claim and angered the Jewish leaders who had condemned Jesus to death for blasphemy. They would not tolerate Stephen's words, so they mobbed him and killed him. People may not kill us for witnessing about Christ, but they will let us know they don't want to hear the truth and will often try to silence us. Keep honoring God in your conduct and words; though many will turn against you and your message, some will turn to Christ.

7:58 When Luke introduces Paul, Paul is hating and persecuting Jesus' followers. This is a great contrast to the Paul about whom Luke will write for most of the rest of the book of Acts—a devoted follower of Christ and a gifted gospel preacher. Paul was uniquely qualified to talk to the Jews about Jesus because he had once opposed him, and he understood how the opposition felt about him. In other translations, the name here is "Saul," which was his Hebrew name; Paul, his Greek name, was used after his conversion.

●**7:59** The penalty for blasphemy, speaking irreverently about God, was death by stoning (Leviticus 24:14). The religious leaders, in a rage and without trial or verdict, had Stephen stoned. They did not understand that Stephen's words were truth, because they were

not seeking the truth. They only wanted support for their own views. Stephen did not have widespread public support as Jesus had, so the leaders felt secure in stoning him.

●**7:60** As Stephen died, he repeated what Jesus had said as he died on the cross (Luke 23:34). The early believers were glad to suffer as Jesus had suffered, because that meant they were counted worthy (5:41). Stephen was ready to suffer like Jesus, even to the point of asking forgiveness for his murderers. Such a forgiving response comes only from the Holy Spirit. The Spirit can also help us respond as Stephen did and love our enemies (Luke 6:27). How would you respond if someone hurt you because of what you believe?

8:1–4 Persecution forced the Christians out of Jerusalem and into Judea and Samaria—thus fulfilling the next part of Jesus' command (see 1:8). The persecution helped spread the gospel. All the believers suffered, but God would bring great results from their suffering.

8:4 Persecution forced the believers out of their homes in Jerusalem, and with them went the gospel. Often we have to become uncomfortable before we'll move. Discomfort may be unwanted, but it is not undesirable, for out of our hurting, God works his purposes. The next time you are tempted to complain about uncomfortable or painful circumstances, stop and ask if God may be preparing you for a special task.

Philip and Simon the sorcerer

8:9
Acts 5:36; 13:6

8:12
Acts 1:3; 2:38

9, 10, 11A man named Simon had formerly been a sorcerer there for many years; he was a very influential, proud man because of the amazing things he could do—in fact, the Samaritan people often spoke of him as the Messiah. 12But now they believed Philip's message that Jesus was the Messiah, and his words concerning

8:9-11 *the Messiah,* literally, "this man is that Power of God which is called great."

MISSIONARIES OF THE NEW TESTAMENT AND THEIR JOURNEYS	Name	Journey Purpose	Scripture Reference in Acts
	Philip	One of the first to preach the gospel outside Jerusalem	8:4–40
	Peter and John	Visited new Samaritan believers to encourage them	8:14–25
	Paul (journey to Damascus)	Set out to capture Christians but was captured by Christ	9:1–25
	Peter	Led by God to one of the first Gentile families to become Christian—Cornelius' family	9:32—10:48
	Barnabas	Went to Antioch as an encourager; traveled on to Troas to bring Paul back to Jerusalem from Antioch	11:25–30
	Barnabas, Paul, John Mark	Left Antioch for Cyprus, Pamphylia, and Galatia on the first missionary journey	13:1—14:28
	Barnabas and John Mark	After a break with Paul, they left Antioch for Cyprus	15:36–41
	Paul, Silas, Timothy, Luke	Left Antioch to revisit churches in Galatia, then traveled on to Asia, Macedonia, and Achaia on a second missionary journey	15:36—18:22
	Apollos	Left Alexandria for Ephesus; learned the complete gospel story from Priscilla and Aquila; preached in Athens and Corinth	18:24–28
	Paul, Timothy, Erastus	Third major missionary journey revisiting churches in Galatia, Asia, Macedonia, and Achaia	18:23; 19:1—21:14

PHILIP'S MINISTRY

To escape persecution in Jerusalem, Philip fled to Samaria, where he continued preaching the gospel. While he was there, an angel commanded him to meet an Ethiopian official on the road between Jerusalem and Gaza. The official became a believer before continuing to Ethiopia. Philip then went from Azotus to Caesarea.

north, Samaria in the middle, and Judea in the south. The city of Samaria (in the region of Samaria) had been the capital of the Northern Kingdom of Israel in the days of the divided kingdom, before it was conquered by Assyria in 722 B.C. The Assyrian king took many captives, leaving only the poorest people in the land and resettling it with foreigners. These foreigners intermarried with the Jews who were left, and the mixed race became known as Samaritans. The Samaritans were considered half-breeds by the "pure" Jews in the Southern Kingdom of Judah, and there was intense hatred between the two groups. But Jesus himself went into Samaria (John 4), and he commanded his followers to spread the gospel even there (1:8).

8:7 Jesus encountered and cast out many demons during his ministry on earth. Demons, or evil spirits, are ruled by Satan. They are probably fallen angels who joined Satan in his rebellion against God, and they can cause a person to be mute, deaf, blind, or insane. They also tempt people to sin. Demons are real and active, but Jesus has authority over them, and he gave this authority to his followers. Although he permits Satan to work in our world, God is in complete control. His power can cast demons out and end their destructive work in people's lives. Eventually Satan and his demons will be bound forever, ending their evil work in the world (Revelation 20:10).

8:9–11 In the days of the early church, sorcerers and magicians were numerous and influential. They worked wonders, performed healings and exorcisms, and practiced astrology. Simon the sorcerer had done so many wonders that some even thought he was the Messiah, but his powers did not come from God (see 8:18–24).

● **8:5** This is not the apostle Philip (see John 1:43, 44), but a Greek-speaking Jew, "wise and full of the Holy Spirit," who was one of the seven deacons chosen to help with the food distribution program in the church (6:5).

8:5 Israel was divided into three main regions—Galilee in the

the Kingdom of God; and many men and women were baptized. ¹³Then Simon himself believed and was baptized and began following Philip wherever he went, and was amazed by the miracles he did.

¹⁴When the apostles back in Jerusalem heard that the people of Samaria had accepted God's message, they sent down Peter and John. ¹⁵As soon as they arrived, they began praying for these new Christians to receive the Holy Spirit, ¹⁶for as yet he had not come upon any of them. For they had only been baptized in the name of the Lord Jesus. ¹⁷Then Peter and John laid their hands upon these believers, and they received the Holy Spirit.

¹⁸When Simon saw this—that the Holy Spirit was given when the apostles placed their hands upon people's heads—he offered money to buy this power.

¹⁹"Let me have this power too," he exclaimed, "so that when I lay my hands on people, they will receive the Holy Spirit!"

²⁰But Peter replied, "Your money perish with you for thinking God's gift can be bought! ²¹You can have no part in this, for your heart is not right before God. ²²Turn from this great wickedness and pray. Perhaps God will yet forgive your evil thoughts— ²³for I can see that there is jealousy and sin in your heart."

²⁴"Pray for me," Simon exclaimed, "that these terrible things won't happen to me."

²⁵After testifying and preaching in Samaria, Peter and John returned to Jerusalem, stopping at several Samaritan villages along the way to preach the Good News to them too.

Philip and the Ethiopian official

²⁶But as for Philip, an angel of the Lord said to him, "Go over to the road that runs from Jerusalem through the Gaza Desert, arriving around noon." ²⁷So he did, and who should be coming down the road but the Treasurer of Ethiopia, a eunuch of great authority under Candace the queen. He had gone to Jerusalem to worship, ²⁸and was now returning in his chariot, reading aloud from the book of the prophet Isaiah.

²⁹The Holy Spirit said to Philip, "Go over and walk along beside the chariot."

8:23 *jealousy,* literally, "the gall of bitterness."

Cross-references:
8:13 Acts 19:11
8:14 Acts 8:1
8:15 Acts 2:38; 19:2
8:16 Acts 10:48
8:17 Acts 2:4
8:20 Mic 3:11,12; Mt 10:8; Acts 2:38
8:21 Jer 17:9; Eph 5:5
8:22 Isa 55:7; Dan 4:27
8:23 Heb 12:15
8:24 Gen 20:7; Ex 8:8; Num 21:7; Job 42:8; Jas 5:16
8:26 Ps 91:11; Heb 1:14
8:27 1 Kgs 8:41,42; Ps 68:29; Isa 43:6; 53:7; 56:3; Zeph 3:10

8:14 Peter and John were sent to Samaria to find out whether or not the Samaritans were truly becoming believers. The Jewish Christians, even the apostles, were still unsure whether Gentiles (non-Jews) and half-Jews could receive the Holy Spirit. It wasn't until Peter's experience with Cornelius (chapter 10) that the apostles became fully convinced that the Holy Spirit was for all people. It was John who had asked Jesus if they should call fire down from heaven to burn up a Samaritan village which refused to welcome them (Luke 9:49–55). Now he and Peter went to the Samaritans to pray with them.

● **8:15–17** This was a crucial moment in the spread of the gospel and the growth of the church, and the apostles, Peter and John, had to go to Samaria to help keep this new group of believers from becoming segregated from other believers. When Peter and John saw the Holy Spirit working in these people, they were assured that the Holy Spirit worked through all believers—Gentiles and mixed races as well as the "pure" Jews.

8:17–20 "Everything has a price" seems to be true in our world of bribes, wealth, and materialism. Simon thought he could buy the Holy Spirit's power, but Peter harshly rebuked him. The only way to receive God's power is to do as Peter told Simon—turn from sin, ask God for forgiveness, and be filled with his Spirit. No amount of money can buy salvation, forgiveness of sin, or God's power. These are only gained by repentance and belief in Christ as Savior.

8:24 Do you remember the last time a parent or friend rebuked you harshly? Were you hurt? Angry? Defensive? Learn a lesson from Simon and his reaction to Peter's rebuke. He exclaimed, "Pray for me!" If you are rebuked for a serious mistake, it is for your good. Admit your error, repent quickly, and ask for prayer.

● **8:26** Philip had a successful preaching ministry to great crowds in Samaria (8:5–7), but he obediently left that ministry to go to a desert road. Because Philip went where God sent him, Ethiopia was opened to the gospel. Follow God's leading, even if it appears to be a demotion. You may not understand his plans at first, but the results will leave no doubt of the rightness of following wherever he leads.

● **8:27** Ethiopia was located in Africa south of Egypt. The eunuch was obviously very dedicated to God because he came such a long distance to worship in Jerusalem. The Jews had contact with Ethiopia in ancient days (Psalm 68:31; Jeremiah 38:7), so this man may have been a Gentile convert to Judaism. Because he was the treasurer of Ethiopia, his conversion brought Christianity into the power structures of another government. This is the beginning of the witness "to the ends of the earth" (1:8). Isaiah had prophesied that Gentiles and eunuchs would be blessed (Isaiah 56:3–5).

8:29–35 Philip found the Ethiopian man reading the Scriptures, and he took advantage of this opportunity to explain the gospel by asking if the man understood what he was reading. Philip (1) followed the Spirit's leading, (2) began the discussion from where the man was—immersed in the prophecies of Isaiah, and (3)

30Philip ran over and heard what he was reading and asked, "Do you understand it?"

8:31
2 Cor 3:14

31"Of course not!" the man replied. "How can I when there is no one to instruct me?" And he begged Philip to come up into the chariot and sit with him.

8:32,33
Isa 53:7,8
Phil 2:7,8

32The passage of Scripture he had been reading from was this:

"He was led as a sheep to the slaughter, and as a lamb is silent before the shearers, so he opened not his mouth; 33in his humiliation, justice was denied him; and who can express the wickedness of the people of his generation? For his life is taken from the earth."

34The eunuch asked Philip, "Was Isaiah talking about himself or someone else?"

8:35
Lk 24:27
Acts 18:28

35So Philip began with this same Scripture and then used many others to tell him about Jesus.

36As they rode along, they came to a small body of water, and the eunuch said, "Look! Water! Why can't I be baptized?"

8:37
Mt 16:16; 28:19
Mk 16:16
Jn 6:69; 11:27
Rom 10:10

37"You can," Philip answered, "if you believe with all your heart."

And the eunuch replied, "I believe that Jesus Christ is the Son of God."

8:39
1 Kgs 18:12
2 Kgs 2:16
Ezek 3:12

38He stopped the chariot, and they went down into the water and Philip baptized him. 39And when they came up out of the water, the Spirit of the Lord caught away Philip, and the eunuch never saw him again, but went on his way rejoicing. 40Meanwhile, Philip found himself at Azotus! He preached the Good News there and in every city along the way, as he traveled to Caesarea.

Paul is converted on the way to Damascus

9:1
Acts 8:3
Gal 1:13
1 Tim 1:13

9:2
Acts 22:5; 26:10

9 But Paul, threatening with every breath and eager to destroy every Christian, went to the High Priest in Jerusalem. 2He requested a letter addressed to synagogues in Damascus, requiring their cooperation in the persecution of any believers he found there, both men and women, so that he could bring them in chains to Jerusalem.

8:33 *who can express the wickedness of the people of his generation,* implied. Literally, "Who can declare his generation?" Alternatively, "Who will be able to speak of his posterity? For . . ."   **8:37** Many ancient manuscripts omit vs 37 wholly or in part.

---

explained how Jesus Christ fulfilled Isaiah's prophecies. When we share the gospel, we should start where the other person's concerns are focused. Then we can bring the gospel to bear on those concerns.

8:30, 31 The eunuch begged Philip to explain a passage of Scripture which he did not understand. When we do not understand the Bible, we should ask others to help us. We must never let our pride get in the way of understanding God's Word.

8:35 Some think the Old Testament is not relevant today, but Philip led this man to faith in Jesus Christ by using Old Testament Scripture. Jesus Christ is found in the pages of both the Old and New Testaments. God's entire Word is applicable to all people in all ages. We must not neglect to use the Old Testament, because it too is God's Word.

8:39, 40 Why was Philip suddenly transported to a different city? This miraculous sign showed the urgency of bringing the Gentiles to belief in Christ.

9:2 Why would the Jews in Jerusalem want to persecute Christians as far away as Damascus? There are several possibilities: (1) to seize the Christians who had fled, (2) to contain and prevent the spread of Christianity to other major cities, (3) to keep the Christians from provoking any problems with Rome, (4) to advance Paul's career and build his reputation as a true Pharisee zealous for the law, (5) to unify the factions of Judaism by giving them a common enemy.

PAUL TRAVELS TO DAMASCUS
Many Christians fled Jerusalem when persecution began after Stephen's death, seeking refuge in other cities and countries. Paul tracked them down, even traveling 150 miles to Damascus in Syria to bring Christians back in chains to Jerusalem. But as he neared the ancient city, he discovered that God had other plans for him (9:15).

³As he was nearing Damascus on this mission, suddenly a brilliant light from heaven spotted down upon him! ⁴He fell to the ground and heard a voice saying to him, "Paul! Paul! Why are you persecuting me?"

9:3
Acts 22:6,7
26:12,13
1 Cor 15:8

GREAT ESCAPES IN THE BIBLE

Who escaped	Reference	What happened	What the escape accomplished	Application
Jacob	Genesis 31:1–55	Left his father-in-law, Laban, after almost 20 years of service	Allowed Jacob to return home for Isaac's death and for reconciliation with Esau, his brother	A time away from home often puts the really important things into perspective
Moses	Exodus 2:11–15	Fled Egypt after killing an Egyptian in defense of a fellow Israelite	Saved his own life and began another part of God's training	God even fits our mistakes into his plan
Israelites	Exodus 12:28–42	Escaped Egypt after 430 years, most of that time in slavery	God confirmed his choice of Abraham's descendants	God will not forget his promises
Spies	Joshua 2:1–24	Escaped searchers in Jericho by hiding in Rahab's house	Prepared the destruction of Jericho, preserved Rahab who would become one of David's ancestors—as well as an ancestor of Jesus	God's plan weaves lives together in a pattern beyond our understanding
Ehud	Judges 3:15–30	Assassinated the Moabite King Eglon, but escaped undetected	Broke the control of Moab over Israel and began 80 years of peace	Punishments by God are often swift and deadly
Samson	Judges 16:1–3	Escaped a locked city by ripping the gates from their hinges	Merely postponed Samson's self-destruction because of his lack of self-control	Without dependence on God and his guidance, even great ability is wasted
Elijah	1 Kings 19:1–18	Fled into the desert out of fear of Queen Jezebel	Preserved Elijah's life, but also displayed his human weakness	Even at moments of real success, our personal weaknesses are our greatest challenges
Paul	Acts 9:25	Lowered over the wall in a basket to get out of Damascus	Saved this new Christian for great service to God	God has a purpose for every life, which becomes a real adventure for those willing to cooperate
Peter	Acts 12:1–11	Freed from prison by an angel	Saved Peter for God's further plans for his life	God can use extraordinary means to carry out his plan—often when we least expect it
Paul and Silas	Acts 16:22–40	Chains loosened and doors opened by an earthquake, but they chose not to leave the prison	Pointed out the powerlessness of men before God	When our dependence and attention are focused on God rather than our problems, he is able to offer help in unexpected ways

●**9:3** Damascus, a key commercial city, was located about 150 miles northeast of Jerusalem in the Roman province of Syria. Several trade routes linked Damascus to other cities throughout the Roman world. Paul may have thought that by stamping out Christianity in Damascus, he could prevent its spread to other areas.

●**9:2, 3** As Paul traveled to Damascus, pursuing Christians, he was confronted by the risen Christ and brought face to face with the truth of the gospel. Sometimes God breaks into a life in a spectacular manner, and sometimes conversion is a quiet experience. Beware of people who insist you must have a particular type of conversion experience. The right way to come to faith in Jesus is whatever way God brings you.

●**9:3** Paul refers to this experience as the start of his new life in Christ (1 Corinthians 9:1; 15:8; Galatians 1:15, 16). At the center of this wonderful experience was Jesus Christ—Paul did not see a vision, he saw the risen Christ himself (9:17). Paul recognized

9:5
Acts 5:39

9:7
Dan 10:7
Acts 22:9; 26:14

9:10
Acts 10:3;
11:5; 12:9; 22:12

9:11
Acts 21:39

5"Who is speaking, sir?" Paul asked.

And the voice replied, "I am Jesus, the one you are persecuting! 6Now get up and go into the city and await my further instructions."

7The men with Paul stood speechless with surprise, for they heard the sound of someone's voice but saw no one! 8, 9As Paul picked himself up off the ground, he found that he was blind. He had to be led into Damascus and was there three days, blind, going without food and water all that time.

10Now there was in Damascus a believer named Ananias. The Lord spoke to him in a vision, calling, "Ananias!"

"Yes, Lord!" he replied.

11And the Lord said, "Go over to Straight Street and find the house of a man named Judas and ask there for Paul of Tarsus. He is praying to me right now, for

PHILIP

Jesus' last words to his followers were a command to take the gospel everywhere, but they seemed reluctant to leave Jerusalem. It took intense persecution to scatter the believers from Jerusalem and into Judea and Samaria, where Jesus had instructed them to go. Philip, one of the deacons in charge of food distribution, left Jerusalem and, like most Jewish Christians, spread the gospel wherever he went; but unlike most of them, he did not limit his audience to other Jews. He went directly to Samaria, the last place many Jews would go, due to age-old prejudice.

The Samaritans responded in large numbers. When word got back to Jerusalem, Peter and John were sent to evaluate Philip's ministry. They quickly became involved themselves, seeing firsthand God's acceptance of those who previously were considered unacceptable.

In the middle of all this success and excitement, God directed Philip out to the desert for an appointment with an Ethiopian eunuch, another foreigner, who had been in Jerusalem. Philip went immediately. His effectiveness in sharing the gospel with this man placed a Christian in a significant position in a distant country, and may well have had an effect on an entire nation.

Philip ended up in Caesarea, where events allowed him to be Paul's host many years later. Paul, who as the leading persecutor of the Christians had been instrumental in pushing Philip and others out of Jerusalem, had himself become an effective believer. The conversion of the Gentiles begun by Philip was continued across the entire Roman empire by Paul.

Whether or not you are a follower of Christ, Philip's life presents a challenge. To those still outside the gospel, he is a reminder that the gospel is for you also. To those who have accepted Christ, he is a reminder that we are not free to disqualify anyone from hearing about Jesus. How much like Philip would your neighbors say you are?

Strengths and accomplishments:
- One of the seven organizers of food distribution in the early church
- Became an evangelist, one of the first traveling missionaries
- One of the first to obey Jesus' command to take the gospel to all people
- A careful student of the Bible who could explain its meaning clearly

Lessons from his life:
- God finds great and various uses for those willing to obey wholeheartedly
- The gospel is universal Good News
- The whole Bible, not just the New Testament, helps us understand more about Jesus
- Both mass response (the Samaritans) and individual response (the man from Ethiopia) to the gospel are valuable

Vital statistics:
- Occupation: Deacon, evangelist
- Relatives: Four daughters
- Contemporaries: Paul, Stephen, the apostles

Key verse:
"So Philip began with this same Scripture and then used many others to tell him about Jesus" (Acts 8:35).

Philip's story is told in Acts 6:1–7; 8:5–40; 21:8–10.

Jesus as Lord, realized his own sin, surrendered his life to Jesus, and resolved to obey. True conversion comes from a personal encounter with Jesus Christ and leads to a new life in relationship with him.

9:5 Paul thought he was persecuting heretics, but he was persecuting Jesus himself. Anyone who persecutes believers today is also guilty of persecuting Jesus (see Matthew 25:45), because believers are the body of Christ on earth.

12I have shown him a vision of a man named Ananias coming in and laying his hands on him so that he can see again!"

13"But Lord," exclaimed Ananias, "I have heard about the terrible things this man has done to the believers in Jerusalem! 14And we hear that he has arrest warrants with him from the chief priests, authorizing him to arrest every believer in Damascus!"

15But the Lord said, "Go and do what I say. For Paul is my chosen instrument to take my message to the nations and before kings, as well as to the people of Israel. 16And I will show him how much he must suffer for me."

17So Ananias went over and found Paul and laid his hands on him and said, "Brother Paul, the Lord Jesus, who appeared to you on the road, has sent me so that you may be filled with the Holy Spirit and get your sight back."

18Instantly (it was as though scales fell from his eyes) Paul could see, and was immediately baptized.

19Then he ate and was strengthened.

Paul preaches boldly

He stayed with the believers in Damascus for a few days 20and went at once to the synagogue to tell everyone there the Good News about Jesus—that he is indeed the Son of God!

21All who heard him were amazed. "Isn't this the same man who persecuted Jesus' followers so bitterly in Jerusalem?" they asked. "And we understand that he came here to arrest them all and take them in chains to the chief priests."

22Paul became more and more fervent in his preaching, and the Damascus Jews couldn't withstand his proofs that Jesus was indeed the Christ.

23After a while the Jewish leaders determined to kill him. 24But Paul was told about their plans, that they were watching the gates of the city day and night prepared to murder him. 25So during the night some of his converts let him down in a basket through an opening in the city wall!

26Upon arrival in Jerusalem he tried to meet with the believers, but they were all afraid of him. They thought he was faking! 27Then Barnabas brought him to the apostles and told them how Paul had seen the Lord on the way to Damascus, what the Lord had said to him, and all about his powerful preaching in the name of Jesus. 28Then they accepted him, and after that he was constantly with the believers 29and preached boldly in the name of the Lord. But then some Greek-speaking Jews with whom he had argued plotted to murder him. 30However, when the other believers

9:13
Acts 26:10
9:14
1 Cor 1:2
9:15
Acts 13:2
22:21; 26:1-18
Rom 1:1,5
11:13
Gal 1:15,16
Eph 3:7
1 Tim 2:7
2 Tim 1:11
9:16
Acts 20:23
21:11
2 Cor 11:23-27
9:17
Acts 2:4; 13:52
22:12,13
9:19
Acts 26:20

9:21
Acts 8:3
Gal 1:13
9:22
Acts 18:28
9:23
Gal 1:17,18
9:24
Acts 20:3; 23:12
25:3
2 Cor 11:32
9:25
Josh 2:15
1 Sam 19:12
9:26
Acts 22:17,18
9:27
Acts 4:36
11:24; 13:2

● **9:13** "Not him, Lord, that's impossible. He could never become a Christian!" This was the essence of Ananias' response when God told him of Paul's conversion. After all, Paul had pursued believers to their death. Despite these understandable feelings, Ananias obeyed God and ministered to Paul. We must not limit God. He can do anything. We must obey, following God's leading even to difficult people and places.

9:15, 16 Christianity involves not only great blessings but often great suffering too. Paul would suffer for his faith (see 2 Corinthians 11:23–27). God calls us to commitment, not to comfort. He promises to be with us through suffering and hardship, not to spare us from them.

9:17 Ananias found Paul, as he had been instructed, and greeted him as "Brother Paul." Ananias feared this meeting; after all, Paul had come to Damascus to persecute the believers and take them in chains to Jerusalem (9:2). Yet in obedience to the Holy Spirit he greeted Paul lovingly. It is not always easy to show love to others, especially if we are afraid of them or doubt their motives. Nevertheless, we must follow Jesus' command (John 13:34) and Ananias' example, showing loving acceptance to other believers.

9:20 Immediately after receiving his sight, Paul went to the synagogue to tell the Jews about Jesus Christ. Some Christians

counsel new believers to wait until they are thoroughly grounded in their faith before attempting to share the gospel. Paul took time alone to learn about Jesus before beginning his worldwide ministry, but he did not wait to witness. Although we should not rush into a ministry unprepared, we do not need to wait before telling others what has happened to us.

9:23 According to Galatians 1:17, 18, Paul left Damascus and traveled to Arabia, the desert region just southeast of Damascus, where he lived for three years. It is unclear whether his three-year stay occurred between verses 22 and 23, or between verses 25 and 26. Some commentators say that "a while" could mean a long period of time. They suggest that when Paul returned to Damascus, the governor under Aretas ordered his arrest (2 Corinthians 11:32), probably trying to keep peace with influential Jews.

The other possibility is that Paul's night escape occurred during his first stay in Damascus, just after his conversion when the Pharisees were especially upset over his defection from their ranks. He would have fled to Arabia to let the Jewish religious leaders cool down as well as to spend time alone with God. Regardless of which theory is correct, there was a period of at least three years between Paul's conversion (9:3–6) and his trip to Jerusalem (9:26).

PAUL

No person, apart from Jesus himself, shaped the history of Christianity like the apostle Paul. Even before he was a believer, his actions were significant. His frenzied persecution of Christians following Stephen's death got the church started in obeying Christ's final command to take the gospel worldwide. Paul's personal encounter with Jesus changed his life. He never lost his fierce intensity, but from then on it was channeled for the gospel.

Paul was very religious. His training under Gamaliel was the finest available. His intentions and efforts were sincere. He was a good Pharisee, knew the Bible, and sincerely believed that this Christian movement was dangerous to Judaism. Thus Paul hated the Christian faith and persecuted Christians without mercy.

Paul got permission to travel to Damascus to capture Christians and bring them back to Jerusalem. But God stopped him in his hurried tracks on the Damascus road. Paul personally met Jesus Christ, and his life was never the same.

Until Paul's conversion, little had been done about carrying the gospel to non-Jews. Philip had preached in Samaria and to an Ethiopian man; Cornelius, a Gentile, was converted under Peter; and in Antioch in Syria, some Greeks had joined the believers. When Barnabas was sent from Jerusalem to check on this situation, he went to Tarsus to find Paul and bring him to Antioch, and together they worked among the believers there. They were then sent on a missionary journey, the first of three Paul would take, that would carry the gospel across the Roman Empire.

The thorny issue of whether Gentile believers had to obey Jewish laws before they could become Christians caused many problems in the early church. Paul worked hard to convince the Jews that Gentiles were acceptable to God, but he spent even more time convincing the Gentiles that they were acceptable to God. The lives Paul touched were changed and challenged by meeting Christ through him.

God did not waste any part of Paul—his background, his training, his citizenship, his mind, or even his weaknesses. Are you willing to let God do the same for you? You will never know all he can do with you until you allow him to have all that you are!

Strengths and accomplishments:
- Transformed by God from a persecutor of Christians to a preacher for Christ
- Preached for Christ throughout the Roman Empire on three missionary journeys
- Wrote letters to various churches, which became part of the New Testament
- Was never afraid to face an issue head-on and deal with it
- Was sensitive to God's leading and, despite his strong personality, always did as God directed
- Is often called the apostle to the Gentiles

Weaknesses and mistakes:
- Witnessed and approved of Stephen's stoning
- Set out to destroy Christianity by persecuting Christians

Lessons from his life:
- The Good News is that forgiveness and eternal life are a gift of God's grace received by faith in Christ and available to all people
- Obedience results from a relationship with God, but obedience will never create or earn that relationship
- Real freedom doesn't come until we no longer have to prove our freedom
- God does not waste our time—he will use our past and present so we may serve him with our future

Vital statistics:
- Where: Born in Tarsus, but became a world traveler for Christ
- Occupations: Trained as a Pharisee, learned the tentmaking trade, served as a missionary
- Contemporaries: Gamaliel, Stephen, the apostles, Luke, Barnabas, Timothy

Key verses:
"For to me, living means opportunities for Christ, and dying—well, that's better yet! But if living will give me more opportunities to win people to Christ, then I really don't know which is better, to live or die" (Philippians 1:21, 22).

Paul's story is told in Acts 7:58—28:31 and throughout his New Testament letters.

9:27 It is difficult to change your reputation, and Paul had a terrible reputation with the Christians. But Barnabas, one of the Jewish converts mentioned in 4:36, became the bridge between Paul and the apostles. New Christians especially need sponsors, people who will come alongside, encourage, teach, and introduce them to other believers. Find ways that you can become a Barnabas to new believers.

9:27 Galatians 1:18, 19 tells us that Paul was in Jerusalem only 15 days and that he met only with Peter and James.

heard about his danger, they took him to Caesarea and then sent him to his home in Tarsus.

³¹Meanwhile, the church had peace throughout Judea, Galilee and Samaria, and grew in strength and numbers. The believers learned how to walk in the fear of the Lord and in the comfort of the Holy Spirit.

9:31
Acts 5:11; 8:1

Peter heals Aeneas and Dorcas

³²Peter traveled from place to place to visit them, and in his travels came to the believers in the town of Lydda. ³³There he met a man named Aeneas, paralyzed and bedridden for eight years.

9:32
Acts 8:14

³⁴Peter said to him, "Aeneas! Jesus Christ has healed you! Get up and make your bed." And he was healed instantly. ³⁵Then the whole population of Lydda and Sharon turned to the Lord when they saw Aeneas walking around.

9:34
Mt 9:6
Jn 5:8
Acts 3:6; 4:10

³⁶In the city of Joppa there was a woman named Dorcas ("Gazelle"), a believer who was always doing kind things for others, especially for the poor. ³⁷About this time she became ill and died. Her friends prepared her for burial and laid her in an upstairs room. ³⁸But when they learned that Peter was nearby at Lydda, they sent two men to beg him to return with them to Joppa. ³⁹This he did; as soon as he arrived, they took him upstairs where Dorcas lay. The room was filled with weeping widows who were showing one another the coats and other garments Dorcas had made for them. ⁴⁰But Peter asked them all to leave the room; then he knelt and prayed. Turning to the body he said, "Get up, Dorcas," and she opened her eyes! And when she saw Peter, she sat up! ⁴¹He gave her his hand and helped her up and called in the believers and widows, presenting her to them.

9:35
Acts 11:21
9:36
Prov 31:31
1 Tim 2:9,10
5:10
Tit 3:8
Jas 1:27

9:40
1 Kgs 17:19-23
2 Kgs 4:32-36
Mt 9:25
Mk 5:41,42
Jn 11:43

9:32 *to visit them,* implied.   **9:40** *Dorcas,* literally, "Tabitha," her name in Hebrew.

PAUL'S RETURN TO TARSUS
At least three years elapsed between Acts 9:22 and 9:26. After time alone in Arabia (see Galatians 1:16–18), Paul returned to Damascus and then to Jerusalem. The apostles were reluctant to believe that this former persecutor could be one of them. He escaped this time to Caesarea where he caught a ship and returned to Tarsus, his hometown.

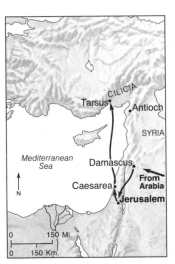

9:31 Paul's visit to Tarsus helped quiet conflicts with the Jews and allowed Paul time to prove his commitment. After Paul, the most zealous persecutor, was converted, the church enjoyed a brief time of relative peace.

9:36 The important harbor city of Joppa sits 125 feet above sea level overlooking the Mediterranean Sea. Joppa was the town into which the cedars of Lebanon were floated to be shipped to Jerusalem and used in the Temple construction (2 Chronicles 2:16; Ezra 3:7). The prophet Jonah left the port of Joppa on his ill-fated trip (Jonah 1:3).

9:36–42 Dorcas made an enormous impact on her community by "always doing kind things for others, especially for the poor." When she died, the room was filled with mourners, people she had helped. And when she was brought back to life, the news raced through the town. God uses great preachers like Peter and Paul, but he also uses those who have gifts of kindness like Dorcas. Rather than wishing you had other gifts, make good use of the gifts God has given you.

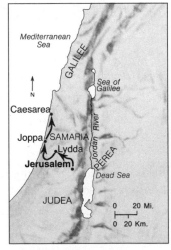

PETER'S MINISTRY
Peter traveled to the ancient crossroads town of Lydda, where he healed crippled Aeneas. The believers in Joppa, an old port city, sent for him after a wonderful woman died, and Peter brought her back to life. While in Joppa, Peter had a vision that led him to open the gospel to Cornelius, a Gentile, in Caesarea.

9:42
Jn 11:45; 12:11

42The news raced through the town, and many believed in the Lord. 43And Peter stayed a long time in Joppa, living with Simon, the tanner.

Peter and Cornelius

10:1
Acts 8:40; 27:1

10:2
Gen 18:19
Josh 24:15

10:3
Ps 34:7
Acts 11:13
Heb 1:14

10:4
2 Chron 7:15
Ps 65:1,2
141:2
Prov 15:29
Heb 6:10; 13:16
Jas 5:16
1 Pet 3:2
Rev 5:8; 8:4

10:6
Acts 9:43; 11:14

10:9
Ps 55:17
Acts 11:5

10:11
Ezek 1:1-3
Mt 3:16
Acts 7:56
Rev 19:11

10:14
Lev 11:4-7
20:25
Deut 14:3-5
Ezek 4:14

10:15
Mt 15:11
Rom 14:14,17,
20
1 Cor 10:25
1 Tim 4:4
Tit 1:15

10:19
Acts 8:29; 11:12

10:20
Mt 28:19
Mk 16:15
Acts 15:7

10 In Caesarea there lived a Roman army officer, Cornelius, a captain of an Italian regiment. 2He was a godly man, deeply reverent, as was his entire household. He gave generously to charity and was a man of prayer. 3While wide awake one afternoon he had a vision—it was about three o'clock—and in this vision he saw an angel of God coming toward him.

"Cornelius!" the angel said.

4Cornelius stared at him in terror. "What do you want, sir?" he asked the angel.

And the angel replied, "Your prayers and charities have not gone unnoticed by God! 5, 6Now send some men to Joppa to find a man named Simon Peter, who is staying with Simon, the tanner, down by the shore, and ask him to come and visit you."

7As soon as the angel was gone, Cornelius called two of his household servants and a godly soldier, one of his personal bodyguard, 8and told them what had happened and sent them off to Joppa.

9, 10The next day, as they were nearing the city, Peter went up on the flat roof of his house to pray. It was noon and he was hungry, but while lunch was being prepared, he fell into a trance. 11He saw the sky open, and a great canvas sheet, suspended by its four corners, settle to the ground. 12In the sheet were all sorts of animals, snakes and birds [forbidden to the Jews for food].

13Then a voice said to him, "Go kill and eat any of them you wish."

14"Never, Lord," Peter declared, "I have never in all my life eaten such creatures, for they are forbidden by our Jewish laws."

15The voice spoke again, "Don't contradict God! If he says something is kosher, then it is."

16The same vision was repeated three times. Then the sheet was pulled up again to heaven.

17Peter was very perplexed. What could the vision mean? What was he supposed to do?

Just then the men sent by Cornelius had found the house and were standing outside at the gate, 18inquiring whether this was the place where Simon Peter lived!

19Meanwhile, as Peter was puzzling over the vision, the Holy Spirit said to him, "Three men have come to see you. 20Go down and meet them and go with them. All is well, I have sent them."

10:11 *a great canvas sheet*, implied.

9:43 In Joppa, Peter stayed at the home of Simon, a tanner. Tanners made animal hides into leather. It is significant that Peter was at Simon's house, because tanning involved contact with dead animals, and Jewish law considered it an unclean job. Peter was already beginning to break down his prejudice against people and customs that did not adhere to Jewish religious tradition.

10:1 This Caesarea, sometimes called Palestinian Caesarea, was located on the coast of the Mediterranean Sea, 32 miles north of Joppa. The largest and most important port city on the Mediterranean in Palestine, it served as the capital of the Roman province of Judea. This was the first city to have Gentile Christians and a non-Jewish church.

10:1 This Roman officer was a *centurion*, a commander of 100 soldiers. Although stationed in Caesarea, Cornelius would probably soon return to Rome. Thus his conversion was a major stepping stone for spreading the gospel to the capital city.

● **10:2** "What about the heathen who have never heard about

Christ?" This is a common question asked about God's justice. Cornelius wasn't a Christian, but he was seeking God, and he was a reverent and generous man. Therefore God sent Peter to tell Cornelius about Jesus. Cornelius is an example that God "rewards those who sincerely look for him" (Hebrews 11:6). Those who sincerely seek God will find him! God made Cornelius' knowledge complete.

10:12 According to Jewish law, certain foods were forbidden (see Leviticus 11). The food laws made it hard for Jews to eat with Gentiles without risking defilement. In fact, the Gentiles themselves were often seen as "unclean." Peter's vision meant that he was not to look upon the Gentiles as inferior people whom God would not redeem. Before having the vision, Peter would have thought a Gentile Roman officer could not accept Christ. Afterward, he understood that he should go with the messengers into a Gentile home and tell Cornelius the Good News of salvation in Jesus Christ.

21So Peter went down. "I'm the man you're looking for," he said. "Now what is it you want?"

22Then they told him about Cornelius the Roman officer, a good and godly man, well thought of by the Jews, and how an angel had instructed him to send for Peter to come and tell him what God wanted him to do.

10:22
Acts 10:2

23So Peter invited them in and lodged them overnight.

The next day he went with them, accompanied by some other believers from Joppa.

10:23
Acts 10:45; 11:12

24They arrived in Caesarea the following day, and Cornelius was waiting for him, and had called together his relatives and close friends to meet Peter. 25As Peter entered his home, Cornelius fell to the floor before him in worship.

10:24
Acts 8:40; 10:1

26But Peter said, "Stand up! I'm not a god!"

10:26
Lk 4:8
Acts 14:14
Col 2:18
Rev 19:10; 22:9

27So he got up and they talked together for a while and then went in where the others were assembled.

28Peter told them, "You know it is against the Jewish laws for me to come into a Gentile home like this. But God has shown me in a vision that I should never think of anyone as inferior. 29So I came as soon as I was sent for. Now tell me what you want."

10:28
Jn 4:9
Acts 11:3; 15:9
Gal 2:12

30Cornelius replied, "Four days ago I was praying as usual at this time of the afternoon, when suddenly a man was standing before me clothed in a radiant robe! 31He told me, 'Cornelius, your prayers are heard and your charities have been noticed by God! 32Now send some men to Joppa and summon Simon Peter, who is staying in the home of Simon, a tanner, down by the shore.' 33So I sent for you at once, and you have done well to come so soon. Now here we are, waiting before the Lord, anxious to hear what he has told you to tell us!"

10:30
Acts 10:3-6

10:31
Prov 14:31
Dan 10:12
Mt 6:4; 10:42
Heb 6:10

Peter preaches in Cornelius' house

34Then Peter replied, "I see very clearly that the Jews are not God's only favorites! 35In every nation he has those who worship him and do good deeds and are acceptable to him. 36, 37I'm sure you have heard about the Good News for the people of Israel—that there is peace with God through Jesus, the Messiah, who is Lord of all creation. This message has spread all through Judea, beginning with John the Baptist in Galilee. 38And you no doubt know that Jesus of Nazareth was anointed by God with the Holy Spirit and with power, and he went around doing good and healing all who were possessed by demons, for God was with him.

10:34
Rom 2:11
Col 3:11,25

10:35
Rom 3:9-24
Eph 2:13; 3:6

10:36
Rom 5:1
Eph 2:17

10:38
Lk 4:18,19

39"And we apostles are witnesses of all he did throughout Israel and in Jerusalem, where he was murdered on a cross. 40, 41But God brought him back to life again three days later and showed him to certain witnesses God had selected beforehand—not to the general public, but to us who ate and drank with him after he rose from the dead. 42And he sent us to preach the Good News everywhere and to testify that Jesus is ordained of God to be the Judge of all—living and dead. 43And all the prophets have written about him, saying that everyone who believes in him will have their sins forgiven through his name."

10:39
Lk 24:40

10:40,41
Jn 21:13

10:42
Mt 28:19
2 Cor 5:10

10:43
Isa 53:11
Jer 31:34

44Even as Peter was saying these things, the Holy Spirit fell upon all those listening! 45The Jews who came with Peter were amazed that the gift of the Holy

10:44
Acts 11:15; 15:8

10:34, 35 Perhaps the greatest barrier to the spread of the gospel in the first century was the Jewish-Gentile conflict. Most of the early believers were Jewish, and to them it was scandalous even to think of associating with Gentiles. But God told Peter to take the gospel to a Roman, and Peter obeyed despite his background and personal feelings. (Later he struggled with this again—see Galatians 2:12.) But God was making it clear that the Good News of Christ is for everyone! We should not allow any barrier—language, culture, prejudice, geography, economic class, or education—to keep us from spreading the gospel.

10:35 In every nation there are hearts bent toward God, ready to receive the gospel—but someone must take it to them. Seeking God is not enough—people must find him. How then shall seekers find God without someone to point the way? Is God asking you to show someone the way to him? (See Romans 10:14, 15.)

10:43 Two examples of prophets writing about Jesus and his forgiveness of sin are Isaiah 52:13—53:1 and Ezekiel 36:25, 26.

●**10:45** Cornelius and Peter were two very different people. Cornelius was wealthy, a Gentile, a military man. Peter was a Jewish fisherman turned preacher. But God's plan included both of them. In Cornelius' house that day, a new chapter in Christian history was written as a Jewish Christian leader and a Gentile Christian convert each discovered something significant about God at work in the other person. Cornelius needed Peter and his gospel to know he could be saved. Peter needed Cornelius and his salvation experience to know Gentiles were included in God's

10:46
Acts 2:4,19:6

10:47
Acts 8:36; 11:17

10:48
Acts 2:38
8:16; 19:5

Spirit would be given to Gentiles too! 46, 47But there could be no doubt about it, for they heard them speaking in tongues and praising God.

Peter asked, "Can anyone object to my baptizing them, now that they have received the Holy Spirit just as we did?" 48So he did, baptizing them in the name of Jesus, the Messiah. Afterwards Cornelius begged him to stay with them for several days.

10:46, 47 *But there could be no doubt about it,* implied.

CORNELIUS

The early days of Christianity were exciting as God's Spirit moved and people's lives were changed. Converts were pouring in from surprising backgrounds. Even the dreaded Saul (Paul) became a Christian, and non-Jews were responding to the Good News about Jesus. Among the first of these was the Roman centurion, Cornelius.

Because of frequent outbreaks of violence, Roman soldiers had to be stationed to keep peace throughout Israel. But most Romans, hated as conquerors, did not get along well in the nation. As an army officer, Cornelius was in a difficult position. He represented Rome, but his home was in Caesarea. During his years in Israel, he had himself been conquered by the God of Israel. He had a reputation as a godly man who put his faith into action, and he was respected by the Jews.

Four significant aspects of Cornelius' character are noted in Acts. He actively sought after God, he revered God, he was generous in meeting other people's needs, and he prayed. God told him to send for Peter, because Peter would give him more knowledge about the God he was already seeking to please.

When Peter entered Cornelius' home, he broke a whole list of Jewish rules. Peter confessed he wasn't comfortable, but here was an eager audience and he couldn't hold back his message. He had no sooner started sharing the gospel when God gave overwhelming approval by filling that Roman family with his Holy Spirit. Peter saw he had no choice but to baptize them and welcome them as equals in the growing Christian church. Another step had been taken in carrying the gospel to the whole world.

Cornelius is a welcome example of God's willingness to use extraordinary means to reach those who desire to know him. He does not play favorites, and he does not hide from those who want to find him. God sent his Son because he loves the whole world— and that includes Peter, Cornelius, and you.

Strengths and accomplishments:
- A godly and generous Roman
- Although an officer in the occupying army, he seems to have been well-respected by the Jews
- He responded to God and encouraged his family to do the same
- His conversion helped the young church realize that the Good News was for all people, both Jews and Gentiles

Lessons from his life:
- God reaches those who want to know him
- The gospel is open to all people
- There are those eager to believe everywhere
- When we are willing to seek the truth and be obedient to the light God gives us, God will reward us richly

Vital statistics:
- Where: Caesarea
- Occupation: Roman centurion
- Contemporaries: Peter, Philip, the apostles

Key verse:
"He was a godly man, deeply reverent, as was his entire household. He gave generously to charity and was a man of prayer" (Acts 10:2).

Cornelius' story is told in Acts 10:1—11:18.

plan. You and another believer may also need each other to understand how God works!

10:48 Cornelius wanted Peter to stay with him for several days. He was a new believer and realized his need for teaching and fellowship. Are you as eager to learn more about Jesus? Recognize your need to be with more mature Christians, and strive to learn from them.

Peter defends his preaching to Gentiles

11 Soon the news reached the apostles and other brothers in Judea that Gentiles also were being converted! 2But when Peter arrived back in Jerusalem, the Jewish believers argued with him.

3"You fellowshiped with Gentiles and even ate with them," they accused. 4Then Peter told them the whole story. 5"One day in Joppa," he said, "while I was praying, I saw a vision—a huge sheet, let down by its four corners from the sky. 6Inside the sheet were all sorts of animals, reptiles and birds [which we are not to eat]. 7And I heard a voice say, 'Kill and eat whatever you wish.'

8" 'Never, Lord,' I replied. 'For I have never yet eaten anything forbidden by our Jewish laws!'

9"But the voice came again, 'Don't say it isn't right when God declares it is!'

10"This happened *three times* before the sheet and all it contained disappeared into heaven. 11Just then three men who had come to take me with them to Caesarea arrived at the house where I was staying! 12The Holy Spirit told me to go with them and not to worry about their being Gentiles! These six brothers here accompanied me, and we soon arrived at the home of the man who had sent the messengers. 13He told us how an angel had appeared to him and told him to send messengers to Joppa to find Simon Peter! 14'He will tell you how you and all your household can be saved!' the angel had told him.

15"Well, I began telling them the Good News, but just as I was getting started with my sermon, the Holy Spirit fell on them, just as he fell on us at the beginning! 16Then I thought of the Lord's words when he said, 'Yes, John baptized with water, but you shall be baptized with the Holy Spirit.' 17And since it was *God* who gave these Gentiles the same gift he gave us when we believed on the Lord Jesus Christ, who was I to argue?"

18When the others heard this, all their objections were answered and they began praising God! "Yes," they said, "God has given to the Gentiles, too, the privilege of turning to him and receiving eternal life!"

The Gentile church in Antioch

19Meanwhile, the believers who fled from Jerusalem during the persecution after Stephen's death traveled as far as Phoenicia, Cyprus, and Antioch, scattering the Good News, but only to Jews. 20However, some of the believers who went to Antioch from Cyprus and Cyrene also gave their message about the Lord Jesus to some Greeks. 21And the Lord honored this effort so that large numbers of these Gentiles became believers.

11:3
Mt 9:11
Acts 10:28
Gal 2:12
11:5
Acts 10:9,10
11:8
Ezek 4:14
11:12
Jn 16:13
Acts 10:23; 15:7
11:13
Acts 10:30
11:14
Acts 10:2; 16:15
18:8
1 Cor 1:16
11:15
Acts 2:4
11:16
Isa 44:3
Joel 2:28
Mt 3:11
Jn 1:26,33
11:17
Acts 10:47
15:8,9
11:18
Rom 10:12; 15:9
11:19
Acts 8:1; 13:1
14:25-27; 15:3
11:20
Acts 6:1
11:21
Lk 1:66

11:6 *which we are not to eat,* implied.   **11:16** *baptized with,* or, "baptized in."

11:1 A Gentile was anyone who was not a Jew. Most Jewish believers thought God offered salvation only to the Jews because God had given his law to them (Exodus 19, 20). One group in Jerusalem believed that Gentiles could be saved, but only if they followed all the Jewish laws and traditions—in essence, if they became Jews. Both groups were mistaken. God chose the Jews and taught them his laws so they could bring the message of salvation to *all* people (see Genesis 12:3; Psalm 22:27; Isaiah 42:4; 49:6; 56:3; 60:1–3; Jeremiah 16:19–21; Zechariah 2:11; Malachi 1:11; Romans 15:9–12).

11:2–18 When Peter brought the news of Cornelius' conversion back to Jerusalem, the believers were shocked that he had eaten with Gentiles. After they heard the whole story, however, they began praising God (11:18). Their reactions teach us how to handle disagreements with other believers. Before judging the behavior of fellow believers, it is important to hear them out. The Holy Spirit may have something important to teach us through them.

11:8 God had promised throughout Scripture that he would reach the Gentiles. This began with his general promise to Abraham (Genesis 12:3; 18:18) and became very specific in Malachi's

statement that God's name "will be honored by the Gentiles from morning till night" (Malachi 1:11). But this was an extremely difficult truth for Jews, even Jewish believers, to accept. The Jewish believers understood how certain prophecies were fulfilled in Christ, but they overlooked other Old Testament teachings. Too often we are inclined to accept only the parts of God's Word that appeal to us, ignoring the teachings we don't like. We must accept all of God's Word as absolute truth.

11:12ff Peter's defense for eating with Gentiles was a simple restatement of what happened. He brought six witnesses with him to back him up, and then he quoted Jesus' promise about the coming of the Holy Spirit (11:16). These Gentiles' lives had been changed, and that was all the evidence Peter and the other believers needed. Changed lives are an equally powerful evidence today.

11:18 The intellectual questions ended and the theological discussion stopped with the report that God had given the Holy Spirit to the Gentiles. This was a turning point for the early church. They had to accept those whom God had chosen, even if they were Gentiles. But joy over the conversion of Gentiles was not unanimous. Throughout the first century this continued to be a struggle for some Jewish Christians.

11:22
Acts 9:27
13:43; 14:22,23

11:23
Deut 10:20
1 Cor 15:58
Col 2:6

11:24
Acts 2:4,47
5:14

11:25
Acts 9:30

11:27
Acts 2:17; 13:1
1 Cor 16:1
2 Cor 9:1

11:28
Acts 21:10

11:29
Rom 15:25,26

11:30
1 Pet 5:1

22When the church at Jerusalem heard what had happened, they sent Barnabas to Antioch to help the new converts. 23When he arrived and saw the wonderful things God was doing, he was filled with excitement and joy, and encouraged the believers to stay close to the Lord, whatever the cost. 24Barnabas was a kindly person, full of the Holy Spirit and strong in faith. As a result large numbers of people were added to the Lord.

25Then Barnabas went on to Tarsus to hunt for Paul. 26When he found him, he brought him back to Antioch; and both of them stayed there for a full year, teaching the many new converts. (It was there at Antioch that the believers were first called "Christians.")

27During this time some prophets came down from Jerusalem to Antioch, 28and one of them, named Agabus, stood up in one of the meetings to predict by the Spirit that a great famine was coming upon the land of Israel. (This was fulfilled during the reign of Claudius.) 29So the believers decided to send relief to the Christians in Judea, each giving as much as he could. 30This they did, consigning their gifts to Barnabas and Paul to take to the elders of the church in Jerusalem.

11:28 *the land of Israel*, literally, "upon the earth."

BARNABAS AND PAUL IN ANTIOCH
Persecution spread the believers into Phoenicia, Cyprus, and Antioch, and the gospel went with them. Most spoke only to Jews, but in Antioch, some Gentile Greeks were converted. The church sent Barnabas to investigate, and he was pleased with what he found. Barnabas went to Tarsus to bring Paul back to Antioch.

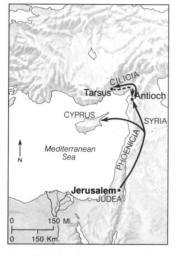

commercial center—the gateway to the eastern world. Antioch was a key city both to Rome and to the early church.

11:22–26 Barnabas gives us a wonderful example of how to help new Christians. He demonstrated strong faith; he ministered joyfully with kindness and encouragement; and he taught them further lessons about God. Remember Barnabas when you see new believers, and think of ways to help them grow in their faith.

11:25 Paul had been sent to his home in Tarsus to protect him from danger (9:30). He stayed there for several years before Barnabas brought him to help the church at Antioch.

11:26 The young church at Antioch was a curious mixture of Jews (who spoke Greek or Aramaic) and Gentiles. It is significant that this is the first place where the believers were called Christians, because all they had in common was Christ—not race, culture, or even language. Christ can cross all boundaries and unify all people.

11:26 Barnabas and Paul stayed at Antioch for a full year, teaching the new believers. They could have left for new cities, but they saw the importance of follow-through and training. Have you helped someone believe in God? Spend time teaching and encouraging that person. Are you a new believer? Remember, you are just beginning your Christian life. Your faith needs to grow and mature through consistent Bible study and learning.

11:19–21 When the church accepted Peter's testimony that the gospel was also for Gentiles, Christianity exploded into Gentile areas and large numbers became believers. The seeds of this missionary work had been sown after Stephen's death when many believing Jews were persecuted and scattered, settling in faraway cities and spreading the gospel.

11:20, 21 It was in Antioch that Christianity was launched on its worldwide mission and where the believers aggressively preached to the Gentiles. Philip had preached in Samaria, but the Samaritans were already partly Jewish (8:5); Peter preached to Cornelius, but he already worshiped God (10:46, 47). Believers who scattered after the outbreak of persecution in Jerusalem spread the gospel to other Jews in the lands they fled to (11:19). But now the believers began actively sharing the Good News with Gentiles.

11:22 With the exception of Jerusalem, Antioch played a more important role in the early church than any other city. After Rome and Alexandria, Antioch was the largest city in the Roman world. In Antioch, the first Gentile church was founded, and the believers were first called Christians. Paul used the city as his home base during his missionary journeys. Antioch was the center of worship for several pagan cults, promoting much sexual immorality and other forms of evil common to pagan religions. It was also a vital

11:27 Prophets were found not only in the Old Testament, but also in the early church. Their role was to present God's will to the people and to instruct them in God's Word. Sometimes they, like Agabus, also had the gift of predicting the future.

11:28, 29 There were serious food shortages during the reign of the Roman emperor Claudius (A.D. 41–54) because of a drought that extended across much of the Roman empire for many years. It is significant that the church in Antioch assisted the church in Jerusalem. The daughter church had grown enough to be able to help the established church.

11:29 The people of Antioch were motivated to give generously because they cared about the needs of others. This is "cheerful giving," which the Bible commends (2 Corinthians 9:7). Reluctant giving reflects a lack of concern for people. Focus your concern on the needy, and you will be motivated to give.

11:30 Elders were appointed to manage the affairs of the congregation. At this point, not much is known about their responsibilities, but it appears that their main role was to respond to the believers' needs.

An angel rescues Peter from prison

12 About that time King Herod moved against some of the believers, ²and killed the apostle James (John's brother). ³When Herod saw how much this pleased the Jewish leaders, he arrested Peter during the Passover celebration ⁴and imprisoned him, placing him under the guard of sixteen soldiers. Herod's intention was to deliver Peter to the Jews for execution after the Passover. ⁵But earnest prayer was going up to God from the church for his safety all the time he was in prison.

⁶The night before he was to be executed, he was asleep, double-chained between two soldiers with others standing guard before the prison gate, ⁷when suddenly there was a light in the cell and an angel of the Lord stood beside Peter! The angel slapped him on the side to awaken him and said, "Quick! Get up!" And the chains fell off his wrists! ⁸Then the angel told him, "Get dressed and put on your shoes." And he did. "Now put on your coat and follow me!" the angel ordered.

⁹So Peter left the cell, following the angel. But all the time he thought it was a dream or vision, and didn't believe it was really happening. ¹⁰They passed the first and second cell blocks and came to the iron gate to the street, and this opened to them of its own accord! So they passed through and walked along together for a block, and then the angel left him.

¹¹Peter finally realized what had happened! "It's really true!" he said to himself. "The Lord has sent his angel and saved me from Herod and from what the Jews were hoping to do to me!"

¹²After a little thought he went to the home of Mary, mother of John Mark, where many were gathered for a prayer meeting.

¹³He knocked at the door in the gate, and a girl named Rhoda came to open it. ¹⁴When she recognized Peter's voice, she was so overjoyed that she ran back inside to tell everyone that Peter was standing outside in the street. ¹⁵They didn't believe her. "You're out of your mind," they said. When she insisted they decided, "It must be his angel. [They must have killed him.]"

¹⁶Meanwhile Peter continued knocking. When they finally went out and opened the door, their surprise knew no bounds. ¹⁷He motioned for them to quiet down and

12:2 *and killed the apostle,* implied.   **12:15** *They must have killed him,* implied.

12:1	Mt 10:17
12:2	Mt 4:21; 20:20-23; Mk 10:39
12:3	Ex 12:14,15
12:4	Jn 21:18
12:5	2 Cor 1:11; Eph 6:18
12:7	Acts 5:19; 21:33; Heb 1:14
12:9	Ps 126:1; Acts 10:3
12:10	Acts 5:19; 16:26
12:11	Job 5:19; Ps 33:18,19; 34:7; 97:10; Dan 3:28; 6:22; 2 Pet 2:9
12:12	Acts 12:25; 13:5 15:37; Col 4:10; 1 Pet 5:13
12:15	Mt 18:10
12:17	Acts 15:35; 21:18

●**12:1** This King Herod was Herod Agrippa I, the son of Aristobulus and grandson of Herod the Great. His sister was Herodias, who was responsible for the death of John the Baptist (see Mark 6:17–28). He was partly Jewish. The Romans had appointed him to rule over most of Palestine, including the territories of Galilee, Perea, Judea, and Samaria. He moved against the Christians in order to please the Jewish leaders who opposed them, hoping that would solidify his position. Agrippa I died suddenly in A.D. 44 (see 12:20–23). His death is also recorded by the historian Josephus.

●**12:2** James and John were two of the original 12 disciples who followed Jesus. James and John had asked Jesus for special recognition in his kingdom (Mark 10:35–37). Jesus said that recognition in his kingdom often means suffering for him (drink from the same cup—Mark 10:38, 39). James and John did indeed suffer—Herod executed James, and John was later exiled (see Revelation 1:9).

●**12:2–12** Why did God allow James to die and yet miraculously save Peter? Life is full of difficult questions like this. Why is one child physically handicapped and another child athletically gifted? Why do people die before realizing their potential? These are questions we cannot possibly answer in this life because we do not see all that God sees. He has chosen to allow evil in this world for a time, but we can trust his leading because he has promised to destroy all evil one day. In the meantime, we know he will help us use our suffering in a way that strengthens us and glorifies him. For more on this question, see the notes on Job 1:1ff; 2:10; 3:23–26.

12:3 Peter was arrested during the Passover because there were more Jews in the city than usual. Herod could impress the most people by making the arrest at this time.

●**12:5** In the midst of the plots, execution, and arrest, Luke injects the very important word "but." Herod's plan was to execute Peter, *but* the believers were praying for Peter's safety. The earnest prayer of the church significantly affected the outcome of these events. We know from the testimony of the Bible that prayer changes attitudes and events. So pray often and pray with confidence.

12:7 God sent an angel to rescue Peter. Angels are God's messengers. They are divinely created beings with supernatural powers, and they sometimes take on human appearance in order to talk to people. Angels should not be worshiped because they, too, serve God.

12:12 John Mark wrote the Gospel of Mark. His mother's house was large enough to accommodate a meeting of many believers. An upstairs room in this house may have been the location of Jesus' last supper with his disciples.

●**12:13–15** The prayers of the little group of believers were answered, even as they prayed. But when the answer arrived at the door, they didn't believe it. We should be people of faith who believe that God answers the prayers of those who seek his will. When you pray, believe you'll get an answer—and when the answer comes, don't be surprised!

12:17 This James was Jesus' brother, who became a leader in the Jerusalem church (Galatians 1:19). The James who was killed (12:2) was John's brother and one of the original 12 disciples.

told them what had happened and how the Lord had brought him out of jail. "Tell James and the others what happened," he said—and left for safer quarters.

12:19
Acts 8:40; 16:27

18At dawn, the jail was in great commotion. What had happened to Peter? 19When Herod sent for him and found that he wasn't there, he had the sixteen guards arrested, court-martialed and sentenced to death. Afterwards he left to live in Caesarea for a while.

The judgment of Herod

20While he was in Caesarea, a delegation from Tyre and Sidon arrived to see him. He was highly displeased with the people of those two cities, but the delegates

---

HEROD AGRIPPA I

For good or evil, families have lasting and powerful influence on their children. Traits and qualities are passed on to the next generation, and often the mistakes and sins of the parents are repeated by the children. Four generations of the Herod family are mentioned in the Bible. Each leader left his evil mark: Herod the Great murdered Bethlehem's children; Herod Antipas was involved in Jesus' trial and had John the Baptist executed; Herod Agrippa I murdered the apostle James; and Herod Agrippa II was one of Paul's judges.

Herod Agrippa I related fairly well to his Jewish subjects. Because he had a Jewish grandmother of royal blood (Mariamne), he was grudgingly accepted by the people. Although as a youth he had been temporarily imprisoned by the emperor Tiberias, he was now trusted by Rome and got along well with the emperors Caligula and Claudius.

An unexpected opportunity for Herod to gain new favor with the Jews was created by the Christian movement. Gentiles began to be accepted into the church in large numbers. Many Jews had been tolerating this new movement as a sect within Judaism, but its rapid growth alarmed them. Persecution of Christians was revived, and even the apostles were not spared. James was killed, and Peter was thrown into prison.

But soon, Herod made a fatal error. During a visit to Caesarea, the people called him a god and he accepted their praise. Herod was immediately struck with a painful disease, and he died within a week.

Like his grandfather, uncle, and son after him, Herod Agrippa I came close to the truth but missed it. Because religion was important only as an aspect of politics, he had no reverence and no qualms about taking praise that only God should receive. His mistake is a common one. Whenever we are proud of our own abilities and accomplishments, not recognizing them as gifts from God, we repeat Herod's sin.

Strengths and accomplishments:
• Capable administrator and negotiator
• Managed to maintain good relations with the Jews in his region and with Rome

Weaknesses and mistakes:
• Arranged the murder of the apostle James
• Imprisoned Peter with plans to execute him
• Allowed the people to praise him as a god

Lessons from his life:
• Those who set themselves against God are doomed to ultimate failure
• There is great danger in accepting praise that only God deserves
• Family traits can influence children toward great good or great evil

Vital statistics:
• Where: Jerusalem
• Occupation: Roman-appointed King of the Jews
• Relatives: Grandfather: Herod the Great. Father: Aristobulus. Uncle: Herod Antipas. Sister: Herodias. Wife: Cypros. Son: Herod Agrippa II. Daughters: Bernice, Mariamne, Drusilla.
• Contemporaries: Emperors Tiberias, Caligula, and Claudius. James, Peter, the apostles.

Key verse:
"Instantly, an angel of the Lord struck Herod with a sickness so that he was filled with maggots and died—because he accepted the people's worship instead of giving the glory to God" (Acts 12:23).

Herod Agrippa I's story is told in Acts 12:1–23.

12:19 Under Roman law, if guards allowed their prisoner to escape, they were subject to the same punishment the prisoner was to receive. Thus these 16 guards were sentenced to death.

12:20 The Jews considered Jerusalem their capital, but the Romans made Caesarea their headquarters in Palestine. This is where Herod Agrippa lived.

made friends with Blastus, the royal secretary, and asked for peace, for their cities were economically dependent upon trade with Herod's country. 21An appointment with Herod was granted, and when the day arrived he put on his royal robes, sat on his throne and made a speech to them. 22At its conclusion the people gave him a great ovation, shouting, "It is the voice of a god and not of a man!"

23Instantly, an angel of the Lord struck Herod with a sickness so that he was filled with maggots and died—because he accepted the people's worship instead of giving the glory to God.

24God's Good News was spreading rapidly and there were many new believers.

25Barnabas and Paul now visited Jerusalem and, as soon as they had finished their business, returned to Antioch, taking John Mark with them.

12:23
Deut 28:58,59
1 Sam 25:37,38
2 Sam 24:16
2 Kgs 19:35
Isa 42:8; 48:11
Dan 4:30-37
Rev 15:3,4
12:24
Isa 55:11
Acts 6:7; 19:20
12:25
Acts 11:29,30
15:37

B. PAUL'S MINISTRY (13:1—28:31)
The book focuses now on the ministry to the Gentiles and the spread of the church around the world, and Paul replaces Peter as the central figure in the book. Paul completes three missionary journeys and ends up being imprisoned in Jerusalem and transported to Rome. The book of Acts ends abruptly, showing that the history of the church is not yet complete. We are to be a part of the sequel.

1. First missionary journey
Barnabas and Paul are sent out to preach

13 Among the prophets and teachers of the church at Antioch were Barnabas and Symeon (also called "The Black Man"), Lucius (from Cyrene), Manaen (the foster-brother of King Herod), and Paul. 2One day as these men were worshiping and fasting the Holy Spirit said, "Dedicate Barnabas and Paul for a special job I have for them." 3So after more fasting and prayer, the men laid their hands on them—and sent them on their way.

13:1
Acts 11:22
Rom 16:21
13:2
Eph 3:7-9
13:3
Acts 6:6

Paul curses a sorcerer in Cyprus

4Directed by the Holy Spirit they went to Seleucia and then sailed for Cyprus.

12:25 *returned to Antioch,* implied.

12:23 Herod died a horrible death with intense pain; he was literally eaten alive, from the inside out, by maggots or worms. Pride is a serious sin, and in this case, God chose to punish it immediately. God does not immediately judge all sin, but he will judge it (Hebrews 9:27). Accept Christ's offer of forgiveness today. No one can afford to wait.

12:25 John Mark was Barnabas' nephew. His mother, Mary, often opened her home to the apostles, so John Mark would have been exposed to most of the great men and teachings of the early church. John Mark later joined Paul and Barnabas on their first missionary journey, but for unknown reasons, left them in the middle of the trip. John Mark was criticized for abandoning the mission, but he wrote the Gospel of Mark and was later acclaimed by Paul as a vital help in the growth of the early church.

13:1 What variety there is in the church! The common thread among these five men was their deep faith in Christ. We must never exclude anyone whom Christ has called to follow him.

13:2, 3 The church dedicated Barnabas and Paul to the work God had for them. *Dedicating* means setting apart for a special purpose. We too should dedicate our pastors, missionaries, and Christian workers for their tasks. We can also dedicate ourselves with our time, money, and talents for God's work. Ask God what he wants you to dedicate to him.

13:2, 3 This was the beginning of Paul's first missionary journey. The church was involved in sending Paul and Barnabas, but it was God's plan. Why did Paul and Barnabas go where they did? (1) The Holy Spirit led them. (2) They followed the communication routes of the Roman empire—this made travel easier. (3) They visited key population and cultural centers to reach as many

MINISTRY IN CYPRUS
The leaders of the church in Antioch chose Paul and Barnabas to take the gospel westward. Along with John Mark, they boarded ship at Seleucia and set out across the Mediterranean for Cyprus. They preached in Salamis, the largest city, and went across the island to Paphos.

people as possible. (4) They went to cities with synagogues, speaking first to the Jews in hopes that they would see Jesus as the Messiah and help spread the Good News to everyone.

13:4 Located in the Mediterranean Sea, the island of Cyprus, with a large Jewish population, was Barnabas' home. Their first stop was into familiar territory.

13:5
Acts 9:20; 12:25
1 Pet 5:13

13:6
Ex 7:11
Mt 7:15
Acts 8:9
2 Tim 3:8

⁵There, in the town of Salamis, they went to the Jewish synagogue and preached. (John Mark went with them as their assistant.)

⁶, ⁷Afterwards they preached from town to town across the entire island until finally they reached Paphos where they met a Jewish sorcerer, a fake prophet named Bar-Jesus. He had attached himself to the governor, Sergius Paulus, a man of considerable insight and understanding. The governor invited Barnabas and Paul

JOHN MARK

Mistakes are effective teachers. Their consequences have a way of making lessons painfully clear. But those who learn from their mistakes are likely to develop wisdom. John Mark was a good learner who just needed some time and encouragement.

Mark was eager to do the right thing, but he had trouble staying with a task. In his Gospel, Mark mentions a young man (probably referring to himself) who fled in such fear during Jesus' arrest that he left his clothes behind. This tendency to run was to reappear later when Paul and Barnabas took him as their assistant on their first missionary journey. At their second stop, Mark left them and returned to Jerusalem. It was a decision Paul did not easily accept. In preparing for their second journey two years later, Barnabas again suggested Mark as a traveling companion, but Paul flatly refused. As a result, the team was divided. Barnabas took Mark with him, and Paul chose Silas. Barnabas was patient with Mark, and the young man repaid his investment. Paul and Mark were later reunited, and the older apostle became a close friend of the young disciple.

Mark was a valuable companion to three early Christian leaders—Barnabas, Paul, and Peter. The material in Mark's Gospel seems to have come mostly from Peter. Mark's role as a serving assistant allowed him to be an observer. He heard Peter's accounts of the years with Jesus over and over, and he was one of the first to put Jesus' life in writing.

Barnabas played a key role in Mark's life. He stood beside the young man despite his failure, giving him patient encouragement. Mark challenges us to learn from our mistakes and appreciate the patience of others. Is there a Barnabas in your life you need to thank for his or her encouragement to you?

Strengths and accomplishments:
● Wrote the Gospel of Mark
● He and his mother provided their home as one of the main meeting places for the Christians in Jerusalem
● Persisted beyond his youthful mistakes
● Was an assistant and traveling companion to three of the greatest early missionaries

Weaknesses and mistakes:
● Probably the nameless young man described in the Gospel of Mark who fled in panic when Jesus was arrested
● Left Paul and Barnabas for unknown reasons during the first missionary journey

Lessons from his life:
● Personal maturity usually comes from a combination of time and mistakes
● Mistakes are not usually as important as what can be learned from them
● Effective living is not measured as much by what we accomplish as by what we overcome in order to accomplish it
● Encouragement can change a person's life

Vital statistics:
● Where: Jerusalem
● Occupation: Missionary-in-training, Gospel writer, traveling companion
● Relatives: Mother: Mary. Uncle: Barnabas.
● Contemporaries: Paul, Peter, Timothy, Luke, Silas

Key verse:
"Only Luke is with me. Bring Mark with you when you come, for I need him" (Paul writing in 2 Timothy 4:11).

John Mark's story is told in Acts 12:25—13:13 and 15:36–39. He is also mentioned in Colossians 4:10, 11; 2 Timothy 4:11; Philemon 1:24; 1 Peter 5:13.

13:6, 7 Governors often kept private wizards. Bar-Jesus realized   that if Sergius Paulus believed in Jesus, he'd soon be out of a job.

to visit him, for he wanted to hear their message from God. 8But the sorcerer, Elymas (his name in Greek), interfered and urged the governor to pay no attention to what Paul and Barnabas said, trying to keep him from trusting the Lord.

9Then Paul, filled with the Holy Spirit, glared angrily at the sorcerer and said, 10"You son of the devil, full of every sort of trickery and villainy, enemy of all that is good, will you never end your opposition to the Lord? 11And now God has laid his hand of punishment upon you, and you will be stricken awhile with blindness."

Instantly mist and darkness fell upon him, and he began wandering around begging for someone to take his hand and lead him. 12When the governor saw what happened he believed and was astonished at the power of God's message.

13:9
Acts 2:4; 4:8
13:10
Mt 13:38
Jn 8:44
2 Pet 2:15
1 Jn 3:8
13:11
2 Kgs 6:18

Paul preaches to the Jews in Antioch in Pisidia

13Now Paul and those with him left Paphos by ship for Turkey, landing at the port town of Perga. There John deserted them and returned to Jerusalem. 14But Barnabas and Paul went on to Antioch, a city in the province of Pisidia.

On the Sabbath they went into the synagogue for the services. 15After the usual readings from the Books of Moses and from the Prophets, those in charge of the service sent them this message: "Brothers, if you have any word of instruction for us come and give it!"

16So Paul stood, waved a greeting to them and began. "Men of Israel," he said,

13:13
Acts 14:24,25
15:38
13:14
Acts 14:19,21
24
13:15
Lk 14:16
Acts 15:21
2 Cor 3:14
13:16
Acts 10:2,13:26

13:13 *Turkey,* literally, "Pamphylia." *deserted them,* literally, "departed from them." See 15:38.   **13:16** *waved a greeting to them,* literally, "beckoning with the hand." *Let me begin my remarks with a bit of history,* implied.

●**13:13** No reason is given why John Mark left Paul and Barnabas. Some suggestions are: (1) he was homesick, (2) he resented the change in leadership from Barnabas (his uncle) to Paul, (3) he became ill (this may have affected all of them—see Galatians 4:13), (4) he was unable to withstand the rigors and dangers of the missionary journey, (5) he may have planned to go only that far but had not communicated this to Paul and Barnabas. Paul accused John Mark of lacking courage and commitment, calling him a deserter (see 15:38). It is clear from Paul's later letters, however, that Paul grew to respect Mark (Colossians 4:10) and needed him in his work (2 Timothy 4:11).

13:14 This is Antioch of Pisidia, different from Antioch of Syria where there was already a flourishing church (11:26). Antioch of Pisidia was a hub of good roads and trade and had a large Jewish population.

●**13:14** What happened in a synagogue service? First the *Shema* was recited (see Numbers 15:37–41; Deuteronomy 6:4–9; 11:13–21). Certain prayers were given; then there was a reading from the Law (the books of Genesis through Deuteronomy), a reading from the Prophets intending to illustrate the Law, and a sermon. The synagogue leader decided who was to lead the service and give the sermon. A different person was chosen to lead each week. Since it was customary for the synagogue leader to invite visiting rabbis to speak, Paul and Barnabas usually had an open door when they first went to a synagogue. But as soon as they spoke about Jesus as Messiah, the door slammed. They were usually not invited back by the religious leaders, and sometimes they were thrown out of town!

13:14 When they went to a new town to witness for Christ, Paul and Barnabas went first to the synagogue. The Jews who went to the synagogue believed in God and diligently studied the Scriptures. Tragically, however, many could not accept Jesus as the promised Messiah because they had the wrong idea of what kind of Messiah he would be. He was not a military king who would overthrow Rome's control, but a servant king who would overthrow

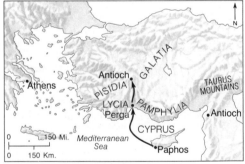

MINISTRY IN PAMPHYLIA AND GALATIA Paul, Barnabas, and John Mark left Paphos and landed at Perga in the humid region of Pamphylia, a narrow strip of land between the sea and the Taurus Mountains. John Mark deserted them in Perga, but Paul and Barnabas traveled up the steep road into the higher elevation of Pisidia in Galatia. When the Jews rejected his message, Paul preached to Gentiles, and the Jews drove Paul and Barnabas out of the Pisidian city of Antioch.

sin in people's hearts. (Only later, when he returns, will he overthrow the nations of the world.) Paul and Barnabas did not separate themselves from the synagogues but tried to show clearly that the Scriptures the Jews studied pointed to Jesus.

13:16ff Paul's message to the Jews in the synagogue in Antioch began with an emphasis on God's covenant with Israel. He began with a point of agreement, for all Jews were proud to be God's chosen people. Then Paul went on to explain how the gospel fulfilled this covenant, and some Jews found this message hard to take.

"and all others here who reverence God, [let me begin my remarks with a bit of history].

13:17
Deut 7:6-8
Acts 7:36
13:19,20
Deut 7:1
Judg 2:16

13:21
1 Sam 8:5; 10:1

17"The God of this nation Israel chose our ancestors and honored them in Egypt by gloriously leading them out of their slavery. 18And he nursed them through forty years of wandering around in the wilderness. 19, 20Then he destroyed seven nations in Canaan, and gave Israel their land as an inheritance. Judges ruled for about 450 years, and were followed by Samuel the prophet.

21"Then the people begged for a king, and God gave them Saul (son of Kish), a

BARNABAS

Every group needs an "encourager," because everyone needs encouragement at one time or another. However, the value of encouragement is often missed because it tends to be private rather than public. In fact, people most need encouragement when they feel most alone. A man named Joseph was such an encourager that he earned the nickname "son of encouragement," or Barnabas, from the Jerusalem Christians.

Barnabas was drawn to people he could encourage, and he was a great help to those around him. It is delightful that wherever Barnabas encouraged Christians, non-Christians flocked to become believers!

Barnabas' actions were crucial to the early church. In a way, we can thank him for most of the New Testament. God used his relationship with Paul at one point and with Mark at another to keep these two men going when either might have failed. Barnabas did wonders with encouragement!

When Paul arrived in Jerusalem for the first time following his conversion, the local Christians were understandably reluctant to welcome him. They thought his story was a trick to capture more Christians. Only Barnabas proved willing to risk his life to meet with Paul and then convince the others that their former enemy was now a vibrant believer in Jesus. We can only wonder what might have happened to Paul without Barnabas.

It was Barnabas who encouraged Mark to go with him and Paul to Antioch. Mark joined them on their first missionary journey, but decided during the trip to return home. Later, Barnabas wanted to invite Mark to join them for another journey, but Paul would not agree. As a result, the partners went separate ways, Barnabas with Mark and Paul with Silas. This actually doubled the missionary effort. Barnabas' patient encouragement was confirmed by Mark's eventual effective ministry. Paul and Mark were later reunited in missionary efforts.

As Barnabas' life shows, we are rarely in a situation where there isn't someone we can encourage. Our tendency, however, is to criticize instead. It may be important at times to point out someone's shortcomings, but before we have the right to do this, we must build that person's trust through encouragement. Are you prepared to encourage those with whom you come in contact today?

Strengths and accomplishments:
- One of the first to sell possessions to help the Christians in Jerusalem
- First to travel with Paul as a missionary team
- Was an encourager, as his nickname shows, and thus one of the most quietly influential people in the early days of Christianity
- Called an apostle, although not one of the original Twelve

Weaknesses and mistakes:
- With Peter, temporarily stayed aloof from Gentile believers until Paul corrected him

Lessons from his life:
- Encouragement is one of the most effective ways to help
- Sooner or later, true obedience to God will involve risk
- There is always someone who needs encouragement

Vital statistics:
- Where: Cyprus, Jerusalem, Antioch
- Occupation: Missionary, teacher
- Relatives: Sister: Mary. Nephew: John Mark.
- Contemporaries: Peter, Silas, Paul, Herod Agrippa I

Key verses:
"When he arrived and saw the wonderful things God was doing, he was filled with excitement and joy, and encouraged the believers to stay close to the Lord, whatever the cost. Barnabas was a kindly person, full of the Holy Spirit and strong in faith. As a result large numbers of people were added to the Lord" (Acts 11:23, 24).

Barnabas' story is told in Acts 9:27—15:39. He is also mentioned in 1 Corinthians 9:6; Galatians 2:1, 9, 13; Colossians 4:10.

man of the tribe of Benjamin, who reigned for forty years. 22But God removed him
and replaced him with David as king, a man about whom God said, 'David (son of
Jesse) is a man after my own heart, for he will obey me.' 23And it is one of King
David's descendants, Jesus, who is God's promised Savior of Israel!

24"But before he came, John the Baptist preached the need for everyone in Israel
to turn from sin to God. 25As John was finishing his work he asked, 'Do you think
I am the Messiah? No! But he is coming soon—and in comparison with him, I am
utterly worthless.'

26"Brothers—you sons of Abraham, and also all of you Gentiles here who
reverence God—this salvation is for all of us! 27The Jews in Jerusalem and their
leaders fulfilled prophecy by killing Jesus; for they didn't recognize him, or realize
that he is the one the prophets had written about, though they heard the prophets'
words read every Sabbath. 28They found no just cause to execute him, but asked
Pilate to have him killed anyway. 29When they had fulfilled all the prophecies
concerning his death, he was taken from the cross and placed in a tomb.

30"But God brought him back to life again! 31And he was seen many times during
the next few days by the men who had accompanied him to Jerusalem from
Galilee—these men have constantly testified to this in public witness.

32, 33"And now Barnabas and I are here to bring you this Good News—that God's
promise to our ancestors has come true in our own time, in that God brought Jesus
back to life again. This is what the second Psalm is talking about when it says
concerning Jesus, 'Today I have honored you as my Son.'

34"For God had promised to bring him back to life again, no more to die. This is
stated in the Scripture that says, 'I will do for you the wonderful thing I promised
David.' 35In another Psalm he explained more fully, saying, 'God will not let his
Holy One decay.' 36This was not a reference to David, for after David had served
his generation according to the will of God, he died and was buried, and his body
decayed. 37[No, it was a reference to another]—someone God brought back to life,
whose body was not touched at all by the ravages of death.

38"Brothers! Listen! In this man Jesus, there is forgiveness for your sins! 39Ev-
eryone who trusts in him is freed from all guilt and declared righteous—something
the Jewish law could never do. 40Oh, be careful! Don't let the prophets' words
apply to you. For they said, 41'Look and perish, you despisers [of the truth], for I
am doing something in your day—something that you won't believe when you hear
it announced.' "

42As the people left the synagogue that day, they asked Paul to return and speak
to them again the next week. 43And many Jews and godly Gentiles who worshiped
at the synagogue followed Paul and Barnabas down the street as the two men urged
them to accept the mercies God was offering.

Paul turns to the Gentiles

44The following week almost the entire city turned out to hear them preach the
Word of God.

45But when the Jewish leaders saw the crowds, they were jealous, and cursed and
argued against whatever Paul said.

46Then Paul and Barnabas spoke out boldly and declared, "It was necessary that

13:22
1 Sam 16:1,13

13:23
Isa 11:1
Lk 1:32; 2:11

13:24
Mk 1:1-14

13:25
Mt 3:11
Mk 1:7
Lk 3:16
Jn 1:26,27

13:27
Acts 3:17
1 Cor 2:8

13:28
Acts 3:14

13:29
Lk 23:52,53

13:30
Mt 28:6
Acts 2:24

13:31
Lk 24:48
Acts 1:11
1 Cor 15:5

13:32
Rom 1:2-4
Gal 3:16

13:33
Ps 2:7
Heb 1:5; 5:5

13:34
Isa 55:3

13:35
Ps 16:10

13:36
1 Kgs 2:10

13:37
Acts 2:24
1 Cor 15:42

13:38
Jer 31:34
Col 1:13,14

13:39
Isa 53:11
Rom 3:28; 10:4
Gal 2:16

13:41
Hab 1:5

13:45
Acts 14:2; 18:6
1 Thess 2:15,16
Jude 10

13:46
Deut 32:21
Rom 1:16; 10:19

13:33 Today I have honored you as my Son, literally, "This day have I begotten you." **13:37** No, it was a reference
to another, implied. was not touched at all by the ravages of death, literally, "saw no corruption." **13:41** of the truth,
implied. **13:45** the Jewish leaders, literally, "the Jews." cursed, or "blasphemed."

13:38, 39 This is the Good News of the gospel—that forgiveness
of sins and freedom from guilt are available to all people through
faith in Christ—including you. Have you received this forgiveness?
Are you refreshed by it each day?

13:42–45 The Jewish leaders brought theological arguments
against Paul and Barnabas, but the Bible tells us that the real
reason for their denunciation was jealousy (5:17). When we see
others succeeding where we haven't or receiving the affirmation
we crave, it is hard to rejoice with them. Jealousy is our natural

reaction. But how tragic when our own jealous feelings make us try
to stop God's work. If a work is God's work, rejoice in it—no matter
who is doing it.

13:46 Why was it necessary for the gospel to go first to the Jews?
God planned that through the Jewish nation all the world would
come to know God (Genesis 12:3). Paul, a Jew himself, loved his
people (Romans 9:1–3) and wanted to give them every opportunity
to join him in proclaiming God's salvation. Unfortunately, many
Jews did not recognize Jesus as Messiah, and they did not

this Good News from God should be given first to you Jews. But since you have rejected it, and shown yourselves unworthy of eternal life—well, we will offer it to Gentiles. ⁴⁷For this is as the Lord commanded when he said, 'I have made you a light to the Gentiles, to lead them from the farthest corners of the earth to my salvation.' "

⁴⁸When the Gentiles heard this, they were very glad and rejoiced in Paul's message; and as many as wanted eternal life, believed. ⁴⁹So God's message spread all through that region.

⁵⁰Then the Jewish leaders stirred up both the godly women and the civic leaders of the city and incited a mob against Paul and Barnabas, and ran them out of town. ⁵¹But they shook off the dust of their feet against the town and went on to the city of Iconium. ⁵²And their converts were filled with joy and with the Holy Spirit.

Paul and Barnabas preach boldly at Iconium

14 At Iconium, Paul and Barnabas went together to the synagogue and preached with such power that many—both Jews and Gentiles—believed. ²But the Jews who spurned God's message stirred up distrust among the Gentiles against Paul and Barnabas, saying all sorts of evil things about them. ³Nevertheless, they stayed there a long time, preaching boldly, and the Lord proved their message was from him by giving them power to do great miracles. ⁴But the people of the city were divided in their opinion about them. Some agreed with the Jewish leaders, and some backed the apostles.

⁵, ⁶When Paul and Barnabas learned of a plot to incite a mob of Gentiles, Jews, and Jewish leaders to attack and stone them, they fled for their lives, going to the cities of Lycaonia, Lystra, Derbe, and the surrounding area, ⁷and preaching the Good News there.

Paul heals a cripple in Lystra

⁸While they were at Lystra, they came upon a man with crippled feet who had been that way from birth, so he had never walked. ⁹He was listening as Paul

13:47
Isa 42:6; 49:6
Lk 2:32

13:48
Rom 8:29,30
Eph 1:4,5,11
1 Pet 1:2

13:51
Mt 10:14
Lk 9:5
Acts 18:6
2 Tim 3:11

13:52
1 Pet 1:8

14:2
2 Tim 3:11

14:3
Mk 16:20
Rom 15:19
Heb 2:4

14:4
Acts 27:4,5
19:9; 28:24

14:5
Acts 14:19; 16:1
1 Thess 2:14-16

14:8
Acts 3:2

13:48 *wanted,* or, "were disposed to," or, "ordained to."   **13:52** *their converts,* literally, "the disciples."

---

understand that in Jesus God was offering salvation to anyone, Jew or Gentile, who comes to him in faith.

13:47 God had planned for Israel to be this light (Isaiah 49:6). Through Israel came Jesus, the light of the nations (Luke 2:32). This light would spread out and enlighten the Gentiles.

13:50 Instead of hearing the truth, the Jewish leaders ran Paul and Barnabas out of town. When confronted by a disturbing truth, people often turn away and refuse to listen. When God's Spirit points out needed changes in our lives, we must listen to him, or else we risk pushing the truth so far away that it no longer affects us.

13:51 Jesus had told his disciples to shake from their feet the dust of any village that would not accept or listen to them (Mark 6:11). The disciples were not to blame if the message was rejected as long as they had faithfully presented it. When we share Christ carefully and sensitively, God does not hold us responsible for the other person's decision.

14:3, 4 We may wish we could perform a miraculous act that would convince everyone once and for all that Jesus is the Lord, but we see here that even if we could, it wouldn't convince everyone. God gave these men power to do great miracles as proof, but people were still divided. Don't spend your time and energy wishing for miracles. Sow your seeds of Good News on the best ground you can find in the best way you can, and leave the convincing to the Holy Spirit.

14:5, 6 Iconium, Lystra, and Derbe were three cities Paul visited in the region of Galatia. Paul wrote a letter to these churches—the letter to the Galatians—because many Jewish Christians were

CONTINUED MINISTRY IN GALATIA Paul and Barnabas, thrown out of Antioch in Pisidia, descended the mountains, going east into Lycaonia. They went first to Iconium, a commercial center on the road between Asia and Syria. After preaching there, they had to flee to Lystra, 25 miles south. Paul was stoned in Lystra, but he and Barnabas traveled the 50 miles to Derbe, a frontier town. The pair then boldly retraced their steps.

claiming that non-Jewish Christians couldn't be saved unless they followed Jewish laws and customs. Paul's letter refuted this and brought the believers back to a right understanding of faith in Jesus (see Galatians 3:3, 5). Paul wrote his letter soon after leaving the region (see the note on 14:28).

preached, and Paul noticed him and realized he had faith to be healed. 10So Paul called to him, "Stand up!" and the man leaped to his feet and started walking!

11When the listening crowd saw what Paul had done, they shouted (in their local dialect, of course), "These men are gods in human bodies!" 12They decided that Barnabas was the Greek god Jupiter, and that Paul, because he was the chief speaker, was Mercury! 13The local priest of the Temple of Jupiter, located on the outskirts of the city, brought them cartloads of flowers and prepared to sacrifice oxen to them at the city gates before the crowds.

14But when Barnabas and Paul saw what was happening they ripped at their clothing in dismay and ran out among the people, shouting, 15"Men! What are you doing? We are merely human beings like yourselves! We have come to bring you the Good News that you are invited to turn from the worship of these foolish things and to pray instead to the living God who made heaven and earth and sea and everything in them. 16In bygone days he permitted the nations to go their own ways, 17but he never left himself without a witness; there were always his reminders—the kind things he did such as sending you rain and good crops and giving you food and gladness."

18But even so, Paul and Barnabas could scarcely restrain the people from sacrificing to them!

19Yet only a few days later, some Jews arrived from Antioch and Iconium and turned the crowds into a murderous mob that stoned Paul and dragged him out of the city, apparently dead. 20But as the believers stood around him, he got up and went back into the city!

Paul and Barnabas appoint elders on the return trip home

The next day he left with Barnabas for Derbe. 21After preaching the Good News there and making many disciples, they returned again to Lystra, Iconium and Antioch, 22where they helped the believers to grow in love for God and each other. They encouraged them to continue in the faith in spite of all the persecution, reminding them that they must enter into the Kingdom of God through many tribulations. 23Paul and Barnabas also appointed elders in every church and prayed for them with fasting, turning them over to the care of the Lord in whom they trusted.

24Then they traveled back through Pisidia to Pamphylia, 25preached again in Perga, and went on to Attalia.

26Finally they returned by ship to Antioch, where their journey had begun, and where they had been committed to God for the work now completed.

27Upon arrival they called together the believers and reported on their trip, telling

14:10
Isa 35:6
Acts 3:8

14:11
Acts 28:6

14:13
Dan 2:46

14:15
Ex 20:11
Deut 32:21
Jer 14:22
Mt 16:16
1 Thess 1:9
Rev 14:7; 19:10

14:16
Ps 81:12

14:17
Deut 11:14
Ps 65:10-12
147:8
Acts 17:27
Rom 1:19,20

14:19
Acts 13:45
2 Cor 1:8; 11:25
2 Tim 3:11

14:20
Acts 14:6

14:22
Mt 10:38 16:24
Jn 15:18
Rom 8:17
2 Tim 2:11; 3:12

14:23
Tit 1:5

14:24
Acts 13:13,14

14:26
Acts 11:26
13:1-3

14:27
1 Cor 16:9
Col 4:3
Rev 3:8

14:11, 12 Jupiter and Mercury were two popular gods in the Roman world. People from Lystra claimed that Jupiter and Mercury had once visited their city. According to legend, no one offered them hospitality except an old couple, so Jupiter and Mercury killed the rest of the people and rewarded the old couple. When the citizens of Lystra saw the miracles of Paul and Barnabas, they assumed that Jupiter and Mercury were revisiting them. Remembering what had happened to their citizens before, they immediately hailed Paul and Barnabas.

14:15-18 Responding to the people of Lystra, Paul and Barnabas reminded them that God never leaves himself "without a witness." Rain and crops, for example, are evidence of his goodness. Later Paul wrote that this evidence in nature leaves people without an excuse for unbelief (Romans 1:20). When in doubt about God, look around and you will see abundant evidence that he is at work in our world.

●**14:18-20** Paul and Barnabas were persistent in their preaching of the Good News. They considered the cost to themselves to be nothing in comparison with obedience to Christ. They had just narrowly escaped being stoned at Iconium (14:1-7). However, Jews from Antioch and Iconium tracked Paul down and stoned him.

They thought he was dead. But Paul got up and went back into the city to preach the Good News—that's true commitment! Being a disciple of Christ calls for costly commitment. As Christians, we no longer belong to ourselves, but to our Lord, for whom we are called to suffer.

14:21, 22 Paul and Barnabas returned to visit the believers in all the cities where they had recently been threatened and physically attacked. They knew the dangers they faced, yet they believed they had a responsibility to encourage the new believers. No matter how inconvenient or uncomfortable the task may seem, we must never fail to support new believers who need our help and encouragement. It was not convenient or comfortable for Jesus to go to the cross for us!

●**14:23** Part of the reason Paul and Barnabas took their lives in their hands to return to these cities was to organize the churches' leadership. They were not just following up on a loosely knit group; they were helping the believers get organized with Spirit-led leaders who could help them grow. Churches grow under Spirit-led leaders, both laypersons and pastors. Pray for your church leaders and support them; and if God urges you, humbly accept the responsibility of a leadership role in your church.

how God had opened the door of faith to the Gentiles too. 28And they stayed there with the believers at Antioch for a long while.

2. Meeting of the church council
The leaders meet in Jerusalem

15:1
Gen 17:9-11
Lev 12:3
Gal 5:2
Phil 3:2,3

15:2
Gal 2:1-10

15:3
Acts 14:27

15 While Paul and Barnabas were at Antioch, some men from Judea arrived and began to teach the believers that unless they adhered to the ancient Jewish custom of circumcision, they could not be saved. 2Paul and Barnabas argued and discussed this with them at length, and finally the believers sent them to Jerusalem, accompanied by some local men, to talk to the apostles and elders there about this question. 3After the entire congregation had escorted them out of the city the delegates went on to Jerusalem, stopping along the way in the cities of

---

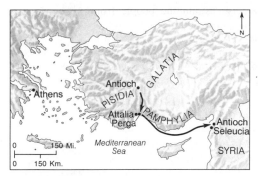

THE END OF THE FIRST JOURNEY From Antioch in Pisidia, Paul and Barnabas went down the mountains back to Pamphylia on the coast. Stopping first in Perga, where they had landed, they went west to Attalia, the main port that sent goods from Asia to Syria and Egypt. There they found a ship bound for Seleucia, the port of Antioch in Syria. This ended their first missionary journey.

14:28 Paul probably wrote his letter to the Galatians while he was staying in Antioch (A.D. 48 or 49) after completing his first missionary journey. There are several theories as to what part of Galatia Paul was addressing, but most agree that Iconium, Lystra, and Derbe were part of that region. Galatians was probably written before the Jerusalem Council (Acts 15), because in the letter the question of whether Gentile believers should be required to follow Jewish law was not yet resolved. The Council met to solve that problem.

●**15:1ff** The delegates to the council at Jerusalem came from the churches in Jerusalem and Antioch. The conversion of Gentiles was raising an urgent question for the early church—do the Gentiles have to adhere to the laws of Moses and other Jewish traditions to be saved? One group of Jewish Christians insisted that following the law, including circumcision, was necessary for salvation. The Gentiles did not think they needed to become Jewish first in order to become Christians. So Paul and Barnabas discussed this problem with the leaders of the church. The council upheld the convictions expressed by Paul and Barnabas that following the Jewish laws, including circumcision, was not essential for salvation and that Jewish and Gentile Christians could eat together without the Jews' becoming defiled.

●**15:1** The real problem for the Jewish Christians was not over whether Gentiles could be saved, but whether Gentiles had to adhere to the laws of Moses. The test of following these laws was

circumcision. The Jewish Christians were worried because soon there would be more Gentile than Jewish Christians, and the Jews were afraid of weakening moral standards among believers if they did not follow Jewish laws. Paul, Barnabas, and the other church leaders believed that the Old Testament law was very important, but it was not a prerequisite to salvation. The law cannot save; only faith in Jesus Christ is what one needs to be saved.

●**15:2, 3** It is helpful to see how the churches in Antioch and Jerusalem resolved their conflict: (1) they sent a delegation to help seek a solution; (2) they met with the church leaders to give their reports and set another date to continue the discussion; (3) Paul and Barnabas gave their report; (4) James summarized the reports and made the decision; (5) everyone abided by the decision; (6) the council sent a letter with delegates back to Antioch to report the decision.

This is a wise way to handle conflicts within the church. Problems must be confronted, and all sides of the argument must be given a fair hearing. The discussion should be held before leaders who are spiritually mature and trusted to make wise decisions. Everyone should then abide by the decisions.

THE JERUSALEM COUNCIL A dispute arose when some Judeans taught that Gentile believers had to be circumcised to be saved. Paul and Barnabas went to Jerusalem to discuss this situation with the leaders there. After the Jerusalem council made its decision, Paul and Barnabas returned to Antioch with the news.

Phoenicia and Samaria to visit the believers, telling them—much to everyone's joy—that the Gentiles, too, were being converted.

4Arriving in Jerusalem, they met with the church leaders—all the apostles and elders were present—and Paul and Barnabas reported on what God had been doing through their ministry. 5But then some of the men who had been Pharisees before their conversion stood to their feet and declared that all Gentile converts must be circumcised and required to follow all the Jewish customs and ceremonies.

6So the apostles and church elders set a further meeting to decide this question.

7At the meeting, after long discussion, Peter stood and addressed them as follows: "Brothers, you all know that God chose me from among you long ago to preach the Good News to the Gentiles, so that they also could believe. 8God, who knows men's hearts, confirmed the fact that he accepts Gentiles by giving them the Holy Spirit, just as he gave him to us. 9He made no distinction between them and us, for he cleansed their lives through faith, just as he did ours. 10And now are you going to correct God by burdening the Gentiles with a yoke that neither we nor our fathers were able to bear? 11Don't you believe that all are saved the same way, by the free gift of the Lord Jesus?"

12There was no further discussion, and everyone now listened as Barnabas and Paul told about the miracles God had done through them among the Gentiles.

13When they had finished, James took the floor. "Brothers," he said, "listen to me. 14Peter has told you about the time God first visited the Gentiles to take from them a people to bring honor to his name. 15And this fact of Gentile conversion agrees with what the prophets predicted. For instance, listen to this passage from the prophet Amos:

16'Afterwards' [says the Lord], 'I will return and renew the broken contract with David, 17so that Gentiles, too, will find the Lord—all those marked with my name.'

18That is what the Lord says, who reveals his plans made from the beginning.

19"And so my judgment is that we should not insist that the Gentiles who turn to God must obey our Jewish laws, 20except that we should write to them to refrain from eating meat sacrificed to idols, from all fornication, and also from eating unbled meat of strangled animals. 21For these things have been preached against in Jewish synagogues in every city on every Sabbath for many generations."

The council sends a letter to Gentile believers

22Then the apostles and elders and the whole congregation voted to send delegates to Antioch with Paul and Barnabas, to report on this decision. The men chosen were two of the church leaders—Judas (also called Barsabbas) and Silas. 23This is the letter they took along with them:

15:5
1 Cor 7:18
Gal 5:2-11
15:7
Acts 10:19-29
15:8
1 Chron 28:9
Jer 17:10
Acts 10:44,47
Heb 4:13
15:9
Acts 10:43
Rom 10:11,12
15:10
Mt 23:4
Gal 5:1
15:11
Rom 3:23,24
5:15
2 Cor 13:14
Eph 1:7,8; 2:8
15:12
Acts 14:27; 15:4
15:13
Acts 12:17
15:15
Isa 11:10
54:1-5

15:16
Amos 9:11,12
15:18
Isa 45:21
15:19
Acts 21:15
15:20
Gen 9:4
Ex 20:3,4
Lev 3:17
Deut 12:16
Ezek 20:30
Dan 1:8
1 Cor 8:7; 10:7
1 Thess 4:3,4
15:21
Acts 13:15

15:22
Acts 1:23
15:27; 16:19
17:4
1 Pet 5:12

15:15 *from the prophet Amos,* implied. See Amos 9:11, 12. **15:16** *says the Lord,* implied. *renew the broken contract with David,* literally, "rebuild the tabernacle of David which is fallen."

15:10 If the law was a yoke that the Jews could not bear, how did having the law help them throughout their history? Paul wrote that the law was a teacher and guide that pointed out their sins so they could repent and return to God and right living (see Galatians 3:24, 25). It was, and still is, impossible to obey the law completely.

15:13 This James is Jesus' brother. He became the leader of the church in Jerusalem and wrote the book of James.

●**15:20** Gentile believers did not have to abide by the Jewish law of circumcision, but they were asked by the council to stay away from idolatry, sexual immorality (a common part of idol worship), and eating meat of unbled animals (reflecting the biblical teaching that the life is in the blood—Leviticus 17:14). If Gentile Christians would abstain from these three practices, they would please God and get along better with fellow Jewish Christians. Of course, there were

other actions inappropriate for believers, but the Jews were especially concerned about these three. This compromise helped the church grow unhindered by the cultural differences of Jews and Gentiles. When we share our message across cultural and economic boundaries, we must be sure that the requirements for faith we set up are God's, not people's.

15:22 Apostleship was not a church office, but a position and function based on specific gifts. Elders were appointed to lead and manage the church. In this meeting, apostles submitted to the decision of an elder—James, Jesus' brother.

15:22 Silas would later accompany Paul on his second missionary journey in place of Barnabas, who visited different cities.

●**15:23–29** This letter answered their questions and brought great joy to the Gentile Christians in Antioch (15:31). Beautifully written, it

"*From:* The apostles, elders and brothers at Jerusalem.

"*To:* The Gentile brothers in Antioch, Syria and Cilicia. Greetings!

15:24
Gal 1:7; 2:4; 5:12
Tit 1:10

24"We understand that some believers from here have upset you and questioned your salvation, but they had no such instructions from us. 25So it seemed wise to us, having unanimously agreed on our decision, to send to you these two official representatives, along with our beloved Barnabas and Paul. 26These men—Judas and Silas, who have risked their lives for the sake of our Lord Jesus Christ—will confirm orally what we have decided concerning your question.

15:26
Acts 13:50
14:19
1 Cor 15:30
2 Cor 11:23,26

27, 28, 29"For it seemed good to the Holy Spirit and to us to lay no greater burden of Jewish laws on you than to abstain from eating food offered to idols and from unbled meat of strangled animals, and, of course, from fornication. If you do this, it is enough. Farewell."

15:29
Lev 17:14
Acts 21:25
Rev 2:14

30The four messengers went at once to Antioch, where they called a general meeting of the Christians and gave them the letter. 31And there was great joy throughout the church that day as they read it.

15:32
Acts 13:1

32Then Judas and Silas, both being gifted speakers, preached long sermons to the

15:24 *questioned your salvation,* literally, "subverted your souls." **15:27-29** *and from unbled meat of strangled animals,* literally, "and from blood." **15:32** *gifted speakers,* or, "prophets."

THE FIRST CHURCH CONFERENCE	Group	Position	Reasons
	Judaizers (some Jewish Christians)	Gentiles must become Jewish first to be eligible for salvation	1. These were devout, practicing Jews who found it difficult to set aside a tradition of gaining merit with God by keeping the law 2. They thought grace was too easy for the Gentiles 3. They were afraid of seeming too non-Jewish in their new faith—which could lead to death 4. The demands on the Gentiles were a way of maintaining control and authority in the movement
	Gentile Christians	Faith in Christ as Savior is the only requirement for salvation	1. To submit to Jewish demands would be to doubt what God had already done for them by faith alone 2. They resisted exchanging a system of Jewish rituals for their pagan rituals—neither of which had power to save 3. They sought to obey Christ by baptism (rather than by circumcision) as a sign of their new faith
	Peter and James	Faith is the only requirement, but there must be evidence of change by rejecting parts of the old lifestyle	1. Tried to distinguish between what was still true from God's Word and what was just human tradition 2. Had Christ's command to preach to all the world 3. Wanted to preserve unity 4. Saw that Christianity could never survive as just a sect within Judaism

As long as most of the first Christians were Jewish, there was little difficulty in welcoming new believers. However, Gentiles (non-Jews) began to accept Jesus' offer of salvation. The evidence from their lives and the presence of God's Spirit in them showed that God was accepting them. Some of the early Christians believed that non-Jewish Christians needed to meet certain conditions before they could be worthy to accept Christ. The issue could have destroyed the church, so a conference was called in Jerusalem and the issue was formally settled there, although it continued to be a problem for many years following. Above is an outline of the three points of view at the conference.

appeals to the Holy Spirit's guidance and explains what is to be done as though the readers already know it. It is helpful when believers learn to be careful not only in what they say, but also in how they say it. We may be correct in our content, but we can lose our audience by our tone of voice or attitude.

●**15:31** The debate over circumcision could have split the church,

but Paul, Barnabas, and the Jews in Antioch made the right decision—they sought counsel from the apostles and God's Word. Our differences should be settled the same way, by seeking wise counsel and abiding by the decisions. Don't let disagreements divide you from other believers. Third-party assistance is a sound or resolving problems and preserving unity.

believers, strengthening their faith. 33They stayed several days, and then Judas and Silas returned to Jerusalem taking greetings and appreciation to those who had sent them. 34, 35Paul and Barnabas stayed on at Antioch to assist several others who were preaching and teaching there.

15:33
Mt 4:24
Acts 6:9; 11:20
15:41
Gal 1:21

3. Second missionary journey

Paul and Barnabas separate

36Several days later Paul suggested to Barnabas that they return again to Turkey, and visit each city where they had preached before, to see how the new converts were getting along. 37Barnabas agreed, and wanted to take along John Mark. 38But Paul didn't like that idea at all, since John had deserted them in Pamphylia. 39Their disagreement over this was so sharp that they separated. Barnabas took Mark with him and sailed for Cyprus, 40, 41while Paul chose Silas and, with the blessing of the believers, left for Syria and Cilicia, to encourage the churches there.

15:36
Acts 13:4,13,
14,51
14:5,6,24-28
15:37
Col 4:10
2 Tim 4:11

15:38
Acts 13:13

Timothy joins Paul and Silas at Lystra

16 Paul and Silas went first to Derbe and then on to Lystra where they met Timothy, a believer whose mother was a Christian Jewess but his father a Greek. 2Timothy was well thought of by the brothers in Lystra and Iconium, 3so Paul asked him to join them on their journey. In deference to the Jews of the area, he circumcised Timothy before they left, for everyone knew that his father was a Greek [and hadn't permitted this before]. 4Then they went from city to city, making

16:1
Acts 14:5,6
Phil 2:19-22
2 Tim 1:2,5; 3:15
16:3
1 Cor 9:20
Gal 2:3; 5:2

15:33 *stayed several days,* literally, "spent some time." **15:36** *return again to Turkey, and visit each city where they had preached before,* implied. Literally, "return now and visit every city wherein we proclaimed the word of the Lord." **16:3** *and hadn't permitted this before,* implied.

15:37–39 Paul and Barnabas disagreed sharply over Mark. Paul didn't want to take him along because he had left them earlier (13:13). This disagreement caused the two great preachers to lead two teams, opening up two missionary endeavors instead of one. God works even through conflict and disagreements. Later, Mark became vital to Paul's ministry (Colossians 4:10). Christians do not always agree, but problems can be solved by agreeing to disagree and letting God work his will.

15:40 Paul's second missionary journey, this time with Silas as his partner, began approximately three years after his first one ended. The two visited many of the cities covered on Paul's first journey, plus others. This journey laid the groundwork for the church in Greece.

15:40 Silas was involved in the Jerusalem council and was one of the two men chosen to represent the Jerusalem church by taking the letter and decision back to Antioch (15:22). Paul, from the Antioch church, chose Silas, from the Jerusalem church, and they traveled together to many cities to spread the Good News. This teamwork revealed the church's unity after the Jerusalem council's decision.

16:1 Timothy is the first second-generation Christian mentioned in the New Testament. His mother, Eunice, and grandmother, Lois (2 Timothy 1:5), had become believers and had faithfully influenced him for the Lord. Although Timothy's father apparently was not a Christian, the faithfulness of his mother and grandmother prevailed. Never underestimate the far-reaching consequences of raising one small child to love the Lord.

16:2, 3 Timothy and his mother, Eunice, were from Lystra. Eunice had probably heard Paul's preaching when he was there during his first missionary journey (Acts 14:5, 6). Timothy was the son of a Jewish mother and Greek father—to the Jews, a half-breed like a Samaritan. So Paul asked Timothy to be circumcised to erase some of the stigma he may have had with Jewish believers. Timothy was not required to be circumcised (the Jerusalem council had decided that—chapter 15), but he voluntarily did this to overcome any barriers to his witness for Christ. Sometimes we need to go beyond the minimum requirements in order to help our audience receive our testimony.

THE SECOND JOURNEY BEGINS Paul and Silas set out on a second missionary journey to visit the cities Paul had preached in earlier. This time they set out by land rather than sea, traveling the Roman road through Cilicia and the Cilician Gates—a gorge through the Taurus Mountains—then northwest toward Derbe, Lystra, and Iconium. The Spirit told them not to go into Asia, so they turned northward toward Bithynia. Again the Spirit said no, so they turned west through Mysia to the harbor city of Troas.

16:5
Acts 9:31

known the decision concerning the Gentiles, as decided by the apostles and elders in Jerusalem. 5So the church grew daily in faith and numbers.

Paul has a vision directing them to Macedonia

16:7
Rom 8:9
Gal 2:20
Phil 1:19

16:8
2 Cor 2:12
2 Tim 4:13

16:9
Num 12:6
Acts 10:3,30
Rom 15:26
18:5; 20:3

6Next they traveled through Phrygia and Galatia, because the Holy Spirit had told them not to go into the Turkish province of Asia Minor at that time. 7Then going along the borders of Mysia they headed north for the province of Bithynia, but again the Spirit of Jesus said no. 8So instead they went on through Mysia province to the city of Troas.

9That night Paul had a vision. In his dream he saw a man over in Macedonia, Greece, pleading with him, "Come over here and help us." 10Well, that settled it. We would go to Macedonia, for we could only conclude that God was sending us to preach the Good News there.

Lydia is converted in Philippi

16:11
2 Cor 2:12

16:12
Acts 20:6
1 Thess 2:2

11We went aboard a boat at Troas, and sailed straight across to Samothrace, and the next day on to Neapolis, 12and finally reached Philippi, a Roman colony just inside the Macedonian border, and stayed there several days.

13On the Sabbath, we went a little way outside the city to a river bank where we understood some people met for prayer; and we taught the Scriptures to some women who came.

16:9 *That night,* literally, "in the night."   **16:12** *Roman,* implied.

16:6 We don't know how the Holy Spirit told Paul that he and his men were not to go into Asia. It may have been through a prophet, a vision, an inner conviction, or some other circumstance. To know God's will does not mean we must hear his voice. He leads in different ways. When seeking God's will (1) make sure your plan is in harmony with God's Word; (2) ask mature Christians for their advice; (3) check your own motives—are you seeking to do what you want or what you think God wants?—and (4) pray for God to open and close the doors of circumstances.

16:7–9 The Spirit of Jesus is another name for the Holy Spirit (16:6). The Holy Spirit closed the door twice for Paul, so he must have wondered which geographical direction he should take in spreading the gospel. Then, in a vision (16:9), Paul was given definite direction, and he and his companions obediently traveled into Greece. The Holy Spirit guides us to the right places, but he also guides us away from the wrong places. As we seek God's will, it is important to know what God wants us to do and where he wants us to go, but it is equally important to know what God does not want us to do and where he does not want us to go.

16:10 The use of the pronoun *we* indicates that Luke, the author of the Gospel of Luke and of this book, joined Paul, Silas, and Timothy on their journey. He was an eyewitness to most of the remaining incidents in this book.

16:12 Philippi was the key city in the region of Macedonia (northern Greece today). Paul founded a church during this visit (A.D. 50–51). Later Paul wrote a letter to the church, the book of Philippians, probably from a prison in Rome (A.D. 61). The letter was personal and tender, showing Paul's deep love and friendship for the believers there. In his letter to them he thanked them for a gift they had sent, alerted them to a coming visit by Timothy and Epaphroditus, urged the church to clear up any disunity, and encouraged the believers not to give in to persecution.

16:13 Inscribed on the arches outside the city of Philippi was a prohibition against bringing an unrecognized religion into the city; therefore, this prayer meeting was held outside the city, beside the river.

●**16:13, 14** After following the Holy Spirit's leading into Macedonia, Paul made his first evangelistic contact with a small group of

women. Paul never allowed sexual or cultural boundaries to keep him from preaching the gospel. He preached to these women; and Lydia, an influential merchant, believed. This threw open the door for ministry in that region. In the early church God often worked in and through women.

16:13ff Luke highlights the stories of three individuals who became believers through Paul's ministry in Philippi: Lydia, the influential businesswoman (16:14), the demon-possessed slave girl (16:18), and the jailer (16:29). The gospel was affecting all strata of society, just as it does today.

PAUL TRAVELS TO MACEDONIA At Troas, Paul received the Macedonian call (16:9), and he, Silas, Timothy, and Luke boarded a ship. They sailed to the island of Samothrace, then on to Neapolis, the port for the city of Philippi. Philippi sat on the Egnatian Way, a main transportation artery connecting the eastern provinces with Italy.

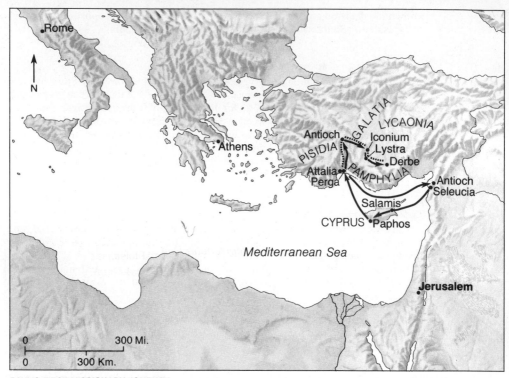

PAUL'S FIRST MISSIONARY JOURNEY

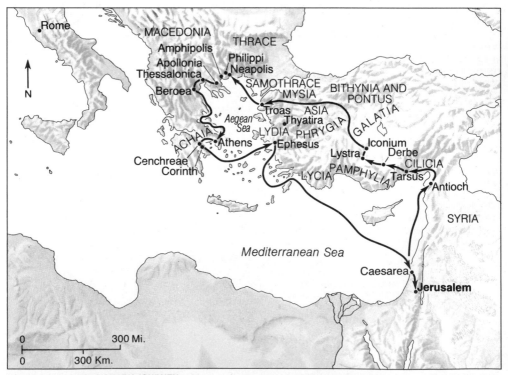

PAUL'S SECOND MISSIONARY JOURNEY

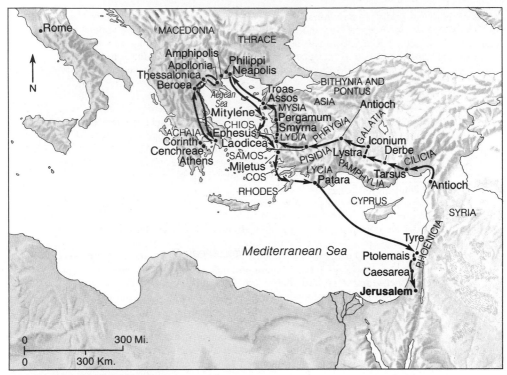

PAUL'S THIRD MISSIONARY JOURNEY

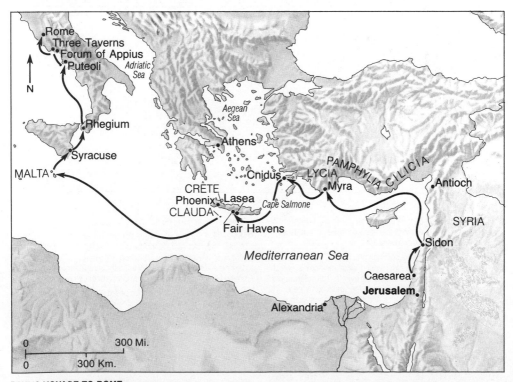

PAUL'S VOYAGE TO ROME

14One of them was Lydia, a saleswoman from Thyatira, a merchant of purple cloth. She was already a worshiper of God and, as she listened to us, the Lord opened her heart and she accepted all that Paul was saying. 15She was baptized along with all her household and asked us to be her guests. "If you agree that I am faithful to the Lord," she said, "come and stay at my home." And she urged us until we did.

16:14
a) Rev 1:11
2:18-29
b) Acts 13:43
18:7
16:15
Acts 16:14

The Philippian jailer is converted

16One day as we were going down to the place of prayer beside the river, we met a demon-possessed slave girl who was a fortune-teller, and earned much money for her masters. 17She followed along behind us shouting, "These men are servants of God and they have come to tell you how to have your sins forgiven."

16:16
Lev 19:31; 20:6
Deut 18:10,11
1 Sam 28:3,7,8

18This went on day after day until Paul, in great distress, turned and spoke to the demon within her. "I command you in the name of Jesus Christ to come out of her," he said. And instantly it left her.

16:18
Mk 1:25,34
16:17

19Her masters' hopes of wealth were now shattered; they grabbed Paul and Silas and dragged them before the judges at the marketplace.

16:19
Mt 10:18
2 Cor 6:5

20,21"These Jews are corrupting our city," they shouted. "They are teaching the people to do things that are against the Roman laws."

16:20,21
Esth 3:8
Acts 16:12; 17:6

22A mob was quickly formed against Paul and Silas, and the judges ordered them stripped and beaten with wooden whips. 23Again and again the rods slashed down across their bared backs; and afterwards they were thrown into prison. The jailer was threatened with death if they escaped, 24so he took no chances, but put them into the inner dungeon and clamped their feet into the stocks.

16:22
2 Cor 11:23
1 Thess 2:2

16:25
Mt 5:10-12
Acts 5:41
Eph 5:19
2 Tim 1:8

25Around midnight, as Paul and Silas were praying and singing hymns to the Lord—and the other prisoners were listening— 26suddenly there was a great earthquake; the prison was shaken to its foundations, all the doors flew open—and the chains of every prisoner fell off! 27The jailer wakened to see the prison doors

16:26
Acts 5:19; 12:7,10

16:27
Acts 12:19

16:23 *if they escaped,* implied.

Book	Approximate Date	Book	Approximate Date	
Galatians	49	Jude	65	**THE BOOKS OF**
James	49	1 Timothy	64	**THE NEW**
1, 2 Thessalonians	51/52	1 Peter	64/65	**TESTAMENT:**
1, 2 Corinthians	55	Titus	64	**WHEN WERE**
Romans	57	Acts	66/68	**THEY WRITTEN?**
Mark	58/60	2 Peter	66/68	
Ephesians	60	2 Timothy	66/67	
Colossians	60	Hebrews	68/70	
Philemon	60	John	85	
Philippians	61	1, 2, 3 John	85/90	
Matthew	61/64	Revelation	95	
Luke	61/64			

16:14 Lydia was a merchant of purple cloth, so she was probably wealthy. Purple cloth was valuable and expensive. It was usually worn as a sign of nobility or royalty.

16:16 Fortune-telling was a common practice in Greek and Roman culture. There were many superstitious methods by which people thought they could foretell future events, from interpreting omens in nature to communicating with the spirits of the dead. This young slave girl had an evil spirit, and she made her master rich by interpreting signs and telling people their fortunes. The master was exploiting her unfortunate condition for personal gain.

16:17 What the slave girl said was true although the source of her knowledge was a demon. Why did a demon announce the truth about Paul, and why did this annoy him? If Paul accepted the demon's words, he would appear to be linking the gospel and demon-related activities. This would damage his message about

Christ. Truth and evil do not mix.

●**16:22-25** Paul and Silas were stripped, beaten, whipped, and placed in stocks in the inner dungeon. Despite this dismal situation, they praised God, praying and singing as the other prisoners listened. No matter what our circumstances, we should praise God. Others may come to Christ because of our example.

16:24 Stocks were made of two boards joined with iron clamps, leaving holes just big enough for the ankles. The prisoner's legs were placed across the lower board and then the upper board was closed over them. Sometimes both wrists and ankles were placed in stocks. Paul, who had committed no crime and was a peaceful man, was put in stocks designed for holding the most dangerous prisoners in absolute security.

16:27 The jailer drew his sword to kill himself because Roman officials had threatened his life if anyone escaped (16:23).

wide open, and assuming the prisoners had escaped, he drew his sword to kill himself.

28But Paul yelled to him, "Don't do it! We are all here!"

29Trembling with fear, the jailer called for lights and ran to the dungeon and fell down before Paul and Silas. 30He brought them out and begged them, "Sirs, what must I do to be saved?"

31They replied, "Believe on the Lord Jesus and you will be saved, and your entire household."

32Then they told him and all his household the Good News from the Lord. 33That

16:30
Acts 2:37

16:31
Jn 3:16,36
Acts 11:14
Rom 10:9

SILAS

The lives of the first Christian missionaries can be described with many words, but "boring" is not one of them. There were days of great excitement as men and women who had never heard of Jesus responded to the gospel. There were dangerous journeys over land and sea. Health risks and hunger were part of the daily routine. And there was open and hostile resistance to Christianity in many cities. Silas was one of the first missionaries, and he found out that serving Jesus Christ was certainly not boring!

The majority of early Christians were Jews who realized Jesus was the fulfillment of God's Old Testament promises to his people; however, the universal application of those promises had been overlooked. Thus, many felt that becoming Jewish was a prerequisite to becoming a Christian. The idea that God could accept a Gentile pagan was too incredible. But Gentiles began to accept Christ as Savior, and the transformation of their lives and the presence of God's Spirit confirmed their conversions. Some Jews were still reluctant, though, and insisted these new Christians take on various Jewish customs. The issue came to a boiling point at the Jerusalem meeting, but was peacefully resolved. Silas was one of the representatives from Jerusalem sent with Paul and Barnabas back to Antioch with an official letter of welcome and acceptance to the Gentile Christians. Having fulfilled this mission, Silas returned to Jerusalem. Within a short time, however, he was back in Antioch at Paul's request to join him on his second missionary journey.

Paul, Silas, and Timothy began a far-ranging ministry that included some exciting adventures. Paul and Silas spent a night singing in a Philippian prison after being severely beaten. Later, they narrowly missed another beating in Thessalonica, prevented by an evening escape. In Beroea there was more trouble, but Silas and Timothy stayed to teach the young believers while Paul traveled on to Athens. The team was finally reunited in Corinth. In each place they visited, they left behind a small group of Christians.

Silas leaves the story as suddenly as he entered it. Peter mentions him as the co-author of 1 Peter, but we do not know when he joined Peter. He was an effective believer before leaving Jerusalem, and he doubtless continued to minister after his work with Paul was completed. He took advantage of opportunities to serve God and was not discouraged by the setbacks and opposition he met along the way. Silas, though not the most famous of the early missionaries, was certainly a hero worth imitating.

Strengths and accomplishments:
● A leader in the Jerusalem church
● Represented the church in carrying the "acceptance letter" prepared by the Jerusalem council to the Gentile believers in Antioch
● Was closely associated with Paul from the second missionary journey on
● When imprisoned with Paul in Philippi, sang songs of praise to God
● Worked as a writing secretary for both Paul and Peter, using "Silvanus" as his pen name

Lessons from his life:
● Partnership is a significant part of effective ministry
● God never guarantees that his servants will not suffer
● Obedience to God will often mean giving up what makes us feel secure

Vital statistics:
● Where: Roman citizen living in Jerusalem
● Occupation: One of the first career missionaries
● Contemporaries: Paul, Timothy, Peter, Mark, Barnabas

Key verse:
"These men—Judas and Silas, who have risked their lives for the sake of our Lord Jesus Christ—will confirm orally what we have decided concerning your question" (Acts 15:26).

Silas' story is told in Acts 15:22—19:10. He is also mentioned in 2 Corinthians 1:19; 1 Thessalonians 1:1; 2 Thessalonians 1:1; 1 Peter 5:12.

same hour he washed their stripes and he and all his family were baptized. 34Then he brought them up into his house and set a meal before them. How he and his household rejoiced because all were now believers! 35The next morning the judges sent police officers over to tell the jailer, "Let those men go!" 36So the jailer told Paul they were free to leave.

16:34
1 Sam 2:1,2
1 Chron 16:10
Ps 119:111
Rom 5:2
1 Pet 1:8

37But Paul replied, "Oh, no they don't! They have publicly beaten us without trial and jailed us—and we are Roman citizens! So now they want us to leave secretly? Never! Let them come themselves and release us!"

16:37
Mt 10:16
Acts 22:25-29

38The police officers reported to the judges, who feared for their lives when they heard Paul and Silas were Roman citizens. 39So they came to the jail and begged them to go, and brought them out and pled with them to leave the city. 40Paul and Silas then returned to the home of Lydia where they met with the believers and preached to them once more before leaving town.

16:38
Acts 22:29

16:40
Acts 16:14,15

Paul preaches in Thessalonica

17 Now they traveled through the cities of Amphipolis and Apollonia and came to Thessalonica, where there was a Jewish synagogue. 2As was Paul's custom, he went there to preach, and for three Sabbaths in a row he opened the Scriptures to the people, 3explaining the prophecies about the sufferings of the Messiah and his coming back to life, and proving that Jesus is the Messiah. 4Some who listened were persuaded and became converts—including a large number of godly Greek men, and also many important women of the city.

17:1
Phil 4:16
1 Thess 1:1
2 Thess 1:1

17:2
Acts 9:20
13:5,14; 14:1
17:10,17; 19:8

17:3
Lk 24:26
Acts 3:18; 9:22
18:5

5But the Jewish leaders were jealous and incited some worthless fellows from the streets to form a mob and start a riot. They attacked the home of Jason, planning to take Paul and Silas to the City Council for punishment.

17:5
Rom 16:21

6Not finding them there, they dragged out Jason and some of the other believers,

17:6
Acts 16:20,21

17:4 *also many important women of the city.* Some manuscripts read, "many of the wives of the leading men."

16:37 Paul refused to take his freedom and run, in order to teach the rulers in Philippi a lesson and to protect the other believers from the treatment he and Silas had received. The word would spread that Paul and Silas had been found innocent and freed by the leaders, and that believers should not be persecuted—especially if they were Roman citizens.

16:38 Roman citizenship carried with it certain privileges. These Philippian authorities were frightened because it was illegal to whip a Roman citizen. In addition, every citizen had the right to a fair trial—which Paul and Silas had not been given.

● **17:1** Thessalonica was one of the wealthiest and most influential cities in Macedonia. This is the first city Paul visited where his teachings attracted a large group of socially prominent citizens. The church he planted grew quickly, but in A.D. 50–51, Paul was forced out of the city by a mob (17:5, 6, 10). Paul later sent Timothy back to Thessalonica to see how the Christians were doing. Soon afterward, Paul wrote 1 and 2 Thessalonians, two letters to the Thessalonian believers, encouraging them to remain faithful and to refuse to listen to false teachers who tried to refute their beliefs.

17:1, 2 A synagogue, a group of Jews who gathered for teaching and prayer, could be established wherever there were ten Jewish males. Paul's regular practice was to preach in synagogues as long as the Jews allowed it. Often those who weren't Jews came to these services and heard Paul's preaching. For what a synagogue service was like, see the note on 13:14.

● **17:2, 3** When Paul spoke in the synagogues, he wisely began by talking about Old Testament writings and explaining how the Messiah fulfilled them, moving from the known to the unknown. This is a good strategy for us. When we witness for Christ, we should begin where people are, affirming the truth they do know, and then present Christ, the One who is Truth.

17:5 The Jewish leaders didn't refute the theology of Paul and Silas, but they were jealous of the popularity of these itinerant

MINISTRY IN MACEDONIA
Luke stayed in Philippi while Paul, Silas, and Timothy continued on the Egnatian Way to Amphipolis, Apollonia, and Thessalonica. But trouble arose in Thessalonica, and they fled to Beroea. When their enemies from Thessalonica pursued them, Paul set out by sea to Athens, leaving Silas and Timothy to encourage the believers.

preachers. Their motives for causing the uproar were rooted in personal jealousy, not doctrinal purity.

● **17:6** What a reputation these early Christians had; they truly "turned the world upside down!" The power of the gospel revolutionized lives, crossed all social barriers, threw open prison doors, caused people to care deeply for one another, and stirred them to worship God. Our world needs to be turned upside down, to be transformed. The gospel is not in the business of merely improving programs and conduct, but of dynamically transforming lives.

and took them before the Council instead. "Paul and Silas have turned the rest of the world upside down, and now they are here disturbing our city," they shouted,

17:7
Lk 23:2

7"and Jason has let them into his home. They are all guilty of treason, for they claim another king, Jesus, instead of Caesar."

8, 9The people of the city, as well as the judges, were concerned at these reports and let them go only after they had posted bail.

Those at Beroea search the Scriptures

10That night the Christians hurried Paul and Silas to Beroea, and, as usual, they

17:10 *as usual,* implied.

LUKE

One of the essential qualities of a good doctor is compassion. People need to know that their doctor cares. Even if he or she doesn't know what is wrong or isn't sure what to do, real concern is always a doctor's good medicine. Doctor Luke was a person of compassion.

Although we know few facts of his life, Luke has left us a strong impression of himself by what he wrote. In his Gospel, he emphasizes Jesus Christ's compassion. He vividly recorded both the power demonstrated by Christ's life and the care with which he treated people. Luke highlighted the relationships Jesus had with women. His writing in Acts is full of sharp verbal pictures of real people caught up in the greatest events of history.

Luke was also a doctor. He had a traveling medical practice as Paul's companion. Since the gospel was often welcomed with whips and stones, the doctor was seldom without patients. It is even possible that Paul's "thorn in the flesh" was some kind of physical ailment that needed Luke's regular attention. Paul deeply appreciated Luke's skills and faithfulness.

God also made special use of Luke as the historian of the early church. Repeatedly, the details of Luke's descriptions have been proven accurate. The first words in his Gospel indicate his interest in the truth.

Luke's compassion reflected his Lord's. His skill as a doctor helped Paul. His passion for the facts as he recorded the life of Christ, the spread of the early church, and the lives of Christianity's missionaries gives us dependable sources for the basis of our faith. He accomplished all this while staying out of the spotlight. Perhaps his greatest example is the challenge to greatness even when we are not the center of attention.

Strengths and accomplishments:
- A humble, faithful, and useful companion of Paul
- A well-educated and trained physician
- A careful and exact historian
- Writer of both the Gospel of Luke and the Acts of the Apostles

Lessons from his life:
- The words we leave behind will be a lasting picture of who we are
- Even the most successful person needs the personal care of others
- Excellence is shown by how we work when no one is noticing

Vital statistics:
- Where: Probably met Paul in Troas
- Occupation: Doctor, historian, traveling companion
- Contemporaries: Paul, Timothy, Silas, Peter

Key verses:
"Dear friend who loves God: Several biographies of Christ have already been written using as their source material the reports circulating among us from the early disciples and other eyewitnesses. However, it occurred to me that it would be well to recheck all these accounts from first to last and after thorough investigation to pass this summary on to you, to reassure you of the truth of all you were taught" (Luke 1:1–4).

Luke includes himself in the *we* sections of Acts 16—28. He is also mentioned in Luke 1:3; Acts 1:1; Colossians 4:14; 2 Timothy 4:11; Philemon 24.

17:7 The Jewish leaders had difficulty manufacturing an accusation that would be heard by the city government. The Romans did not care about theological disagreements between the Jews and these preachers. Treason, however, was a serious offense in the Roman Empire. Although Paul and Silas were not advocating rebellion against Roman law, their loyalty to another king sounded suspicious.

17:8, 9 "Posting bail" was not the process we think of—putting up cash for freedom. Instead Jason had to promise that the trouble would cease or his own property and possibly his life would be taken.

went to the synagogue to preach. ¹¹But the people of Beroea were more open minded than those in Thessalonica, and gladly listened to the message. They searched the Scriptures day by day to check up on Paul and Silas' statements to see if they were really so. ¹²As a result, many of them believed, including several prominent Greek women and many men also.

¹³But when the Jews in Thessalonica learned that Paul was preaching in Beroea, they went over and stirred up trouble. ¹⁴The believers acted at once, sending Paul on to the coast, while Silas and Timothy remained behind. ¹⁵Those accompanying Paul went on with him to Athens, and then returned to Beroea with a message for Silas and Timothy to hurry and join him.

In Athens Paul tells about the unknown God

¹⁶While Paul was waiting for them in Athens, he was deeply troubled by all the idols he saw everywhere throughout the city. ¹⁷He went to the synagogue for discussions with the Jews and the devout Gentiles, and spoke daily in the public square to all who happened to be there.

¹⁸He also had an encounter with some of the Epicurean and Stoic philosophers. Their reaction, when he told them about Jesus and his resurrection, was, "He's a dreamer," or, "He's pushing some foreign religion."

¹⁹But they invited him to the forum at Mars Hill. "Come and tell us more about this new religion," they said, ²⁰"for you are saying some rather startling things and we want to hear more." ²¹(I should explain that all the Athenians as well as the foreigners in Athens seemed to spend all their time discussing the latest new ideas!)

²²So Paul, standing before them at the Mars Hill forum, addressed them as follows:

"Men of Athens, I notice that you are very religious, ²³for as I was out walking I saw your many altars, and one of them had this inscription on it—'To the Unknown God.' You have been worshiping him without knowing who he is, and now I wish to tell you about him.

²⁴"He made the world and everything in it, and since he is Lord of heaven and earth, he doesn't live in man-made temples; ²⁵and human hands can't minister to his needs—for he has no needs! He himself gives life and breath to everything, and

17:11
Isa 34:16
Lk 16:29
Jn 5:39
Acts 26:22,23

17:13
1 Thess 2:15

17:14
Mt 10:23

17:15
Acts 18:5
1 Thess 3:1

17:16
Acts 18:1

17:18
1 Cor 1:20-24
4:10

17:23
Jn 4:22
2 Thess 2:4

17:24
1 Kgs 8:27
Isa 42:5
Acts 7:48,49

17:25
Ps 50:10-12
Dan 4:35
Rom 11:36

17:11 How do you evaluate sermons and teachings? The people in Beroea opened the Scriptures for themselves and searched for truths to verify or disprove the message they heard. Always compare what you hear with what the Bible says. A preacher or teacher who gives God's true message will never contradict or explain away anything in God's Word.

17:15 Athens, with its magnificent buildings and many gods, was a center for Greek culture, philosophy, and education. Philosophers and educated men were always ready to hear something new, so they invited Paul to speak to them at Mars Hill.

17:18 The Epicureans and Stoics were the dominant philosophers in Greek culture. The Epicureans believed that seeking happiness or pleasure was the primary goal of life. By contrast, the Stoics placed thinking above feeling and tried to live in harmony with nature and reason, suppressing their desire for pleasure. Thus they were very disciplined.

17:19 At one time the supreme court met on Mars Hill. As Paul stood on Mars Hill and spoke about the one true God, his audience could look down on the city and see the many idols representing gods Paul claimed were worthless.

●**17:22** Paul was well prepared to speak to this group. He came from Tarsus, an educational center, and had the training and knowledge to present his beliefs clearly and persuasively. Paul was a rabbi, taught by the finest scholar of his day, Gamaliel, and he had spent much of his life thinking and reasoning through the Scriptures.

It is not enough to teach or preach with conviction. Like Paul, we must be prepared. The more we know about the Bible, what it

means, and how to apply it to our lives, the more convincing our words will be. This does not mean we should avoid presenting the gospel until we feel adequately prepared. We should work with what we know, but always want to know more in order to reach more people and answer their questions and arguments more effectively.

●**17:22ff** Paul's address is a good example of how to communicate the gospel. Paul did not begin by reciting Jewish history, as he usually did, for this would have been meaningless to his Greek audience. He began by building a case for the one true God, using examples they understood. Then he established common ground by emphasizing what they agreed about God (17:22, 23). Finally he moved his message to the person of Christ, centering on the resurrection (17:30, 31). When you witness to others, you can use Paul's approach: use examples, establish common ground, and then move people toward a decision about Jesus Christ.

●**17:23** The Athenians built an idol to the unknown god for fear of missing blessings or receiving punishment. Paul's opening statement to the men of Athens was about their unknown god. Paul was not endorsing this god, but using the inscription as a point of entry for his witness to the one true God.

●**17:23** Paul explained the one true God to these educated men of Athens; although they were, in general, very religious, they did not know him. Today we have a "Christian" society, but to most people, God is still unknown. We need to proclaim who he is and make it clear what he did for all mankind through his Son Jesus Christ. We cannot assume that even religious people around us truly know Jesus or understand the importance of faith in him.

17:26
Job 12:23; 14:5

17:27
Jer 23:23,24
Acts 14:17
Rom 1:20

17:28
Job 12:10
Dan 5:23
Col 1:17-19
Heb 1:3

17:29
Isa 40:18-25
Rom 1:23

17:30
Acts 14:16,17
Rom 3:25

17:31
Ps 96:13
Acts 2:24; 10:42
Rom 2:16; 4:25
1 Cor 15

satisfies every need there is. 26He created all the people of the world from one man, Adam, and scattered the nations across the face of the earth. He decided beforehand which should rise and fall, and when. He determined their boundaries.

27"His purpose in all of this is that they should seek after God, and perhaps feel their way toward him and find him—though he is not far from any one of us. 28For in him we live and move and are! As one of your own poets says it, 'We are the sons of God.' 29If this is true, we shouldn't think of God as an idol made by men from gold or silver or chipped from stone. 30God tolerated man's past ignorance about these things, but now he commands everyone to put away idols and worship only him. 31For he has set a day for justly judging the world by the man he has appointed, and has pointed him out by bringing him back to life again."

32When they heard Paul speak of the resurrection of a person who had been dead, some laughed, but others said, "We want to hear more about this later." 33That ended Paul's discussion with them, 34but a few joined him and became believers. Among them was Dionysius, a member of the City Council, and a woman named Damaris, and others.

The governor releases Paul at Corinth

18:2
Hom 16:3
1 Cor 16:19

18:3
Acts 20:34
1 Cor 4:12; 9:15
2 Cor 11:7

18:5
Acts 17:3
18:28

18:6
Ezek 3:18,19
Mt 10:14
27:24,25
Acts 13:46
20:26; 28:26-28

18:8
1 Cor 1:2,14

18:10
Isa 41:10
Jer 1:18
2 Tim 2:19

18 Then Paul left Athens and went to Corinth. 2, 3There he became acquainted with a Jew named Aquila, born in Pontus, who had recently arrived from Italy with his wife, Priscilla. They had been expelled from Italy as a result of Claudius Caesar's order to deport all Jews from Rome. Paul lived and worked with them, for they were tentmakers just as he was.

4Each Sabbath found Paul at the synagogue, trying to convince the Jews and Greeks alike. 5And after the arrival of Silas and Timothy from Macedonia, Paul spent his full time preaching and testifying to the Jews that Jesus is the Messiah. 6But when the Jews opposed him and blasphemed, hurling abuse at Jesus, Paul shook off the dust from his robe and said, "Your blood be upon your own heads—I am innocent—from now on I will preach to the Gentiles."

7After that he stayed with Titus Justus, a Gentile who worshiped God and lived next door to the synagogue. 8However, Crispus, the leader of the synagogue, and all his household believed in the Lord and were baptized—as were many others in Corinth.

9One night the Lord spoke to Paul in a vision and told him, "Don't be afraid! Speak out! Don't quit! 10For I am with you and no one can harm you. Many people

17:26 *Adam,* implied.

● **17:30, 31** Paul did not leave his message unfinished. He confronted his listeners with Jesus' resurrection and its meaning to all people—either blessing or punishment. The Greeks had no concept of judgment. Most of them preferred worshiping many gods over just one, and the concept of resurrection was unbelievable and offensive to them. Paul did not hold back the truth, however, no matter what they might think of it. He changed his approach to fit his audience, but he never changed his basic message.

● **17:32–34** Paul's speech received a mixed reaction: some laughed, some kept searching for more information, and a few believed. Don't hesitate to tell others about Christ because you fear that some will not believe you. And don't expect a unanimously positive response to your witnessing. Even if only a few believe, it's worth the effort.

18:1 Corinth was the political and commercial center of Greece, surpassing Athens in importance. It had a reputation for great wickedness and immorality. A temple to Aphrodite—goddess of love and war—had been built on the large hill behind the city. In this popular religion, people worshiped the goddess by giving money to the temple and taking part in sexual acts with male and

female temple prostitutes. Paul found Corinth a challenge and a great ministry opportunity. Later, he wrote a series of letters to the Corinthians dealing in part with the problems of immorality. The Bible books of 1 and 2 Corinthians are two of those letters.

18:2, 3 Each Jewish boy learned a trade and tried to earn his living with it. Paul and Aquila had been trained in tentmaking, cutting and sewing the woven cloth of goat's hair into tents. Many tents were used to house soldiers, and so these tents may have been sold to the Roman army. As a tentmaker, Paul was able to go wherever God led him, carrying his livelihood with him. The word "tentmaker" in Greek was also used to describe a leather worker.

18:6 Paul told the Jews he had done all he could for them. Since they rejected Jesus as their Messiah, he would go to the Gentiles who would be more receptive.

18:10, 11 Others who became Christians in Corinth were Phoebe (Romans 16:1), Tertius (Romans 16:22), Erastus (Romans 16:23), Quartus (Romans 16:23), Chloe (1 Corinthians 1:11), Gaius (1 Corinthians 1:14), Stephanas and his household (1 Corinthians 16:15), Fortunatus (1 Corinthians 16:17), and Achaicus (1 Corinthians 16:17).

here in this city belong to me." 11So Paul stayed there the next year and a half, teaching the truths of God.

12But when Gallio became governor of Achaia, the Jews rose in concerted action against Paul and brought him before the governor for judgment. 13They accused Paul of "persuading men to worship God in ways that are contrary to Roman law." 14But just as Paul started to make his defense, Gallio turned to his accusers and said, "Listen, you Jews, if this were a case involving some crime, I would be obliged to listen to you, 15but since it is merely a bunch of questions of semantics and personalities and your silly Jewish laws, you take care of it. I'm not interested and I'm not touching it." 16And he drove them out of the courtroom.

17Then the mob grabbed Sosthenes, the new leader of the synagogue, and beat him outside the courtroom. But Gallio couldn't have cared less.

18:12
Rom 15:26
1 Thess 1:7; 2:16

18:15
Acts 23:29
25:19

18:17
Acts 18:8
1 Cor 1:1

18:17 *Then the mob,* implied.

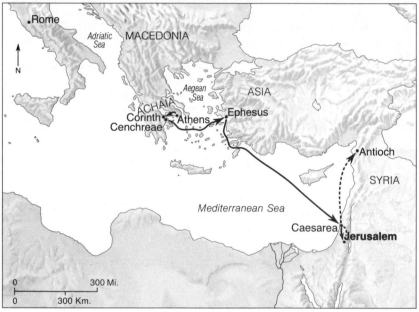

MINISTRY IN CORINTH AND EPHESUS
Paul left Athens and traveled on to Corinth, located on a narrow neck of land offering direct passage between the Aegean and Adriatic seas. When he left from the port of Corinth at Cenchreae, he visited Ephesus. He then traveled to Caesarea, from which he went on to Jerusalem to report on his trip before returning to Antioch.

18:11 During the year and a half that Paul stayed in wicked Corinth, he established a church there and wrote two letters to the believers in Thessalonica (the books of 1 and 2 Thessalonians). Although he had been in Thessalonica for only a short time (17:1–15), he commended the believers there for their loving deeds, strong faith, and steadfast hope. While encouraging them to stay away from immorality, he dealt with the themes of salvation, suffering, and the Second Coming of Jesus Christ. He told them to continue to work hard while they awaited Christ's return.

18:12 Gallio was governor of Achaia and the brother of Seneca the philosopher. He came to power in A.D. 51–52.

● **18:13** Paul was unjustly charged with treason. He was not encouraging obedience to a human king other than Caesar (see 17:7), nor was he speaking against the Roman empire. Instead he was speaking about the eternal Kingdom of Jesus Christ.

18:14–16 This was an important judicial decision for the spread of the gospel in the Roman empire. Judaism was a recognized

religion under Roman law. As long as Christians were seen as part of Judaism, the court refused to hear cases brought against them. If they had claimed to be a new religion, they could easily have been outlawed by the government.

18:17 Crispus had been the leader of the synagogue, but he and his family were converted and joined the Christians (18:8). Sosthenes was chosen to take his place. The mob could have been Greeks venting their feelings against the Jews for causing turmoil. Or they may have been Jews who beat Sosthenes for losing the case and leaving the synagogue worse off than before. A Sosthenes is mentioned in 1 Corinthians 1:1, and many believe this was the same man who, in time, became a convert and companion of Paul.

18:18 This was probably a temporary Nazirite vow that ended with shaving his head and offering the hair as a sacrifice (Numbers 6:18).

The return to Jerusalem and Antioch

18:18
Num 6:2,18
Acts 18:2,26
21:24
Rom 16:1
1 Cor 9:20
18:19
Eph 1:1
Rev 1:11; 2:1

18Paul stayed in the city several days after that and then said good-bye to the Christians and sailed for the coast of Syria, taking Priscilla and Aquila with him. At Cenchreae, Paul had his head shaved according to Jewish custom, for he had taken a vow. 19Arriving at the port of Ephesus, he left us aboard ship while he went over to the synagogue for a discussion with the Jews. 20They asked him to stay for a few days, but he felt that he had no time to lose.

AQUILA, PRISCILLA

Some couples know how to make the most of life. They complement each other, utilize each other's strengths, and form an effective team. Their united efforts affect those around them. Aquila and Priscilla were such a couple. They are never mentioned apart from one another in the Bible. In marriage and ministry, they were always together.

Priscilla and Aquila met Paul in Corinth while Paul was on his second missionary journey. They had just been expelled from Rome by Emperor Claudius' decree against the Jews. The emperor expelled the Jews from Rome for rioting (apparently over questions about the Messiah). Their home was as movable as the tents they made to support themselves. They opened their home to Paul, and he joined them in tentmaking. He shared with them his wealth of spiritual wisdom.

Priscilla and Aquila made the most of their spiritual education. They listened carefully to sermons and evaluated what they heard. When they heard Apollos speak, they were impressed by his ability as an orator, but realized that the content of his message was not complete. Instead of open confrontation, the couple quietly took Apollos home and shared with him what he needed to know. Until then, Apollos had only known John the Baptist's message about Christ. Priscilla and Aquila told him about Jesus' life, death, and resurrection, and the reality of God's indwelling Spirit. Apollos continued to preach powerfully—but now with the full story.

As for Priscilla and Aquila, they went on using their home as a warm place for training and worship. Back in Rome years later, they hosted one of the house churches that developed. The early Christians did not meet in church buildings, but in the homes of its members. This informal atmosphere provided opportunity for intimate fellowship.

In an age when the focus is mostly on what happens *between* husband and wife, Aquila and Priscilla are an example of what can happen *through* husband and wife. Their effectiveness together speaks about their relationship with each other. Their hospitality opened the doorway of salvation to many. The Christian home is still one of the best tools for spreading the gospel. Do guests find Christ in your home?

Strengths and accomplishments:
- Outstanding husband/wife team who ministered in the early church
- Supported themselves by tentmaking while serving Christ
- Close friends of Paul
- Explained to Apollos the full message of Christ

Lessons from their lives:
- Couples can have an effective ministry together ·
- The home is a valuable tool for evangelism
- Every believer needs to be well educated in the faith, whatever his or her role in the church

Vital statistics:
- Where: Originally from Rome, moved to Corinth, then Ephesus
- Occupation: Tentmakers
- Contemporaries: Emperor Claudius, Paul, Timothy, Apollos

Key verses:
"Tell Priscilla and Aquila 'hello.' They have been my fellow workers in the affairs of Christ Jesus. In fact, they risked their lives for me; and I am not the only one who is thankful to them: so are all the Gentile churches" (Romans 16:3, 4).

Their story is told in Acts 18. They are also mentioned in Romans 16:3–5; 1 Corinthians 16:19; 2 Timothy 4:19.

21"I must by all means be at Jerusalem for the holiday," he said. But he promised to return to Ephesus later if God permitted; and so he set sail again.

18:21
Acts 19:1
Jas 4:15

22The next stop was at the port of Caesarea from where he visited the church [at Jerusalem] and then sailed on to Antioch.

18:22
Acts 8:40; 11:19

4. Third missionary journey
Apollos is instructed at Ephesus

23After spending some time there, he left for Turkey again, going through Galatia and Phrygia visiting all the believers, encouraging them and helping them grow in the Lord.

18:23
Isa 35:3
Acts 16:6
Gal 1:2; 4:14

24As it happened, a Jew named Apollos, a wonderful Bible teacher and preacher, had just arrived in Ephesus from Alexandria in Egypt. 25, 26While he was in Egypt, someone had told him about John the Baptist and what John had said about Jesus, but that is all he knew. He had never heard the rest of the story! So he was preaching boldly and enthusiastically in the synagogue, "The Messiah is coming! Get ready to receive him!" Priscilla and Aquila were there and heard him—and it was a powerful sermon. Afterwards they met with him and explained what had happened to Jesus since the time of John, and all that it meant!

18:24
Acts 19:1
1 Cor 1:12
4:1,6; 16:12
Tit 3:13
18:25
Acts 18:2,18
19:3
18:27
1 Cor 3:6

27Apollos had been thinking about going to Greece, and the believers encouraged him in this. They wrote to their fellow-believers there, telling them to welcome him. And upon his arrival in Greece, he was greatly used of God to strengthen the church, 28for he powerfully refuted all the Jewish arguments in public debate, showing by the Scriptures that Jesus is indeed the Messiah.

18:28
Ps 22
Isa 7:14
9:6; 53
Jer 23:5,6
Dan 9:25,26
Mic 5:2
Mal 3:1
Lk 24:27

Christians in Ephesus receive the Holy Spirit

19 While Apollos was in Corinth, Paul traveled through Turkey and arrived in Ephesus, where he found several disciples. 2"Did you receive the Holy Spirit when you believed?" he asked them.

19:1
Acts 28:21
19:2
Jn 7:39
Acts 8:15,16

"No," they replied, "we don't know what you mean. What is the Holy Spirit?" 3"Then what beliefs did you acknowledge at your baptism?" he asked.

And they replied, "What John the Baptist taught."

19:3
Lk 7:29
Acts 18:25,26

4Then Paul pointed out to them that John's baptism was to demonstrate a desire to turn from sin to God and that those receiving his baptism must then go on to believe in Jesus, the one John said would come later.

19:4
Acts 1:5; 11:16
19:5
Acts 8:12,16
10:48
Gal 3:27

5As soon as they heard this, they were baptized in the name of the Lord Jesus. 6Then, when Paul laid his hands upon their heads, the Holy Spirit came on them,

19:6
Acts 2:4; 10:46

18:21 *holiday*, literally, "feast." This entire sentence is omitted in many of the ancient manuscripts. **18:22** *at Jerusalem*, implied. **18:26** *explained what had happened to Jesus since the time of John, and all that it meant!* Literally, "explained to him the way of God more accurately." **19:5** *baptized in*, or, "baptized into."

18:21 This holiday was either Passover or Pentecost.

18:22 This verse marks the end of Paul's second missionary journey and the beginning of the third, which lasted from A.D. 53–57. Leaving the church at Antioch (his home base), Paul headed toward Ephesus, but along the way he revisited the churches in Galatia and Phrygia. The heart of this trip was a lengthy stay (2 to 3 years) in Ephesus. Before returning to Jerusalem, he also visited believers in Macedonia and Greece.

18:25, 26 Apollos had heard only what John the Baptist had said about Jesus (see Luke 3:1–18), so his message was not the complete story. John focused on repentance from sin, the first step to faith in Christ. Apollos did not know about Jesus' life, crucifixion, and resurrection, nor did he know about the coming of the Holy Spirit. Priscilla and Aquila explained this to him.

18:27, 28 Apollos was from Alexandria in Egypt, the second

largest city in the Roman Empire, home of a great university. He was a scholar, orator, and debater, and after his knowledge about Christ was made more complete, God greatly used these gifts to strengthen and encourage the church. Reason is a powerful tool in the right hands and the right situation. Apollos used it to convince many in Greece of the truth of the gospel. You don't have to turn off your mind when you turn to Christ. If you have an ability in logic or debate, use it to bring others to God.

18:27, 28 Not all the work of the minister or missionary is drudgery, setback, or suffering. Chapter 18 is triumphant, showing victories in key cities and the addition of exciting new leaders such as Priscilla, Aquila, and Apollos, to the church. Rejoice in the victories Christ brings, and don't let the hazards create a negative mindset.

and they spoke in other languages and prophesied. 7The men involved were about twelve in number.

19:8
Acts 1:3; 28:23,31

19:10
Acts 16:6;
19:20,22
20:31

19:11
Mk 16:20

19:12
2 Kgs 4:29
Jn 14:12
Acts 5:15

19:13
Mt 12:26-28
Mk 9:38,39
Lk 9:49,50
11:19

Paul ministers powerfully in Ephesus

8Then Paul went to the synagogue and preached boldly each Sabbath day for three months, telling what he believed and why, and persuading many to believe in Jesus. 9But some rejected his message and publicly spoke against Christ, so he left, refusing to preach to them again. Pulling out the believers, he began a separate meeting at the lecture hall of Tyrannus and preached there daily. 10This went on for the next two years, so that everyone in the Turkish province of Asia Minor—both Jews and Greeks—heard the Lord's message.

11And God gave Paul the power to do unusual miracles, 12so that even when his handkerchiefs or parts of his clothing were placed upon sick people, they were healed, and any demons within them came out.

13A team of itinerant Jews who were traveling from town to town casting out demons planned to experiment by using the name of the Lord Jesus. The incantation they decided on was this: "I adjure you by Jesus, whom Paul preaches, to come

19:8 *each Sabbath day,* implied. *telling what he believed and why,* literally, "concerning the Kingdom of God."

PAUL TAKES A THIRD JOURNEY What prompted Paul's third journey may have been the spread of his opponents' message in the churches Paul had planted. So he hurried north, then west, returning to many of the cities he had previously visited. This time, however, he stayed on a more direct westward route toward Ephesus.

19:1 Ephesus was the capital and leading business center of the Roman province of Asia (part of present-day Turkey). A hub of sea and land transportation, it ranked with Antioch in Syria and Alexandria in Egypt as one of the great cities on the Mediterranean Sea. Paul stayed in Ephesus for a little over two years. There he wrote his first letter to the Corinthians to counter several problems they were facing. Later, while imprisoned in Rome, Paul wrote a letter to the Ephesian church (the book of Ephesians).

19:2–4 John's baptism was a sign of repentance from sin only, not a sign of new life in Christ. Like Apollos (18:24–26), these Ephesian believers needed further instruction on the message and ministry of Jesus Christ. By faith they believed in Jesus as the Messiah, but they did not understand the significance of Jesus' death and resurrection or the work of the Holy Spirit. Therefore they had not experienced the presence and power of the Holy Spirit.

In the book of Acts, believers received the Holy Spirit in a variety of ways. Usually the Holy Spirit filled a person as soon as he or she professed faith in Christ. In this case, however, God allowed it to happen later. God was confirming to these believers, who did not initially know about the Holy Spirit, that they too were a part of the church. The Holy Spirit's filling endorsed them as believers.

Pentecost was the formal outpouring of the Holy Spirit to the church. The other outpourings in the book of Acts were God's way of uniting new believers to the church. The mark of the true church is not merely right doctrine, but evidence of the Holy Spirit's working.

19:4 Paul was quick to point out that salvation requires repentance *and* faith. People need to be confronted with their sin and their need to repent, but this is only half the story. They must also accept the Good News of forgiveness and new life through Jesus.

19:6 When Paul laid his hands on these disciples, they received the Holy Spirit just as the disciples did at Pentecost. This also happened when the Holy Spirit came upon Gentiles, or non-Jews (10:46, 47).

19:9 Lecture halls were used in the morning for teaching philosophy, but were empty during the hot part of the day (about 11 a.m. to 4 p.m.). Since many people did not work during those hours, they came to hear Paul's preaching.

19:13 Many Ephesians engaged in exorcism and occult practices for profit, even sending demons from people (see 19:18, 19). The sons of Sceva were impressed by Paul's work, whose power to cast out demons came from God's Holy Spirit, not from witchcraft, and was obviously more powerful than theirs. They discovered, however, that one cannot control or duplicate God's power. These men were calling upon the name without knowing the person. The power to change people is in the person of Jesus Christ. It cannot be tapped by reciting his name like a magic charm. He works his power only through those he chooses.

out!" 14Seven sons of Sceva, a Jewish priest, were doing this. 15But when they tried it on a man possessed by a demon, the demon replied, "I know Jesus and I know Paul, but who are you?" 16And he leaped on two of them and beat them up, so that they fled out of his house naked and badly injured.

19:15
Mt 8:29
Mk 1:24
Lk 4:34
Acts 16:16-18
Jas 2:19

17The story of what happened spread quickly all through Ephesus, to Jews and Greeks alike; and a solemn fear descended on the city, and the name of the Lord Jesus was greatly honored. 18, 19Many of the believers who had been practicing black magic confessed their deeds and brought their incantation books and charms and burned them at a public bonfire. (Someone estimated the value of the books at $10,000.) 20This indicates how deeply the whole area was stirred by God's message.

19:17
Lk 7:16

19:18
Isa 30:22
Jer 3:13

19:20
Acts 6:7; 12:24
19:10

The tradesmen cause a riot

21Afterwards, Paul felt impelled by the Holy Spirit to go across to Greece before returning to Jerusalem. "And after that," he said, "I must go on to Rome!" 22He sent his two assistants, Timothy and Erastus, on ahead to Greece while he stayed awhile longer in Asia Minor.

19:21
Acts 20:1,22
23:11
Rom 15:24-26
1 Cor 16:5

19:22
Acts 16:9
Rom 16:23
2 Tim 4:20

23But about that time, a big blowup developed in Ephesus concerning the Christians. 24It began with Demetrius, a silversmith who employed many craftsmen to manufacture silver shrines of the Greek goddess Diana. 25He called a meeting of his men, together with others employed in related trades, and addressed them as follows:

19:23
2 Cor 1:8

19:24
Acts 16:16,19

19:25
1 Tim 6:10

"Gentlemen, this business is our income. 26As you know so well from what you've seen and heard, this man Paul has persuaded many, many people that handmade gods aren't gods at all. As a result, our sales volume is going down! And this trend is evident not only here in Ephesus, but throughout the entire province! 27Of course, I am not only talking about the business aspects of this situation and our loss of income, but also of the possibility that the temple of the great goddess Diana will lose its influence, and that Diana—this magnificent goddess worshiped not only throughout this part of Turkey but all around the world—will be forgotten!"

19:26
1 Chron 16:26
Ps 115:4
Isa 44:10-20
46:7
Jer 16:20
Acts 17:29
1 Cor 8:4

28At this their anger boiled and they began shouting, "Great is Diana of the Ephesians!"

19:28
Jer 50:38
Hab 2:18-20

19:19 *$10,000,* approximately £3,500.   19:21 *felt impelled by the Holy Spirit,* literally, "purposed in the spirit."

19:18, 19 Ephesus was considered a center for black magic and other occult practices. The people sought spells to give them wealth, happiness, and success in marriage. Superstition and sorcery were commonplace. God clearly forbids such practices (Deuteronomy 18:9–13). You cannot be a believer and hold onto the occult, black magic, or sorcery. Once you begin to dabble in these areas, it is extremely easy to become obsessed by them because Satan is very powerful. But God's power is even greater (1 John 4:4; Revelation 20:10). If you are mixed up in the occult, learn a lesson from the Ephesians and get rid of anything that lures you into such practices.

19:21 Why did Paul say he had to go to Rome? Wherever he went, he could see Rome's influence. Paul wanted to take the message of Christ to the world's center of influence and power.

19:22 Paul mentions Timothy in more detail in the books of 1 and 2 Timothy. Erastus was a committed follower of God who was not only Paul's helpful assistant, but also the city treasurer of Corinth (see Romans 16:23).

●**19:26** When Paul preached in Ephesus, Demetrius and his fellow shrinemakers did not quarrel with his doctrine. Their anger boiled because his preaching threatened their profits. They made statues of the goddess Diana and her temple, and if people started believing in God and discarding their idols, their livelihood would suffer.

Jesus does not promise us escape from persecution, but a way through it. He also promises not to send us through it alone. He said, "I am with you always, even to the end of the world" (Matthew 28:20).

●**19:27** Demetrius' strategy for stirring up a riot was to appeal to the people's love of money and then hide their greed behind the mask of patriotism and religious loyalty. The rioters couldn't see the selfish motives for their rioting—instead they saw themselves as heroes for the sake of their land and beliefs.

19:29 Paul often sought others to help him in his work. On this occasion, his traveling companions were Aristarchus (who would accompany him on other journeys; see 20:3, 4 and 27:1, 2), and Gaius (probably not the same Gaius mentioned in Romans 16:23 or 1 Corinthians 1:14).

19:31 These men were not military officers, but government officials responsible for the religious and political order of the region. Paul's message had reached all levels of society, crossing all social barriers and giving Paul friends in high places.

19:29
Acts 20:4; 27:2
Rom 16:23
1 Cor 1:14
Col 4:10
Philem 24

19:32
Acts 21:34

29A crowd began to gather and soon the city was filled with confusion. Everyone rushed to the amphitheater, dragging along Gaius and Aristarchus, Paul's traveling companions, for trial. 30Paul wanted to go in, but the disciples wouldn't let him. 31Some of the Roman officers of the province, friends of Paul, also sent a message to him, begging him not to risk his life by entering.

32Inside, the people were all shouting, some one thing and some another—everything was in confusion. In fact, most of them didn't even know why they were there.

APOLLOS

Some people have an amazing natural talent for public speaking. A few even have a great message to go along with it. When Apollos arrived in Ephesus shortly after Paul's departure, he made an immediate impact. He spoke boldly in public, interpreting and applying the Old Testament Scriptures effectively. He debated opponents of Christianity forcefully and effectively. It didn't take long for him to be noticed by Priscilla and Aquila.

The couple quickly realized that Apollos did not have the whole story. His preaching was based on the Old Testament and John the Baptist's message. He was probably urging people to repent and prepare for the coming Messiah. Priscilla and Aquila took him home with them and brought him up to date on all that had happened. As they told him of the life of Jesus, his death and resurrection, and the coming of the Holy Spirit, Apollos must have seen Scripture after Scripture become clear. He was filled with new energy and boldness now that he had the complete gospel.

Apollos next decided to travel to Achaia. His friends in Ephesus were able to send along a glowing letter of introduction. He quickly became the verbal champion of the Christians in Corinth, debating the opponents of the gospel in public. As often happens, Apollos' abilities eventually created a problem. Some of the Corinthians began to follow Apollos rather than his message. Paul had to confront the Corinthians about their divisiveness. They had been forming little groups named after their favorite preacher. Apollos left Corinth and hesitated to return. Paul wrote warmly of Apollos as a fellow minister who had "watered" the seeds of the gospel that Paul had planted in Corinth. Paul last mentions Apollos briefly to Titus. He was still a traveling representative of the gospel who deserved Titus' help.

Although his natural abilities could have made him proud, Apollos proved himself willing to learn. God used Priscilla and Aquila, fresh from months of learning from Paul, to give Apollos the complete gospel. Because Apollos did not hesitate to be a student, he became an even better teacher. How much does your willingness to learn affect God's efforts to help you become all he wants you to be?

Strengths and accomplishments:
- A gifted and persuasive preacher and apologist in the early church
- Willing to be taught
- One of the possible candidates for the unknown author of Hebrews

Lessons from his life:
- Effective communication of the gospel includes an accurate message delivered with God's power
- A clear verbal defense of the gospel can be a real encouragement to believers, while convincing non-believers of its truth

Vital statistics:
- Where: From Alexandria in Egypt
- Occupation: Traveling preacher, apologist
- Contemporaries: Priscilla, Aquila, Paul

Key verses:
"While he was in Egypt, someone had told him about John the Baptist and what John had said about Jesus, but that is all he knew. He had never heard the rest of the story! So he was preaching boldly and enthusiastically in the synagogue, 'The Messiah is coming! Get ready to receive him!' Priscilla and Aquila were there and heard him—and it was a powerful sermon. Afterwards they met with him and explained what had happened to Jesus since the time of John, and all that it meant!" (Acts 18:25, 26).

Apollos' story is told in Acts 18:24–28; 19:1. He is also mentioned in 1 Corinthians 1:12; 3:4–6, 22; 4:1, 6; 16:12; Titus 3:13.

33Alexander was spotted among the crowd by some of the Jews and dragged forward. He motioned for silence and tried to speak. 34But when the crowd realized he was a Jew, they started shouting again and kept it up for two hours: "Great is Diana of the Ephesians! Great is Diana of the Ephesians!"

19:33
1 Tim 1:20
2 Tim 4:14

35At last the mayor was able to quiet them down enough to speak. "Men of Ephesus," he said, "everyone knows that Ephesus is the center of the religion of the great Diana, whose image fell down to us from heaven. 36Since this is an indisputable fact, you shouldn't be disturbed no matter what is said, and should do nothing rash. 37Yet you have brought these men here who have stolen nothing from her temple and have not defamed her. 38If Demetrius and the craftsmen have a case against them, the courts are currently in session and the judges can take the case at once. Let them go through legal channels. 39And if there are complaints about other matters, they can be settled at the regular City Council meetings; 40for we are in danger of being called to account by the Roman government for today's riot, since there is no cause for it. And if Rome demands an explanation, I won't know what to say."

41Then he dismissed them, and they dispersed.

Paul raises Eutychus from the dead at Troas

20 When it was all over, Paul sent for the disciples, preached a farewell message to them, said good-bye and left for Macedonia, 2preaching to the believers along the way, in all the cities he passed through. 3He was in Greece three months and was preparing to sail for Syria when he discovered a plot by the Jews against his life, so he decided to go north to Macedonia first.

20:3
Acts 9:24; 20:19
23:12,13
2 Cor 11:26

4Several men were traveling with him, going as far as Turkey; they were Sopater of Beroea, the son of Pyrrhus; Aristarchus and Secundus, from Thessalonica; Gaius, from Derbe; and Timothy; and Tychicus and Trophimus, who were returning to their homes in Turkey, 5and had gone on ahead and were waiting for us at Troas. 6As soon as the Passover ceremonies ended, we boarded ship at Philippi in

20:4
Acts 16:1
19:22,29; 21:29
Eph 6:21
2 Tim 4:12,20
Tit 3:12

20:6
Ex 23:15
2 Cor 2:12

19:35 *is the center,* literally, "is the temple-keeper."   **20:4** *Turkey,* literally, "Asia."

● **19:33, 34** The mob had become anti-Jewish as well as anti-Christian. This Alexander may have been pulled forward by the Jews as a spokesman to explain that the Jews had no part in the Christian community, and thus had no part in the economic problem of the silversmiths.

19:40 The city of Ephesus was under the domination of the Roman empire. The main responsibility of the local city leaders was simply to maintain peace and order. If they failed to control the people, Rome would remove them from office. An additional threat was that the entire town might be put under martial law, taking away many civic freedoms.

19:41 The riot in Ephesus showed Paul that it was time to move on, but it also showed that the law still provided some protection for Christians as they confronted the worship of the goddess Diana, the largest idolatrous religion in Asia.

20:1–3 While in Greece, Paul spent much of his time in Corinth. From there he wrote the letter to the Romans. Although he had not yet been to Rome, believers had already started a church there (2:10; 18:2), and Paul wrote that he planned to visit the Roman believers. The letter to the Romans is a theological essay on the meaning of salvation and faith, an explanation of the relation between Jews and Gentiles in Christ, and a list of practical guidelines for the church.

20:4 These men traveling with Paul represented churches he had started in Asia. Each man was carrying an offering from his home church to the believers in Jerusalem. Paul's strategy of having each man deliver the gift gave the gift a personal touch and promoted the unity of believers. It was also an effective way to

THROUGH MACEDONIA AND ACHAIA
A riot in Ephesus sent Paul to Troas, then through Macedonia to the region of Achaia. In Achaia he went to Corinth to deal with problems there. Paul had planned to sail from there straight to Antioch in Syria, but a plot against his life was discovered. So he retraced his steps through Macedonia.

teach the church about giving, for the men were able to report to their churches what they had seen. Paul discussed this gift in one of his letters to the Corinthian church (see 2 Corinthians 8:1–21).

20:6 Jewish believers celebrated the Passover according to Moses' instructions (see Exodus 12:43–51) even if they couldn't go to Jerusalem.

northern Greece and five days later arrived in Troas, Turkey, where we stayed a week.

20:7
Acts 2:42
1 Cor 10:16,17
11:20-34; 16:2
Rev 1:10

7On Sunday, we gathered for a communion service, with Paul preaching. And since he was leaving the next day, he talked until midnight! 8The upstairs room where we met was lighted with many flickering lamps; 9and as Paul spoke on and on, a young man named Eutychus, sitting on the window sill, went fast asleep and fell three stories to his death below. 10, 11, 12Paul went down and took him into his arms. "Don't worry," he said, "he's all right!" And he was! What a wave of awesome joy swept through the crowd! They all went back upstairs and ate the Lord's Supper together; then Paul preached another long sermon—so it was dawn when he finally left them!

20:10
1 Kgs 17:21
2 Kgs 4:34
Mt 9:23-25
Mk 5:39-42

Paul's farewell to the elders of Ephesus

20:15
Acts 21:4,12
24:17
2 Tim 4:20

13Paul was going by land to Assos, and we went on ahead by ship. 14He joined us there and we sailed together to Mitylene; 15the next day we passed Chios; the next, we touched at Samos; and a day later we arrived at Miletus.

16Paul had decided against stopping at Ephesus this time, as he was hurrying to get to Jerusalem, if possible, for the celebration of Pentecost.

20:18
Acts 18:19
19:1,10
20:21
Lk 24:47
Acts 2:38;
11:18; 26:20

17But when we landed at Miletus, he sent a message to the elders of the church at Ephesus asking them to come down to the boat to meet him.

18When they arrived he told them, "You men know that from the day I set foot in Turkey until now 19I have done the Lord's work humbly—yes, and with tears—and have faced grave danger from the plots of the Jews against my life. 20Yet I never shrank from telling you the truth, either publicly or in your homes. 21I have had one message for Jews and Gentiles alike—the necessity of turning from sin to God through faith in our Lord Jesus Christ.

20:22
Acts 19:21
20:23
Acts 9:16;
21:4,11,33
20:24
Acts 21:13
2 Tim 4:7

22"And now I am going to Jerusalem, drawn there irresistibly by the Holy Spirit, not knowing what awaits me, 23except that the Holy Spirit has told me in city after city that jail and suffering lie ahead. 24But life is worth nothing unless I use it for

20:7 On Sunday, or, "on Saturday night." Literally, "the first day of the week," by Jewish reckoning, from sundown to sundown. **20:22** by the Holy Spirit, or, "by an inner compulsion."

20:7 A fellowship meal—much like a potluck supper—was eaten just before the Lord's Supper was celebrated with the breaking of bread and drinking of the cup (20:10–12).

20:16 Paul had missed attending the Passover feast in Jerusalem, so he was especially interested in arriving on time for Pentecost, which was 50 days after Passover. He was carrying with him gifts for the Jerusalem believers from churches in Asia and Greece (see Romans 15:25, 26; 1 Corinthians 16:1ff; 2 Corinthians 8, 9). The Jerusalem church was experiencing difficult times. Paul may have been anxious to deliver this gift to the believers at Pentecost because it was a day of celebration and thanksgiving to God for his provision.

● **20:18–21** The way of the believer is not an easy road; being a Christian does not solve all problems. Paul sowed humbly and "with tears," but he never quit, never gave up. The message of salvation was so important that he never missed an opportunity to share it. The Christian life will have its rough times, its tears, and its joys, but we should always be ready to tell others what good things God has done for us. His blessings far outweigh life's difficulties.

20:23 The Holy Spirit showed Paul that he would be imprisoned and would suffer. Even knowing this, Paul did not shrink from fulfilling his mission. His strong character was a good example to the Ephesian elders, some of whom would also suffer for Christ.

● **20:24** We often feel that life is a failure unless we're getting a lot out of it: recognition, fun, money, success. But Paul thought life was worth *nothing* unless he used it for God's work. What he put *into* life was far more important than what he got out. Which is more important to you—what you get out of life, or what you put into it?

PAUL TRAVELS FROM TROAS TO MILETUS
From Troas, Paul traveled overland to Assos, then boarded a ship to Mitylene and Samos on its way to Miletus. He summoned the elders of the Ephesian church to say farewell to them, for he knew he would probably not see them again.

20:24 Single-mindedness is a quality needed by anyone who wishes to do God's work. Paul was a single-minded person, and the single most important goal of his life was to tell others about Christ (Philippians 3:13). It is no wonder that Paul was the greatest missionary who ever lived. God is looking for more men and women who focus on that one great task God has given them.

doing the work assigned me by the Lord Jesus—the work of telling others the Good News about God's mighty kindness and love.

25"And now I know that none of you among whom I went about teaching the Kingdom will ever see me again. 26Let me say plainly that no man's blood can be laid at my door, 27for I didn't shrink from declaring all God's message to you.

28"And now beware! Be sure that you feed and shepherd God's flock—his church, purchased with his blood—for the Holy Spirit is holding you responsible as overseers. 29I know full well that after I leave you, false teachers, like vicious wolves, will appear among you, not sparing the flock. 30Some of you yourselves will distort the truth in order to draw a following. 31Watch out! Remember the three years I was with you—my constant watchcare over you night and day and my many tears for you.

32"And now I entrust you to God and his care and to his wonderful words which are able to build your faith and give you all the inheritance of those who are set apart for himself.

33"I have never been hungry for money or fine clothing— 34you know that these hands of mine worked to pay my own way and even to supply the needs of those who were with me. 35And I was a constant example to you in helping the poor; for I remembered the words of the Lord Jesus, 'It is more blessed to give than to receive.'"

36When he had finished speaking, he knelt and prayed with them, 37and they wept aloud as they embraced him in farewell, 38sorrowing most of all because he said that he would never see them again. Then they accompanied him down to the ship.

Paul continues to Jerusalem

21 After parting from the Ephesian elders, we sailed straight to Cos. The next day we reached Rhodes and then went to Patara. 2There we boarded a ship sailing for the Syrian province of Phoenicia. 3We sighted the island of Cyprus, passed it on our left and landed at the harbor of Tyre, in Syria, where the ship unloaded. 4We went ashore, found the local believers and stayed with them a week. These disciples warned Paul—the Holy Spirit prophesying through them—not to go on to Jerusalem. 5At the end of the week when we returned to the ship, the entire congregation including wives and children walked down to the beach with us where we prayed and said our farewells. 6Then we went aboard and they returned home.

7The next stop after leaving Tyre was Ptolemais where we greeted the believers, but stayed only one day. 8Then we went on to Caesarea and stayed at the home of Philip the Evangelist, one of the first seven deacons. 9He had four unmarried daughters who had the gift of prophecy.

21:9 unmarried, literally, "virgins."

20:26 Acts 18:6

20:28 Jn 21:15-17 / 1 Pet 1:19; 5:2 / Rev 5:9

20:29 Ezek 22:27 / Mt 7:15 / Jn 10:10,12

20:31 Acts 19:10

20:32 Jn 17:17 / Acts 9:31; 26:18 / Eph 1:18 / Col 3:24 / 1 Pet 1:4; 2:2

20:33 1 Sam 12:3 / 1 Cor 9:12 / 2 Cor 7:2 / 11:8,9; 12:17

20:34 1 Cor 4:12 / 1 Thess 2:9 / 2 Thess 3:8

20:35 2 Cor 8:9 / 1 Thess 4:11 / 5:14 / Heb 13:1,3

21:4 Acts 20:23; 21:11

21:5 Acts 20:36

21:8 Acts 6:3,5 / 8:26,40 / Eph 4:11

21:9 Joel 2:28 / Acts 2:17

20:28 The Ephesian elders were told to feed the believers under their care by teaching them God's Word, and to shepherd them by being examples of God's love. All leaders of the church carry these two major responsibilities—to nourish others with God's truth and to exemplify God's truth at work in their lives. God's truth must be talked out and lived out.

20:31, 36–38 Paul's relationship with these believers is a beautiful example of Christian fellowship. He had cared for them and loved them, even cried over their needs. They responded with love and care for him and sorrow over his leaving. They had prayed together and comforted one another. Like Paul, you can build strong relationships with other Christians by sharing, caring, sorrowing, rejoicing, and praying with them. You will gather others around you only by giving yourself away to them.

● **20:33** Paul was satisfied with whatever he had, wherever he was, as long as he could do God's work. Examine your attitudes toward wealth and comfort. If you focus more on what you don't have than on what you do have, it's time to reexamine your priorities and put God's work back in first place.

● **20:34** Paul worked to show he was free of covetousness, not to grow rich. He supported himself and others working with him (he also mentions this in some of his letters; see Philippians 4:11–13; 1 Thessalonians 2:9).

20:35 These words of Jesus are not recorded in the Gospels. Obviously, not all of Jesus' words were written down (John 21:25); this saying may have been passed on orally through the apostles.

21:4 Did Paul disobey the Holy Spirit by going to Jerusalem? Probably not. More likely, the Holy Spirit warned these believers about the suffering Paul would face in Jerusalem. They drew the conclusion that he should not go because of that danger. This is supported by 21:10–12 where the local believers, after hearing that Paul would be turned over to the Romans, beg him to turn back.

21:8 This is the Philip mentioned in Acts 6:5 and 8:26–40.

21:9 Obviously the gift of prophecy was given to both men and women. Women actively participated in God's work (2:17;

21:10
Acts 11:28

21:11
Acts 20:23; 21:3
Eph 6:20

21:13
Acts 20:24
2 Cor 4:10
Col 1:24

21:14
Mt 26:42

21:19
Rom 15:18

21:20
Acts 15:1,5
Gal 3:10,11

10During our stay of several days, a man named Agabus, who also had the gift of prophecy, arrived from Judea 11and visited us. He took Paul's belt, bound his own feet and hands with it and said, "The Holy Spirit declares, 'So shall the owner of this belt be bound by the Jews in Jerusalem and turned over to the Romans.' " 12Hearing this, all of us—the local believers and his traveling companions— begged Paul not to go on to Jerusalem.

13But he said, "Why all this weeping? You are breaking my heart! For I am ready not only to be jailed at Jerusalem, but also to die for the sake of the Lord Jesus." 14When it was clear that he wouldn't be dissuaded, we gave up and said, "The will of the Lord be done."

15So shortly afterwards, we packed our things and left for Jerusalem. 16Some disciples from Caesarea accompanied us, and on arrival we were guests at the home of Mnason, originally from Cyprus, one of the early believers; 17and all the believers at Jerusalem welcomed us cordially.

5. Paul on trial

Paul arrives at Jerusalem

18The second day Paul took us with him to meet with James and the elders of the Jerusalem church. 19After greetings were exchanged, Paul recounted the many things God had accomplished among the Gentiles through his work.

20They praised God but then said, "You know, dear brother, how many

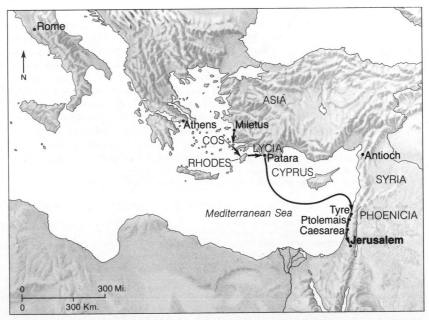

PAUL RETURNS TO JERUSALEM
The ship sailed from Miletus to Cos, Rhodes, and Patara. Paul and his companions then boarded a cargo ship bound for Phoenicia. They passed Cyprus and landed at Tyre, then Ptolemais, and finally Caesarea, where Paul disembarked and returned by land to Jerusalem.

Philippians 4:3). Other women who prophesied include Miriam (Exodus 15:20), Deborah (Judges 4:4), Huldah (2 Kings 22:14), Noadiah (Nehemiah 6:14), Isaiah's wife (Isaiah 8:3), and Anna (Luke 2:36–38).

21:10 This is the Agabus who, 15 years earlier, had predicted the famine in Jerusalem (11:27–29).

21:13, 14 Paul knew he would be imprisoned in Jerusalem. His friends pleaded with him to not go there, but he knew he had to because God wanted him to. No one wants to face hardship or suffering, but a faithful disciple wants above all else to please God. Our desire to please God should overshadow our desire to avoid hardship and suffering. When we really want to do God's will, we must accept all that comes with it—even the pain. Then we can say with Paul, "The will of the Lord be done."

21:18 James, Jesus' brother, was the leader of the Jerusalem church (15:13–21; Galatians 1:19; 2:9). He was called an apostle even though he wasn't one of the original 12 who followed Jesus.

thousands of Jews have also believed, and they are all very insistent that Jewish believers must continue to follow the Jewish traditions and customs. 21Our Jewish Christians here at Jerusalem have been told that you are against the laws of Moses, against our Jewish customs, and that you forbid the circumcision of their children. 22Now what can be done? For they will certainly hear that you have come.

23"We suggest this: We have four men here who are preparing to shave their heads and take some vows. 24Go with them to the Temple and have your head shaved too—and pay for theirs to be shaved.

"Then everyone will know that you approve of this custom for the Hebrew Christians and that you yourself obey the Jewish laws and are in line with our thinking in these matters.

25"As for the Gentile Christians, we aren't asking them to follow these Jewish customs at all—except for the ones we wrote to them about: not to eat food offered to idols, not to eat unbled meat from strangled animals, and not to commit fornication."

26, 27So Paul agreed to their request and the next day went with the men to the Temple for the ceremony, thus publicizing his vow to offer a sacrifice seven days later with the others.

Paul is arrested at the Temple

The seven days were almost ended when some Jews from Turkey saw him in the Temple and roused a mob against him. They grabbed him, 28yelling, "Men of Israel! Help! Help! This is the man who preaches against our people and tells everybody to disobey the Jewish laws. He even talks against the Temple and defiles it by bringing Gentiles in!" 29(For down in the city earlier that day, they had seen him with Trophimus, a Gentile from Ephesus in Turkey, and assumed that Paul had taken him into the Temple.)

30The whole population of the city was electrified by these accusations and a great riot followed. Paul was dragged out of the Temple, and immediately the gates were closed behind him. 31As they were killing him, word reached the commander of the Roman garrison that all Jerusalem was in an uproar. 32He quickly ordered out his soldiers and officers and ran down among the crowd. When the mob saw the troops coming, they quit beating Paul. 33The commander arrested him and ordered him bound with double chains. Then he asked the crowd who he was and what he had done. 34Some shouted one thing and some another. When he couldn't find out anything in all the uproar and confusion, he ordered Paul to be taken to the armory. 35As they reached the stairs, the mob grew so violent that the soldiers lifted Paul to their shoulders to protect him, 36and the crowd surged behind shouting, "Away with him, away with him!"

21:26, 27 *seven days,* literally, "the days of purification." **21:29** *a Gentile,* implied. **21:34** *armory,* literally, "castle," or "fort."

Cross references (margin):

21:21 Acts 16:3 / Gal 2:3
21:23 Acts 18:18
21:24 Num 6:2,13-21 / 1 Cor 9:20
21:25 Acts 15:19-29
21:27 Acts 24:18 / 26:21 / Rom 8:35 / 2 Cor 4:9 / 2 Tim 3:12
21:28 Mt 5:11 / Lk 6:22; 11:49 / 21:12; 23:2 / Jn 15:10 / Acts 6:13 / 16:20,21; 17:6 / 24:5,6 / 1 Cor 4:12
21:29 Acts 20:4 / 2 Tim 4:20
21:32 Acts 23:27
21:33 Acts 20:23; 28:20 / Eph 6:20
21:36 Lk 23:18 / Jn 19:15 / Acts 22:22

● **21:21** The Jerusalem council (Acts 15) settled the issue of circumcision of Gentile believers. Evidently there was a rumor that Paul had gone far beyond their decision, even forbidding Jews to circumcise their children. This, of course, was not true. So Paul willingly submitted to Jewish custom to show that he was not working against the council's decision and that he was still Jewish in his lifestyle. Sometimes we must go the second mile to avoid offending others, especially when offending them would hinder the gospel.

21:23, 24 Paul submitted himself to this Jewish custom to keep peace in the Jerusalem church. Although Paul was a man of strong conviction, he was willing to compromise on nonessential points, becoming all things to all men that he might win some (1 Corinthians 9:19–23). Often a church is split over disagreements about minor issues or traditions. Like Paul, we should remain firm on Christian essentials but flexible on nonessentials. Of course, no one should violate his true convictions, but sometimes we need to exercise the gift of mutual submission for the sake of the gospel.

21:23, 24 There are two ways to think of the Jewish law. Paul rejects one and accepts the other. (1) Paul rejects the idea that the Old Testament law brings salvation to those who keep it. Our salvation is freely given by God's gracious act. We receive it by faith. The law is of no value for salvation except to show us our sin. (2) Paul accepts the view that the Old Testament laws prepared us for and taught us about the coming of Jesus Christ. Christ fulfilled the law and released us from its burden of guilt. But the law still teaches us many valuable principles and gives us guidelines for living. Paul was not observing the law for salvation. He was simply keeping the law as custom to avoid offending those he wished to reach with the gospel (see Romans 3:21–31; 7:4–6; 13:9, 10). For more on the law, see Galatians 3:23–29; 4:21–31.

● **21:28, 29** These men knew how effective Paul's work had been in Asia. Their strategy was to discredit Paul so his work would be weakened. Be alert when you hear accusations against God's workers. Someone may be trying to discredit them or to hinder their work. Keep an open mind and pray for the workers. They will be strengthened by your support.

21:31 Since Jerusalem was under Roman control, an uproar in the city would be investigated by Roman authorities. The ruler at this time was Claudius Lysias (23:26).

Paul speaks to the crowd

37, 38 As Paul was about to be taken inside, he said to the commander, "May I have a word with you?"

"Do you know Greek?" the commander asked, surprised. "Aren't you that Egyptian who led a rebellion a few years ago and took 4,000 members of the Assassins with him into the desert?"

39 "No," Paul replied, "I am a Jew from Tarsus in Cilicia which is no small town. I request permission to talk to these people."

40 The commander agreed, so Paul stood on the stairs and motioned to the people to be quiet; soon a deep silence enveloped the crowd, and he addressed them in Hebrew as follows:

22 "Brothers and fathers, listen to me as I offer my defense." 2(When they heard him speaking in Hebrew, the silence was even greater.) 3"I am a Jew," he said, "born in Tarsus, a city in Cilicia, but educated here in Jerusalem under Gamaliel, at whose feet I learned to follow our Jewish laws and customs very carefully. I became very anxious to honor God in everything I did, just as you have tried to do today. 4And I persecuted the Christians, hounding them to death, binding and delivering both men and women to prison. 5The High Priest or any member of the Council can testify that this is so. For I asked them for letters to the Jewish leaders in Damascus, with instructions to let me bring any Christians I found to Jerusalem in chains to be punished.

6"As I was on the road, nearing Damascus, suddenly about noon a very bright light from heaven shone around me. 7And I fell to the ground and heard a voice saying to me, 'Saul, Saul, why are you persecuting me?'

8" 'Who is it speaking to me, sir?' I asked. And he replied, 'I am Jesus of Nazareth, the one you are persecuting.' 9The men with me saw the light but didn't understand what was said.

10"And I said, 'What shall I do, Lord?'

"And the Lord told me, 'Get up and go into Damascus, and there you will be told what awaits you in the years ahead.'

11"I was blinded by the intense light, and had to be led into Damascus by my companions. 12There a man named Ananias, as godly a man as you could find for obeying the law, and well thought of by all the Jews of Damascus, 13came to me, and standing beside me said, 'Brother Saul, receive your sight!' And that very hour I could see him!

14"Then he told me, 'The God of our fathers has chosen you to know his will and to see the Messiah and hear him speak. 15You are to take his message everywhere, telling what you have seen and heard. 16And now, why delay? Go and be baptized, and be cleansed from your sins, calling on the name of the Lord.'

17, 18"One day after my return to Jerusalem, while I was praying in the Temple, I fell into a trance and saw a vision of God saying to me, 'Hurry! Leave Jerusalem, for the people here won't believe you when you give them my message.'

19" 'But Lord,' I argued, 'they certainly know that I imprisoned and beat those in

21:37, 38 *a few years ago,* literally, "before these days."   **22:14** *Messiah,* literally, "Righteous One."

21:39
Acts 9:11
2 Cor 11:22
Gal 3:5
1 Pet 3:15; 4:16

21:40
Acts 26:14

22:3
Acts 5:34-40
26:5
Rom 10:2
2 Cor 11:22
Gal 1:14
Phil 3:5

22:4
Acts 8:3
1 Tim 1:13

22:5
Acts 9:2,3

22:6
Acts 9:3-8
26:12,13

22:8
Acts 26:15

22:9
Dan 10:7
Acts 9:7; 26:13

22:11
Acts 9:8

22:12,13
Acts 9:10,17,18

22:14
Acts 3:13; 26:16
1 Cor 9:1; 15:8
Gal 1:12

22:15
Acts 26:16

22:16
Ps 116:13
Acts 2:38
Rom 10:13
1 Cor 6:11
Heb 10:22

22:19
Acts 8:3; 22:4
26:11

21:37, 38 By speaking in Greek, Paul showed that he was a cultured man and not just a common rebel starting riots in the streets. The language grabbed the commander's attention and gave Paul protection and the opportunity to give his defense.

21:37, 38 The historian Josephus tells of an Egyptian who led a revolt of 4,000 people in Jerusalem in A.D. 54 and then disappeared. The commander assumed that Paul was this rebel.

●**22:1, 2** Paul was speaking in Hebrew, the language of the Old Testament. He spoke this language not only to communicate in the language of his listeners, but also to show that he was a devout Jew, had respect for the Jewish laws and customs, and was learned in Hebrew. Paul spoke Greek to the Roman officials and Hebrew to the Jews. If you want to minister to people with maximum effectiveness, you must be able to use their language.

●**22:3** Gamaliel was the most honored rabbi of the first century. He was well known and respected as an expert on religious law (5:34) and as a voice for moderation. Paul was showing his credentials as a well-educated man trained under the most respected Jewish rabbi.

●**22:3** When Paul said "just as you have tried to do today," he acknowledged their sincere motives in trying to kill him and recognized that he would have done the same to Christian leaders a few years earlier. Paul always tried to establish a common point of contact with his audience before launching into a full-scale defense of Christianity. When you witness for Christ, first identify yourself with your audience. They are much more likely to listen to you if they feel a common bond with you.

every synagogue who believed on you. 20And when your witness Stephen was
killed, I was standing there agreeing—keeping the coats they laid aside as they
stoned him.'

21"But God said to me, 'Leave Jerusalem, for I will send you far away to the
Gentiles!' "

22The crowd listened until Paul came to that word, then with one voice they
shouted, "Away with such a fellow! Kill him! He isn't fit to live!" 23They yelled
and threw their coats in the air and tossed up handfuls of dust.

Paul reveals his Roman citizenship

24So the commander brought him inside and ordered him lashed with whips to
make him confess his crime. He wanted to find out why the crowd had become so
furious!

25As they tied Paul down to lash him, Paul said to an officer standing there, "Is
it legal for you to whip a Roman citizen who hasn't even been tried?"

26The officer went to the commander and asked, "What are you doing? This man
is a Roman citizen!"

27So the commander went over and asked Paul, "Tell me, are you a Roman
citizen?"

"Yes, I certainly am."

28"I am too," the commander muttered, "and it cost me plenty!"

"But I am a citizen by birth!"

29The soldiers standing ready to lash him, quickly disappeared when they heard
Paul was a Roman citizen, and the commander was frightened because he had
ordered him bound and whipped.

Paul appears before the Sanhedrin

30The next day the commander freed him from his chains and ordered the chief
priests into session with the Jewish Council. He had Paul brought in before them to
try to find out what the trouble was all about.

23 Gazing intently at the Council, Paul began:
"Brothers, I have always lived before God in all good conscience!"

2Instantly Ananias the High Priest commanded those close to Paul to slap him on
the mouth.

3Paul said to him, "God shall slap you, you whitewashed pigpen. What kind of
judge are you to break the law yourself by ordering me struck like that?"

4Those standing near Paul said to him, "Is that the way to talk to God's High
Priest?"

5"I didn't realize he was the High Priest, brothers," Paul replied, "for the
Scriptures say, 'Never speak evil of any of your rulers.' "

6Then Paul thought of something! Part of the Council were Sadducees, and part

23:3 *you whitewashed pigpen,* literally, "you whitewashed wall."

22:20
Acts 7:58-8:1

22:21
Acts 13:2; 18:6
26:17
Rom 15:15,16
1 Tim 2:7

22:22
Acts 21:36
25:24

22:25
Acts 16:37

22:29
Acts 16:38

23:1
1 Cor 4:4
2 Cor 1:12; 4:2
Heb 13:18

23:2
Jn 18:22
Acts 24:1

23:3
Lev 19:15
Ezek 13:10-15
Jn 7:51

23:5
Ex 22:28

●**22:21, 22** These people listened intently to Paul, waiting to trap
and accuse him. The word *Gentile* brought out all their anger and
pride. They were supposed to be a light to the Gentiles, telling
them about the one true God. But they had renounced that mission
by becoming separatist and exclusive. God's plan, however, was
not thwarted; the Gentiles would hear the Good News through
Jewish Christians such as Paul and Peter.

22:25 Paul's question stopped the officers because, by law, a
Roman citizen could not be whipped until he had been proven
guilty of a crime. Paul was born a Roman citizen, whereas the
commander had bought his citizenship. Buying citizenship was a
common practice and a good source of money for the Roman
government, but bought citizenship was considered inferior to
citizenship by birth.

22:30 God used Paul's persecution as an opportunity for him to
witness. Now even his enemies were creating a platform for him to

address the entire Jewish Council. If we are sensitive to the Holy
Spirit's leading, we will notice increased opportunities to share our
faith, even in the heat of opposition.

23:2, 3 Josephus, a respected first-century historian, described
Ananias as profane, greedy, and hot tempered. Paul's outburst
came as a result of the illegal command Ananias had given. He
had violated Jewish law by assuming that Paul was guilty without a
trial and ordering his punishment (see Deuteronomy 19:15). Paul
didn't recognize Ananias as the High Priest, probably because
Ananias' command broke the law he was pledged to represent.
We are pledged to represent Christ. When those around us say, "I
didn't know you were a Christian," we have failed to represent him
as we should. As Christians, we are not merely Christ's followers;
we are Christ's representatives to others, as the High Priest was
the law's representative to the people.

23:6 The Sadducees and Pharisees were both religious leaders,

were Pharisees! So he shouted, "Brothers, I am a Pharisee, as were all my ancestors! And I am being tried here today because I believe in the resurrection of the dead!"

7This divided the Council right down the middle—the Pharisees against the Sadducees— 8for the Sadducees say there is no resurrection or angels or even eternal spirit within us, but the Pharisees believe in all of these.

9So a great clamor arose. Some of the Jewish leaders jumped up to argue that Paul was all right. "We see nothing wrong with him," they shouted. "Perhaps a spirit or angel spoke to him [there on the Damascus road]."

10The shouting grew louder and louder, and the men were tugging at Paul from both sides, pulling him this way and that. Finally the commander, fearing they would tear him apart, ordered his soldiers to take him away from them by force and bring him back to the armory.

11That night the Lord stood beside Paul and said, "Don't worry, Paul; just as you have told the people about me here in Jerusalem, so you must also in Rome."

The plan to kill Paul

12, 13The next morning some forty or more of the Jews got together and bound themselves by a curse neither to eat nor drink until they had killed Paul! 14Then they went to the chief priests and elders and told them what they had done. 15"Ask the

23:8
Mt 22:23
Mk 12:18
Lk 20:27
Acts 24:5
23:9
Prov 16:7
Jn 12:29
Acts 5:39; 22:7
23:11
Ps 46:1
Isa 41:10; 43:2
Acts 18:9
22:1-21
27:23
23:12
Acts 9:23
23:15
Ps 37:32

23:8 *or even eternal spirit within us,* literally, "nor spirit." **23:9** *Jewish leaders,* literally, "scribes." *there on the Damascus road,* implied.

UNSUNG HEROES IN ACTS	Hero	Reference	Heroic action
When we think of the success of the early church, we often think of the work of the apostles. But the church could have died if it hadn't been for the "unsung" heroes, the men and women who through some small but committed act moved the church forward.	Lame beggar	3:9-12	After his healing, he praised God. With the crowds gathering to see what happened, Peter used the opportunity to tell many about Jesus.
	Five deacons	6:2-5	Everyone knows Stephen and many people know Philip, but there were five other men chosen to be deacons. They not only laid the foundation for service in the church, but their hard work gave the apostles the time they needed to preach the gospel.
	Ananias	9:10-19	He had the responsibility of being the first to demonstrate Christ's love to Paul after his conversion.
	Cornelius	10:34, 35	His example showed Peter that the gospel was for *all* people, Jews and Gentiles.
	Rhoda	12:13-15	Her persistence brought Peter inside Mary's home where he would be safe.
	James	15:13-21	He took command of the Jerusalem council and had the courage and discernment to make a decision that would affect literally millions of Christians over generations.
	Lydia	16:13-15	Opened her home to Paul from which he led many to Christ and founded a church in Philippi.
	Jason	17:5-7	Risked his life for the gospel by allowing Paul to stay in his home. He stood up for what was true and right, even though he faced persecution for it.
	Paul's nephew	23:16-24	Saved Paul's life by telling officials of a plot to murder Paul.
	Julius	27:43	Spared Paul's life when the other soldiers wanted to kill him.

---

but with strikingly different beliefs. While the Pharisees believed in a bodily resurrection, the Sadducees did not because they adhered only to the Old Testament books of Genesis through Deuteronomy, which contain no explicit teaching on resurrection. Paul's words moved the debate away from himself and toward their raging controversy about the resurrection. The Jewish Council was split.

23:6 Paul's sudden insight is an example of the power Jesus promised to believers (Mark 13:9-11). God will help us when we

are under fire for our faith. Like Paul, we should always be ready to present our testimony. The Holy Spirit will give us power to speak boldly.

23:14, 15 When the Pharisee-Sadducee controversy died down, the religious leaders refocused their attention on Paul. To these leaders, politics and position had become more important than God. They were ready to plan another murder, as they had done with Jesus. But as always, God was in control.

commander to bring Paul back to the Council again," they requested. "Pretend you want to ask a few more questions. We will kill him on the way."

16But Paul's nephew got wind of their plan and came to the armory and told Paul. **23:16** Job 5:12,13

17Paul called one of the officers and said, "Take this boy to the commander. He has something important to tell him."

18So the officer did, explaining, "Paul, the prisoner, called me over and asked me to bring this young man to you to tell you something."

19The commander took the boy by the hand, and leading him aside asked, "What is it you want to tell me, lad?"

20"Tomorrow," he told him, "the Jews are going to ask you to bring Paul before the Council again, pretending they want to get some more information. 21But don't do it! There are more than forty men hiding along the road ready to jump him and kill him. They have bound themselves under a curse to neither eat nor drink till he is dead. They are out there now, expecting you to agree to their request." **23:21** Ps 10:9 37:12,13,32

22"Don't let a soul know you told me this," the commander warned the boy as he left.

Paul is sent to Caesarea

23, 24Then the commander called two of his officers and ordered, "Get 200 soldiers ready to leave for Caesarea at nine o'clock tonight! Take 200 spearmen and 70 mounted cavalry. Give Paul a horse to ride and get him safely to Governor Felix."

25Then he wrote this letter to the governor:

26"*From:* Claudius Lysias

"*To:* His Excellency, Governor Felix.

"Greetings!

27"This man was seized by the Jews and they were killing him when I sent the soldiers to rescue him, for I learned that he was a Roman citizen. 28Then I took him to their Council to try to find out what he had done. 29I soon discovered it was something about their Jewish beliefs, certainly nothing worthy of imprisonment or death. 30But when I was informed of a plot to kill him, I decided to send him on to you and will tell his accusers to bring their charges before you." **23:27** Acts 21:33 22:25-29 **23:28** Acts 22:30 **23:29** Acts 18:15 25:19; 26:31 28:18 **23:30** Acts 24:8,19 25:16

31So that night, as ordered, the soldiers took Paul to Antipatris. 32They returned

---

IMPRISONMENT IN CAESAREA
Paul brought news of his third journey to the elders of the Jerusalem church, who rejoiced at his ministry. But Paul's presence soon stirred up the Jews, who persuaded the Romans to arrest him. A plot to kill Paul was uncovered, so Paul was taken by night to Antipatris, then transferred to the provincial prison in Caesarea.

23:16–22 It is easy to overlook children, assuming that they aren't old enough to do much for the Lord. But a young boy played an important part in protecting Paul's life. God can use anyone, of any age, who is willing to yield to him. Jesus made it clear that children are important (Matthew 18:2–6). Do you give children the importance God gives them?

●**23:23, 24** The Roman commander ordered Paul sent to Caesarea. Jerusalem was the seat of Jewish government, but Caesarea was the Roman headquarters for the area. God works in amazing and amusing ways. God chose to use the Roman army to deliver Paul from his enemies. God's ways are not our ways—ours are limited, his are not. Don't limit God by asking him to respond your way. When God intervenes, anything can happen, much more and much better than you can anticipate.

23:26 Felix was the Roman procurator or governor of Judea from A.D. 52 to 59. This was the same position Pontius Pilate had held. While the Jews were given much freedom to govern themselves, the governor ran the army, kept the peace, and gathered the taxes.

23:26 How did Luke know what was written in the letter from Claudius Felix? In his concern for historical accuracy, Luke used many documents to make sure his writings were correct (see Luke 1:1–4). This letter was probably read aloud in court when Paul came before Felix to answer the Jews' accusations. Also, a copy may have been given to Paul as a courtesy, because he was a Roman citizen.

to the armory the next morning, leaving him with the cavalry to take him on to Caesarea.

23:33
Acts 8:40
23:34
Acts 21:39
23:35
Acts 24:1,19
25:16

33When they arrived in Caesarea, they presented Paul and the letter to the governor. 34He read it and then asked Paul where he was from.

"Cilicia," Paul answered.

35"I will hear your case fully when your accusers arrive," the governor told him, and ordered him kept in the prison at King Herod's palace.

Paul appears before Felix

24:1
Acts 21:26,27
23:2,24-30

24 Five days later Ananias the High Priest arrived with some of the Jewish leaders and the lawyer Tertullus, to make their accusations against Paul. 2When Tertullus was called forward, he laid charges against Paul in the following address to the governor:

"Your Excellency, you have given quietness and peace to us Jews and have greatly reduced the discrimination against us. 3And for this we are very, very grateful to you. 4But lest I bore you, kindly give me your attention for only a moment as I briefly outline our case against this man. 5For we have found him to be a troublemaker, a man who is constantly inciting the Jews throughout the entire world to riots and rebellions against the Roman government. He is a ringleader of the sect known as the Nazarenes. 6Moreover, he was trying to defile the Temple when we arrested him.

24:5
Mt 5:11
Lk 23:2
Jn 15:20
Acts 16:20,21
17:6; 24:14
1 Thess 2:14-16
2 Tim 3:2
1 Pet 2:12,19
24:6
Jn 18:31
Acts 21:28
24:7
Acts 21:33
24:8
Acts 23:30
24:11
Acts 21:26,27

"We would have given him what he justly deserves, 7but Lysias, the commander of the garrison, came and took him violently away from us, 8demanding that he be tried by Roman law. You can find out the truth of our accusations by examining him yourself."

9Then all the other Jews chimed in, declaring that everything Tertullus said was true.

10Now it was Paul's turn. The governor motioned for him to rise and speak.

24:12
Acts 15:8
24:13
Acts 15:7
24:14
Lk 24:27
Acts 9:2; 26:22
2 Tim 1:3
24:15
Dan 12:2
Mt 22:31,32
Jn 5:28,29
Acts 23:6
26:6-8
1 Thess 4:14
Rev 20:12
24:16
Acts 23:1
24:17
Acts 11:29
Rom 15:25-28
1 Cor 16:3
2 Cor 8:4
24:18
Acts 21:26,27

Paul began: "I know, sir, that you have been a judge of Jewish affairs for many years, and this gives me confidence as I make my defense. 11You can quickly discover that it was no more than twelve days ago that I arrived in Jerusalem to worship at the Temple, 12and you will discover that I have never incited a riot in any synagogue or on the streets of any city; 13and these men certainly cannot prove the things they accuse me of doing.

14"But one thing I do confess, that I believe in the way of salvation, which they refer to as a sect; I follow that system of serving the God of our ancestors; I firmly believe in the Jewish law and everything written in the books of prophecy; 15and I believe, just as these men do, that there will be a resurrection of both the righteous and ungodly. 16Because of this I try with all my strength to always maintain a clear conscience before God and man.

17"After several years away, I returned to Jerusalem with money to aid the Jews, and to offer a sacrifice to God. 18My accusers saw me in the Temple as I was presenting my thank offering. I had shaved my head as their laws required, and there was no crowd around me, and no rioting! But some Jews from Turkey were there 19(who ought to be here if they have anything against me)— 20but look! Ask

24:1 *Jewish leaders*, literally, "elders." *lawyer*, literally, "orator." **24:18** *as I was presenting my thank offering,* implied.

24:1 The accusers arrived—Ananias, the High Priest; Tertullus, the lawyer; and several Jewish leaders. They traveled 60 miles to Caesarea, the Roman center of government, to give their false accusations against Paul. Their murder plot had failed (23:12–15), but they persisted in trying to kill him. This attempted murder was both premeditated and persistent.

24:2ff Tertullus was a special orator called to present the religious leaders' case before the Roman governor. He made three accusations against Paul: (1) he was a renegade, inciting the Jews around the world; (2) he was the ringleader of an unrecognized religious sect, which was against Roman law; and (3) he had

profaned the Temple. The religious leaders hoped that these accusations would persuade Felix to execute Paul to keep the peace in Palestine.

24:10ff Tertullus and the religious leaders seemed to have a strong argument against Paul, but Paul refuted their accusation point by point. Paul was also able to present the gospel message through his defense. Paul's accusers were unable to present specific evidence to support their general accusations. For example, Paul was accused of starting trouble among the Jews in Turkey, but the Jews in Turkey were not present to confirm this.

these men right here what wrongdoing their Council found in me, 21except that I
said one thing I shouldn't when I shouted out, 'I am here before the Council to
defend myself for believing that the dead will rise again!' "

24:21
Acts 23:6

22Felix, who knew Christians didn't go around starting riots, told the Jews to
wait for the arrival of Lysias, the garrison commander, and then he would decide
the case. 23He ordered Paul to prison but instructed the guards to treat him gently
and not to forbid any of his friends from visiting him or bringing him gifts to make
his stay more comfortable.

24:23
Acts 27:3; 28:16

24A few days later Felix came with Drusilla, his legal wife, a Jewess. Sending for
Paul, they listened as he told them about faith in Christ Jesus. 25And as he reasoned
with them about righteousness and self-control and the judgment to come, Felix
was terrified.

"Go away for now," he replied, "and when I have a more convenient time, I'll
call for you again."

24:25
Acts 10:42
Gal 5:23
Tit 2:12
2 Pet 1:6

26He also hoped that Paul would bribe him, so he sent for him from time to time
and talked with him. 27Two years went by in this way; then Felix was succeeded by
Porcius Festus. And because Felix wanted to gain favor with the Jews, he left Paul
in chains.

24:26
Acts 24:17
24:27
Acts 25:9,
24-27; 26:24

Paul appears before Festus

25 Three days after Festus arrived in Caesarea to take over his new responsibilities, he left for Jerusalem, 2where the chief priests and other Jewish leaders
got hold of him and gave him their story about Paul. 3They begged him to bring
Paul to Jerusalem at once. (Their plan was to waylay and kill him.) 4But Festus
replied that since Paul was at Caesarea and he himself was returning there soon,
5those with authority in this affair should return with him for the trial.

25:2
Acts 23:12-21
24:1

6Eight or ten days later he returned to Caesarea and the following day opened
Paul's trial.

7On Paul's arrival in court the Jews from Jerusalem gathered around, hurling
many serious accusations which they couldn't prove. 8Paul denied the charges: "I
am not guilty," he said. "I have not opposed the Jewish laws or desecrated the
Temple or rebelled against the Roman government."

25:7
Esth 3:8
Acts 24:13,27
25:8
Acts 6:13
24:12; 28:17
Rom 13:1-7

9Then Festus, anxious to please the Jews, asked him, "Are you willing to go to
Jerusalem and stand trial before me?"

10, 11But Paul replied, "No! I demand my privilege of a hearing before the
Emperor himself. You know very well I am not guilty. If I have done something
worthy of death, I don't refuse to die! But if I am innocent, neither you nor anyone
else has a right to turn me over to these men to kill me. *I appeal to Caesar.*"

25:10
Acts 25:21
26:32
25:11
Acts 23:11
27:24; 28:19

24:21 *except that I said one thing I shouldn't,* literally, "except it be for this one voice." **24:22** *who knew Christians didn't go around starting riots,* literally, "having more accurate knowledge." **24:24** *his legal wife,* literally, "his own wife."

24:22 Felix had been governor for six years and would have known about the Christians, a topic of conversation among the Roman leaders. The Christians' peaceful lifestyles had shown the Romans that "Christians didn't go around starting riots."

24:25 Paul's talk with Felix became so personal that Felix felt convicted. Felix, like Herod Antipas (Mark 6:17, 18), had taken another man's wife. Paul's words were interesting until they focused on "righteousness and self-control and the judgment to come." Many people will be glad to discuss the gospel with you as long as it doesn't touch their lives too personally. When it does, some will resist or run away. But this is what the gospel is all about—God's power to change lives. The gospel is not effective until it moves from principles and doctrine into a life-changing dynamic. When someone resists or runs from your witness, you have made the gospel personal.

●**24:27** Felix lost his job as governor and was called back to Rome. Porcius Festus took over as governor in late 59 or early 60. He was more just than Felix, who had kept Paul in prison for two years in

order to keep the Jews happy. When Festus came into office, he immediately ordered Paul's trial to resume.

24:27 The Jews were in the majority, and the political leaders wanted to defer to them because their job was to keep the peace. Paul seemed to incite problems among the Jews everywhere he went. By keeping him in prison, Felix left office on good terms with the Jews.

●**25:10, 11** Every Roman citizen had the right to appeal to Caesar. This didn't mean that Caesar himself would hear the case, but that his case would be tried by the highest courts in the empire. Festus saw Paul's appeal as a way to send him out of the country and thus calm the Jews. Paul wanted to go to Rome to preach the gospel (Romans 1:10), and he knew his appeal would give him the opportunity. To go there as a prisoner was better than not to go at all.

25:11 Paul knew he was blameless of the charges against him and could appeal to Caesar's judgment. He knew his rights as a Roman citizen and as an innocent person. Paul had met his

12Festus conferred with his advisors and then replied, "Very well! You have appealed to Caesar, and to Caesar you shall go!"

13A few days later King Agrippa arrived with Bernice for a visit with Festus. 14During their stay of several days Festus discussed Paul's case with the king. "There is a prisoner here," he told him, "whose case was left for me by Felix. 15When I was in Jerusalem, the chief priests and other Jewish leaders gave me their side of the story and asked me to have him killed. 16Of course I quickly pointed out to them that Roman law does not convict a man before he is tried. He is given an opportunity to defend himself face to face with his accusers.

17"When they came here for the trial, I called the case the very next day and ordered Paul brought in. 18But the accusations made against him weren't at all what I supposed they would be. 19It was something about their religion, and about someone called Jesus who died, but Paul insists is alive! 20I was perplexed as to how to decide a case of this kind and asked him whether he would be willing to stand trial on these charges in Jerusalem. 21But Paul appealed to Caesar! So I ordered him back to jail until I could arrange to get him to the Emperor."

22"I'd like to hear the man myself," Agrippa said.

And Festus replied, "You shall—tomorrow!"

Paul witnesses to Agrippa

23So the next day, after the king and Bernice had arrived at the courtroom with great pomp, accompanied by military officers and prominent men of the city, Festus ordered Paul brought in.

24Then Festus addressed the audience: "King Agrippa and all present," he said, "this is the man whose death is demanded both by the local Jews and by those in Jerusalem! 25But in my opinion he has done nothing worthy of death. However, he appealed his case to Caesar, and I have no alternative but to send him. 26But what shall I write the Emperor? For there is no real charge against him! So I have brought him before you all, and especially you, King Agrippa, to examine him and then tell me what to write. 27For it doesn't seem reasonable to send a prisoner to the Emperor without any charges against him!"

26 Then Agrippa said to Paul, "Go ahead. Tell us your story." So Paul, with many gestures, presented his defense:

2"I am fortunate, King Agrippa," he began, "to be able to present my answer before you, 3for I know you are an expert on Jewish laws and customs. Now please listen patiently!

4"As the Jews are well aware, I was given a thorough Jewish training from my earliest childhood in Tarsus and later at Jerusalem, and I lived accordingly. 5If they would admit it, they know that I have always been the strictest of Pharisees when it comes to obedience to Jewish laws and customs. 6But the real reason behind their accusations is something else—it is because I am looking forward to the fulfillment of God's promise made to our ancestors. 7The twelve tribes of Israel strive night and day to attain this same hope I have! Yet, O King, for me it is a crime, they say!

25:13 *arrived with Bernice.* She was his sister.   **26:1** *with many gestures,* literally, "stretched forth his hand." **26:4** *my earliest childhood in Tarsus,* literally, "my own nation."

Cross references (margin)

25:14 Acts 24:27

25:15 Acts 25:2

25:16 Acts 23:30

25:19 Acts 18:15 23:29 1 Cor 15:2-8

25:22 Acts 9:15

25:24 Acts 22:22

25:25 Acts 23:22

26:4 Phil 3:5

26:6 Gen 3:15 22:18; 26:4 Deut 18:15 Isa 7:14; 9:6,7 Jer 23:5,6 33:14 Ezek 34:23 37:24 Dan 9:24 Mal 3:1; 4:2 Acts 13:32,33

26:7 Phil 3:11

---

responsibilities as a Roman, and so he had the opportunity to claim Rome's protection. The good reputation and clear conscience that result from our walk with God can help us remain not only guilt-free before God, but blame-free before the world as well.

25:13 This was Herod Agrippa II, son of Herod Agrippa I, and a descendant of Herod the Great. He had power over the Temple, controlled the Temple treasury, and could appoint and remove the High Priest. Bernice was the sister of Herod Agrippa II. She married her uncle Herod Chalcis, became a mistress to her brother Agrippa II, and then became mistress to the emperor Titus. Here Agrippa and Bernice were making an official visit to Festus.

Agrippa, of Jewish descent, could help clarify this "Jewish situation" to the Roman governor. Agrippa and Festus were anxious to cooperate in governing their neighboring territories.

25:19 Even though Festus knew little about Christianity, he understood that the resurrection was central to Christian belief.

●**25:23** Paul was in prison, but that didn't stop him from making the most of his situation. Military officers and prominent city leaders met in the palace room with Agrippa to hear this case. Paul saw this new audience as yet another opportunity to present the gospel. Rather than complain about your present situation, seek for ways to use every opportunity to serve God and share him with others. Our problems may be opportunities in disguise.

8But is it a crime to believe in the resurrection of the dead? Does it seem incredible to you that God can bring men back to life again?

9"I used to believe that I ought to do many horrible things to the followers of Jesus of Nazareth. 10I imprisoned many of the saints in Jerusalem, as authorized by the High Priests; and when they were condemned to death, I cast my vote against them. 11I used torture to try to make Christians everywhere curse Christ. I was so violently opposed to them that I even hounded them in distant cities in foreign lands.

12"I was on such a mission to Damascus, armed with the authority and commission of the chief priests, 13when one day about noon, sir, a light from heaven brighter than the sun shone down on me and my companions. 14We all fell down, and I heard a voice speaking to me in Hebrew, 'Saul, Saul, why are you persecuting me? You are only hurting yourself.'

15" 'Who are you, sir?' I asked.

"And the Lord replied, 'I am Jesus, the one you are persecuting. 16Now stand up! For I have appeared to you to appoint you as my servant and my witness. You are to tell the world about this experience and about the many other occasions when I shall appear to you. 17And I will protect you from both your own people and the Gentiles. Yes, I am going to send you to the Gentiles 18to open their eyes to their true condition so that they may repent and live in the light of God instead of in Satan's darkness, so that they may receive forgiveness for their sins and God's inheritance along with all people everywhere whose sins are cleansed away, who are set apart by faith in me.'

19"And so, O King Agrippa, I was not disobedient to that vision from heaven! 20I preached first to those in Damascus, then in Jerusalem and through Judea, and also to the Gentiles that all must forsake their sins and turn to God—and prove their repentance by doing good deeds. 21The Jews arrested me in the Temple for preaching this, and tried to kill me, 22but God protected me so that I am still alive today to tell these facts to everyone, both great and small. I teach nothing except what the prophets and Moses said— 23that the Messiah would suffer, and be the First to rise from the dead, to bring light to Jews and Gentiles alike."

24Suddenly Festus shouted, "Paul, you are insane. Your long studying has broken your mind!"

25But Paul replied, "I am not insane, Most Excellent Festus. I speak words of sober truth. 26And King Agrippa knows about these things. I speak frankly for I am sure these events are all familiar to him, for they were not done in a corner! 27King Agrippa, do you believe the prophets? But I know you do—"

28Agrippa interrupted him. "With trivial proofs like these, you expect me to become a Christian?"

29And Paul replied, "Would to God that whether my arguments are trivial or

26:8
Dan 12:2
26:9
Jn 15:21; 16:2
1 Tim 1:13
26:10
Acts 8:3; 22:5
26:11
Acts 9:1; 22:19
26:15
Acts 9:5; 22:8
26:16
Acts 22:15
Gal 1:12
Col 1:25
1 Tim 1:12
26:17
Acts 13:46-48
22:21
Rom 11:13
15:16
Gal 1:15,16
2:7-9
1 Tim 2:7
2 Tim 1:11
26:18
Isa 35:5; 42:6,7
Lk 1:77,79
Eph 1:11; 5:8
Col 1:13
1 Pet 2:9
26:20
Mt 3:8
Acts 9:20,26
13:46
26:21
Acts 21:30
26:22
Jn 5:46
Rom 3:21,22
26:23
Ps 2:7
6:8-11,22
Isa 53:1-12
Lk 24:26,27,46,
47
Rom 1:3,4
1 Cor 15:20
Col 1:18
Rev 1:5
26:24
1 Cor 1:23
26:26
Acts 26:3

26:9 *the followers of Jesus of Nazareth,* literally, "the name."   **26:14** *You are only hurting yourself,* literally, "It is hard for you to kick against the oxgoad."   **26:28** *With trivial proofs like these,* literally, "with little persuasion ."

26:18 Paul took every opportunity to remind his audience that the Gentiles have an equal share in God's inheritance. This inheritance is the promise and blessing of the covenant God made with Abraham (see Ephesians 2:19; 1 Peter 1:3, 4).

26:24 Paul was risking his life for an argument that was offensive to the Jews and unbelievable to the Gentiles. Jesus received the same response to his message (Mark 3:21; John 10:20). To a worldly, materialistic mind, it seems insane to risk so much to gain what seems so little. But as you follow Christ, you discover that temporary possessions look small next to even the smallest eternal reward.

26:26 Paul was appealing to the *facts*—people were still alive who had heard Jesus and seen his miracles; the empty tomb could still be seen; and the Christian message was turning the world upside down (17:6). The history of Jesus' life and the early church are facts that are still open for us to examine. We still have

eyewitness accounts of Jesus' life in the Bible as well as historical and archaeological records of the early church to study. Examine the events and facts as verified by many witnesses. Reconfirm your faith with the truth of these accounts.

● **26:28** Agrippa answered Paul's presentation with a sarcastic remark. Paul didn't react to the brush-off, but made a personal appeal to which he hoped all his listeners would respond. Paul's response is a good example for us as we tell others about God's plan of salvation. A sincere personal appeal or personal testimony can show the depth of our concern and break through hardened hearts.

● **26:28, 29** Paul's heart is revealed here in his words: he was more concerned for the salvation of these strangers than for the removal of his own bonds. Ask God to help you share Paul's burning desire to see others come to him—a desire so strong that it overshadows your problems.

strong, both you and everyone here in this audience might become the same as I am, except for these chains.''

26:31
Acts 23:9; 25:25

30Then the king, the governor, Bernice, and all the others stood and left. 31As they talked it over afterwards they agreed, "This man hasn't done anything worthy of death or imprisonment.''

26:32
Acts 25:11

32And Agrippa said to Festus, "He could be set free if he hadn't appealed to Caesar!''

Paul sails for Rome

27:1
Acts 25:12,25

27:2
Acts 19:29; 20:4
Col 4:10

27:3
Mt 11:21
Acts 24:23
27:43; 28:16

27 Arrangements were finally made to start us on our way to Rome by ship; so Paul and several other prisoners were placed in the custody of an officer named Julius, a member of the imperial guard. 2We left on a boat which was scheduled to make several stops along the Turkish coast. I should add that Aristarchus, a Greek from Thessalonica, was with us.

3The next day when we docked at Sidon, Julius was very kind to Paul and let him go ashore to visit with friends and receive their hospitality. 4Putting to sea from there, we encountered headwinds that made it difficult to keep the ship on course,

27:2 *a boat,* literally, "a ship of Adramyttium." *the Turkish coast,* literally, "the coast of Asia."

HEROD AGRIPPA II

Like great-grandfather, like grandfather, like father, like son—this tells the story of Herod Agrippa II. He inherited the effects of generations of powerful men with flawed personalities. Each son followed his father in weaknesses, mistakes, and missed opportunities. Each generation had a confrontation with God, but each failed to realize the importance of the decision. Herod Agrippa's great-uncle, Herod Antipas, actually met Jesus during his trial, but failed to see Jesus for who he was. Agrippa II heard the gospel from Paul, but considered the message mild entertainment. He found it humorous that Paul actually tried to convince him to become a Christian.

Like so many before and after, Agrippa II stopped within hearing distance of the Kingdom of God. He left himself without excuse. He heard the gospel but decided it wasn't worth responding to personally. Unfortunately, his mistake isn't uncommon. Many who read his story also will not believe. Their problem, like his, is not really that the gospel isn't convincing or that they don't need to know God personally; it is that they choose not to respond.

What has been your response to the gospel? Has it turned your life around and given you the hope of eternal life, or has it been a message to resist or reject? Perhaps it has just been entertainment. It may seem like too great a price to give God control of your life, but it is an even greater price by far to live eternally apart from him because you chose not to be his child.

Strengths and accomplishments:
- Last of the Herod dynasty that ruled parts of Palestine from 40 B.C. to A.D. 100
- Continued his father's success in mediating between Rome and Palestine
- Continued the family tradition of building and improving cities

Weaknesses and mistakes:
- Was not convinced by the gospel and consciously rejected it
- Carried on an incestuous relationship with his sister Bernice

Lessons from his life:
- Families pass on both positive and negative influences to children
- There are no guarantees of multiple opportunities to respond to God

Vital statistics:
- Occupation: Ruler of northern and eastern Palestine
- Relatives: Great-grandfather: Herod the Great. Father: Herod Agrippa I. Great-uncle: Herod Antipas. Sisters: Bernice, Drusilla.
- Contemporaries: Paul, Felix, Festus, Peter, Luke

Key verse:
"Agrippa interrupted him [Paul]. 'With trivial proofs like these, you expect me to become a Christian?' " (Acts 26:28).

Herod Agrippa II's story is told in Acts 25:13—26:32.

27:2 Use of the pronoun *we* indicates that Luke accompanied Paul on this journey. Aristarchus is the man who was dragged into the amphitheater at the beginning of the riot in Ephesus (19:29; 20:4; Philemon 24).

so we sailed north of Cyprus between the island and the mainland, 5and passed along the coast of the provinces of Cilicia and Pamphylia, landing at Myra, in the province of Lycia. 6There our officer found an Egyptian ship from Alexandria, bound for Italy, and put us aboard.

27:6
Acts 28:11

7, 8We had several days of rough sailing, and finally neared Cnidus; but the winds had become too strong, so we ran across to Crete, passing the port of Salome. Beating into the wind with great difficulty and moving slowly along the southern coast, we arrived at Fair Havens, near the city of Lasea. 9There we stayed for several days. The weather was becoming dangerous for long voyages by then, because it was late in the year, and Paul spoke to the ship's officers about it.

10"Sirs," he said, "I believe there is trouble ahead if we go on—perhaps ship-wreck, loss of cargo, injuries, and death." 11But the officers in charge of the prisoners listened more to the ship's captain and the owner than to Paul. 12And since Fair Havens was an exposed harbor—a poor place to spend the winter—most of the crew advised trying to go further up the coast to Phoenix, in order to winter there; Phoenix was a good harbor with only a northwest and southwest exposure.

27:10
Amos 3:7

The storm at sea

13Just then a light wind began blowing from the south, and it looked like a perfect day for the trip; so they pulled up anchor and sailed along close to shore.

14, 15But shortly afterwards, the weather changed abruptly and a heavy wind of typhoon strength (a "northeaster," they called it) caught the ship and blew it out to sea. They tried at first to face back to shore but couldn't, so they gave up and let the ship run before the gale.

16We finally sailed behind a small island named Clauda, where with great

27:7, 8 *Cnidus,* a port on the southeast coast of Turkey.   **27:9** *because it was late in the year,* literally, "because the Fast was now already gone by." It came about the time of the autumn equinox.   **27:12** *exposed,* implied.

Reference	What happened
21:30	When Paul arrived in Jerusalem, a riot broke out. Seeing the riot, Roman soldiers put Paul into protective custody. Paul asked for a chance to defend himself to the people. His speech was interrupted by the crowd when he spoke about the Gentiles.
22:24	A Roman commander ordered a beating to get a confession from Paul. Paul claimed Roman citizenship and escaped the whip.
22:30	Paul was brought before the Jewish Council. Because of his Roman citizenship, he was rescued from the religious leaders who wanted to kill him.
23:10	The Roman commander put Paul back under protective custody.
23:12	Due to a plot to kill Paul, the commander transferred him to Caesarea, which was under Governor Felix's control.
23:35	Paul was in prison until the Jews arrived to accuse him. Paul defended himself before Felix.
24:26	Paul was in prison for two years, speaking occasionally to Felix and Drusilla.
24:27	Felix replaced by Festus.
25:1	New accusations against Paul—Jews wanted him back in Jerusalem for a trial. Paul claimed his right to a hearing before Caesar.
25:12	Festus promised to send him to Rome.
25:13	Festus discussed Paul's case with Agrippa II.
26:1	Agrippa and Festus heard Paul speak. Paul again told his story.
26:24–28	Agrippa interrupted with sarcastic rejection of the gospel.
26:30	Group consensus was that Paul was guilty of nothing and could be released if he had not appealed to Rome.
27:1, 2	Paul left for Rome, by courtesy of the Roman Empire.

PAUL'S JOURNEY TO ROME
One of Paul's most important journeys was to Rome, but he didn't get there the way he expected. It turned out to be more of a legal journey than a missionary journey because through a series of legal trials and transactions, Paul was delivered to Rome where his presentation of the gospel would penetrate even into the walls of the emperor's palace. Sometimes when our plans don't work out as we want them to, they work out even better than we expected.

●**27:9** Ships in ancient times had no compasses and navigated by the stars. Overcast weather made sailing almost impossible and very dangerous. Sailing was doubtful in September and impossible by November. This event occurred in October (A.D. 59).

difficulty we hoisted aboard the lifeboat that was being towed behind us, 17and then banded the ship with ropes to strengthen the hull. The sailors were afraid of being driven across to the quicksands of the African coast, so they lowered the topsails and were thus driven before the wind.

18The next day as the seas grew higher, the crew began throwing the cargo overboard. 19The following day they threw out the tackle and anything else they could lay their hands on. 20The terrible storm raged unabated many days, until at last all hope was gone.

21No one had eaten for a long time, but finally Paul called the crew together and said, "Men, you should have listened to me in the first place and not left Fair Havens—you would have avoided all this injury and loss! 22But cheer up! Not one of us will lose our lives, even though the ship will go down.

23"For last night an angel of the God to whom I belong and whom I serve stood beside me, 24and said, 'Don't be afraid, Paul—for you will surely stand trial before Caesar! What's more, God has granted your request and will save the lives of all those sailing with you.' 25So take courage! For I believe God! It will be just as he said! 26But we will be shipwrecked on an island."

The shipwreck

27About midnight on the fourteenth night of the storm, as we were being driven to and fro on the Adriatic Sea, the sailors suspected land was near. 28They sounded, and found 120 feet of water below them. A little later they sounded again, and found only ninety feet. 29At this rate they knew they would soon be driven ashore;

27:17 *were afraid of being driven across to the quicksands of the African coast*, literally, "fearing lest they should be cast upon the Syrtis." 27:20 *The terrible storm raged unabated many days*, literally, "Neither sun nor stars shone upon us."

27:18
Jonah 1:5
27:21
Acts 27:10
27:23
Acts 18:9; 23:11
27:44
2 Tim 4:17
27:24
Isa 41:10,14
43:1,2
Acts 19:21
23:11; 25:11
27:25
2 Chron 20:20
Lk 1:45
Rom 4:20
Heb 6:17
27:26
Acts 28:1

THE TRIP TOWARD ROME
Paul began his 2,000-mile trip to Rome at Caesarea. To avoid the open seas, the ship went north, following the coastline. At Myra, Paul was put on a vessel bound for Italy. It arrived with difficulty at Cnidus, then went to Crete, landing at the port of Fair Havens. The next stop was Phoenix, but the ship was blown south around the island of Clauda, then drifted for two weeks until it was shipwrecked on the island of Malta.

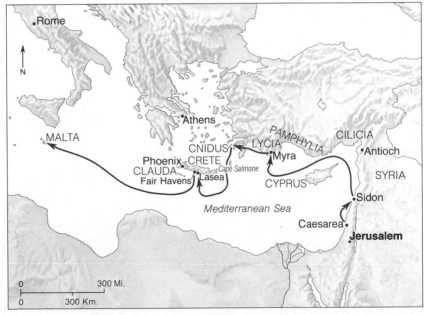

27:21 Why would Paul talk to the crew this way? Paul was not taunting them with an "I told you so," but was reminding them that, with God's guidance, he had predicted this very problem. In the future, they listened to him (27:30–32) and their lives were spared because of it.

27:28 Soundings were made by throwing a weighted, marked line into the water. When the lead hit the bottom, sailors could tell the depth of the water from the marks on the rope.

and fearing rocks along the coast, they threw out four anchors from the stern and prayed for daylight.

³⁰Some of the sailors planned to abandon the ship, and lowered the emergency boat as though they were going to put out anchors from the prow. ³¹But Paul said to the soldiers and commanding officer, "You will all die unless everyone stays aboard." ³²So the soldiers cut the ropes and let the boat fall off.

³³As the darkness gave way to the early morning light, Paul begged everyone to eat. "You haven't touched food for two weeks," he said. ³⁴"Please eat something now for your own good! For not a hair of your heads shall perish!"

³⁵Then he took some hardtack and gave thanks to God before them all, and broke off a piece and ate it. ³⁶Suddenly everyone felt better and began eating, ³⁷all two hundred seventy-six of us—for that is the number we had aboard. ³⁸After eating, the crew lightened the ship further by throwing all the wheat overboard.

³⁹When it was day, they didn't recognize the coastline, but noticed a bay with a beach and wondered whether they could get between the rocks and be driven up onto the beach. ⁴⁰They finally decided to try. Cutting off the anchors and leaving them in the sea, they lowered the rudders, raised the foresail and headed ashore. ⁴¹But the ship hit a sandbar and ran aground. The bow of the ship stuck fast, while the stern was exposed to the violence of the waves and began to break apart.

⁴²The soldiers advised their commanding officer to let them kill the prisoners lest any of them swim ashore and escape. ⁴³But Julius wanted to spare Paul, so he told them no. Then he ordered all who could swim to jump overboard and make for land, ⁴⁴and the rest to try for it on planks and debris from the broken ship. So everyone escaped safely ashore!

Paul is bitten by a snake on Malta

28 We soon learned that we were on the island of Malta. The people of the island were very kind to us, building a bonfire on the beach to welcome and warm us in the rain and cold.

³As Paul gathered an armful of sticks to lay on the fire, a poisonous snake, driven out by the heat, fastened itself onto his hand! ⁴The people of the island saw it hanging there and said to each other, "A murderer, no doubt! Though he escaped the sea, justice will not permit him to live!"

⁵But Paul shook off the snake into the fire and was unharmed. ⁶The people waited for him to begin swelling or suddenly fall dead; but when they had waited

27:41 *a sandbar*, literally, "a place where two seas met." 27:43 *Julius*, implied.

27:34
Mt 10:30
Lk 12:7; 21:18
27:35
Mt 14:19
Jn 6:11
1 Tim 4:4,5
27:38
Jonah 1:5
Acts 27:18

27:41
2 Cor 11:25

27:44
Ps 107:30

28:1
Acts 27:26
28:4
Lk 13:2,4
28:5
Mk 16:18
Lk 10:19
28:6
Acts 14:11

27:42 The soldiers would pay with their own lives if any of their prisoners escaped. Their instinctive reaction was to kill the prisoners so they wouldn't escape. Julius, the centurion, was impressed with Paul and wanted to save his life. This act preserved Paul for his later ministry in Rome and fulfilled Paul's prediction that all people on the ship would be saved (27:22).

28:1 The island of Malta was 60 miles south of Sicily. It had excellent harbors and was ideally located for trade.

●**28:3** God had promised safe passage to Paul, and he would let neither sea nor serpent stop his servant. The snake that bit Paul, though poisonous, was unable to harm him. Our lives are in God's hands, to continue or end in his good timing. God still had work for Paul to do.

28:6 These people were very superstitious and believed in many gods. When they saw that Paul was unhurt by the poisonous snake, they thought he was a god. A similar situation is reported in 14:11–18.

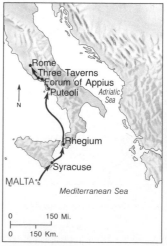

PAUL ARRIVES IN ROME
The shipwreck had occurred on the island of Malta where the ship's company spent three months. Finally another ship gave them passage for the 100 miles to Syracuse, capital of Sicily, then on to Rhegium, finally dropping anchor at Puteoli. Paul was taken along the Appian Way to the Forum, and to the Three Taverns before arriving in Rome.

a long time and no harm came to him, they changed their minds and decided he was a god.

7Near the shore where we landed was an estate belonging to Publius, the governor of the island. He welcomed us courteously and fed us for three days. 8As it happened, Publius' father was ill with fever and dysentery. Paul went in and prayed for him, and laying his hands on him, healed him! 9Then all the other sick people in the island came and were cured. 10As a result we were showered with gifts, and when the time came to sail, people put on board all sorts of things we would need for the trip.

11It was three months after the shipwreck before we set sail again, and this time it was in *The Twin Brothers* of Alexandria, a ship that had wintered at the island. 12Our first stop was Syracuse, where we stayed three days. 13From there we circled around to Rhegium; a day later a south wind began blowing, so the following day we arrived at Puteoli, 14where we found some believers! They begged us to stay with them seven days. Then we went on to Rome.

Paul lives under guard in Rome

15The brothers in Rome had heard we were coming and came to meet us at the Forum on the Appian Way. Others joined us at The Three Taverns. When Paul saw them, he thanked God and took courage.

16When we arrived in Rome, Paul was permitted to live wherever he wanted to, though guarded by a soldier.

17Three days after his arrival, he called together the local Jewish leaders and spoke to them as follows:

"Brothers, I was arrested by the Jews in Jerusalem and handed over to the Roman government for prosecution, even though I had harmed no one nor violated the customs of our ancestors. 18The Romans gave me a trial and wanted to release me, for they found no cause for the death sentence demanded by the Jewish leaders. 19But when the Jews protested the decision, I felt it necessary, with no malice against them, to appeal to Caesar. 20I asked you to come here today so we could get acquainted and I could tell you that it is because I believe the Messiah has come that I am bound with this chain."

21They replied, "We have heard nothing against you! We have had no letters from Judea or reports from those arriving from Jerusalem. 22But we want to hear what you believe, for the only thing we know about these Christians is that they are denounced everywhere!"

23So a time was set and on that day large numbers came to his house. He told them about the Kingdom of God and taught them about Jesus from the Scriptures—from the five books of Moses and the books of prophecy. He began lecturing in the morning and went on into the evening!

28:10 *gifts,* literally, "honors." 28:20 *the Messiah,* literally, "the hope of Israel." But perhaps he is referring here, as in his other defenses, to his belief in the resurrection of the dead. 28:21 *from Jerusalem,* implied.

28:15 Where did the Roman believers come from? The gospel message had spread to Rome by various methods. Many Jews who lived in Rome visited Jerusalem for religious festivals. Some were probably present at Pentecost (chapter 2), believed in Jesus, and brought the message back to Rome. Also, Paul had written his letter to the Romans before he visited there.

28:15 The Forum was a town about 43 miles south of Rome; The Three Taverns was located about 35 miles south of Rome. A *tavern* was a place that provided food and lodging for travelers. The Christians openly went to meet Paul and encourage him.

28:17 The Edict of Claudius expelling Jews from Rome (18:2) must have been temporary because Jewish leaders were back in Rome.

● **28:17–20** Paul wanted to preach the gospel in Rome, and he eventually got there—in chains, through shipwreck, and after many trials. Although he may have wished for an easier passage, he knew that God had blessed him greatly in allowing him to meet the believers in Rome and preach the message to both Jews and Gentiles in that great city. God "worked all things for good" (Romans 8:28) for Paul, and you can trust him to do the same for you. God may not make you comfortable or secure, but he will provide the opportunity to do his work.

28:22 Christians were denounced everywhere by the Romans because they were seen as a threat to the Roman establishment. They believed in one God, whereas the Romans had many gods, including Caesar. The Christians were committed to an authority higher than Caesar.

28:23 Paul used the Old Testament to teach the Jews that Jesus was the Messiah, the fulfillment of God's promises. The book of Romans, written ten years earlier, reveals the ongoing dialogue Paul had with the Jews in Rome.

28:8
Mk 5:23
Acts 19:11
1 Cor 12:9,28
Jas 5:14

28:11
Acts 27:6

28:16
Acts 24:33; 27:3

28:17
Acts 24:12; 25:8

28:18
Acts 23:29

28:19
Acts 25:11; 26:32
28:20
Acts 26:6

28:22
Acts 24:14
1 Pet 2:12; 3:16
4:16

28:23
Lk 24:27
Acts 1:3; 23:11
28:31

24Some believed, and some didn't. 25But after they had argued back and forth among themselves, they left with this final word from Paul ringing in their ears: "The Holy Spirit was right when he said through Isaiah the prophet,

26" 'Say to the Jews, "You will hear and see but not understand, 27for your hearts are too fat and your ears don't listen and you have closed your eyes against understanding, for you don't want to see and hear and understand and turn to me to heal you." ' 28, 29So I want you to realize that this salvation from God is available to the Gentiles too, and they will accept it."

30Paul lived for the next two years in his rented house and welcomed all who visited him, 31telling them with all boldness about the Kingdom of God and about the Lord Jesus Christ; and no one tried to stop him.

28:24
Acts 14:4
28:25-27
Isa 6:9-10
Jn 12:39,40

28:28
Ps 98:3
Lk 2:30-32
Acts 9:15;
13:26,46
28:31
Acts 20:25;
28:23

28:28, 29. Some of the ancient manuscripts add, "And when he had said these words, the Jews departed, having much dissenting among themselves." **28:30** *in his rented house,* or, "at his own expense."

28:27 Paul was quoting from Isaiah 6:9, 10.

28:30 While Paul was under house arrest, he did more than speak to the Jews. He wrote letters, commonly called his Prison Epistles, to the Ephesians, Colossians, and Philippians, as well as personal letters, such as the one to Philemon. Timothy often visited him (Philippians 1:1; Colossians 1:1; Philemon 1), as did Tychicus (Ephesians 6:21), Epaphroditus (Philippians 4:18), and Mark (John Mark, Colossians 4:10). Paul witnessed to the Roman guard (Philippians 1:13) and was involved with the Roman believers.

● **28:30** Tradition says that Paul was released after two years of house arrest in Rome and set off on a fourth missionary journey. Some reasons for this tradition are as follows: (1) Luke does not give us an account of his trial before Caesar, and Luke was a detailed chronicler; (2) the prosecution had two years to bring the case to trial, and time may have run out; (3) in his letter to the Philippians, written during his imprisonment in Rome, Paul implied that he would soon be released and would do further traveling; (4) Paul mentions several places where he intended to take the gospel, but he never visited those places in his first three journeys; and (5) early Christian literature talks plainly about other travels by Paul.

It may be that during Paul's time of freedom, he continued his travels extensively, even going to Spain (see Romans 15:24, 28) and back to the churches in Greece. The books of 1 Timothy and

Titus were written during this time. Later, Paul was imprisoned again, probably in Rome, where he wrote his last epistle (2 Timothy).

28:31 Why does the book of Acts end here? The book is not about the life of Paul, but about the spread of the gospel, and that has been clearly presented. God apparently thought it was not necessary for someone to write an additional book describing the continuing history of the early church. Now that the gospel had been preached and established at the center of trade and government, it would spread across the world.

28:31 The book of Acts deals with the history of the Christian church and its expansion in ever-widening circles touching Jerusalem, Antioch, Ephesus, and Rome—the most influential cities in the western world. Acts also shows the mighty miracles and testimonies of the heroes and martyrs of the early church—Peter, Stephen, James, Paul. All the ministry was prompted and held together by the Holy Spirit working in the lives of ordinary people—merchants, travelers, slaves, jailers, church leaders, males, females, Gentiles, Jews, rich, poor. Many unsung heroes of the faith continued the acts of the Holy Spirit through succeeding generations, changing the world with a changeless message—that Jesus Christ is Savior and Lord for all who call upon him. We today can be the unsung heroes in the continuing story of the spread of the gospel. It is that same message that we Christians are to take to our world, so it too may hear and believe.

It's always exciting to get more than you expect. And that's what you'll find in this Bible study guide—much more than you expect. Our goal was to write thoughtful, practical, dependable, and application-oriented studies of God's Word.

This study guide contains the complete text of the selected Bible book. The commentary is accurate, complete, and loaded with unique charts, maps, and profiles of Bible people.

With the Bible text, extensive notes and helps, and questions to guide discussion, these Life Application Study Guides have everything you need in one place.

The lessons in this Bible study guide will work for large classes as well as small group studies. To get everyone involved in your discussions, encourage participants to answer the questions before each meeting.

Each lesson is divided into five easy-to-lead sections. The section called "Reflect" introduces you and the members of your group to a specific area of life touched by the lesson. "Read" shows which chapters to read and which notes and other features to use. Additional questions help you understand the passage. "Realize" brings into focus the biblical principle to be learned with questions, a special insight, or both. "Respond" helps you make connections with your own situation and personal needs. The questions are designed to help you find areas in your life where you can apply the biblical truths. "Resolve" helps you map out action plans for that day.

Begin and end each lesson with prayer, asking for the Holy Spirit's guidance, direction, and wisdom.

Recommended time allotments for each section of a lesson:

Segment	60 minutes	90 minutes
Reflect on your life	5 minutes	10 minutes
Read the passage	10 minutes	15 minutes
Realize the principle	15 minutes	20 minutes
Respond to the message	20 minutes	30 minutes
Resolve to take action	10 minutes	15 minutes

All five sections work together to help a person learn the lessons, live out the principles, and obey the commands taught in the Bible.

Also, at the end of each lesson, there is a section entitled, "More for studying other themes in this section." These questions will help you lead the group in studying other parts of each section not covered in depth by the main lesson.

And remember, it is a message to obey, not just to listen to. So don't fool yourselves. For if a person just listens and doesn't obey, he is like a man looking at his face in a mirror; as soon as he walks away, he can't see himself anymore or remember what he looks like. But if anyone keeps looking steadily into God's law for free men, he will not only remember it but he will do what it says, and God will greatly bless him in everything he does. (James 1:22-25, TLB)

REFLECT
on your life

1 Give an example of something in your lifetime (trend, political movement, fad) that began very small but then grew rapidly and took the world by storm.

_____

_____

_____

_____

2 What factors caused it to have such a great influence?

_____

_____

_____

READ
the passage

Read the Introduction to Acts and the following notes:

☐1:1   ☐1:3

3 What did the disciples do when Jesus was arrested, tried, and crucified?

_____

_____

_____

4 In Acts we see the disciples as courageous witnesses for Christ. What changed them?

_____

_____

_____

5 At first the church was limited to Jerusalem and the surrounding areas. By the end of Acts, the gospel has spread to most of the Roman world. What factors caused the church to grow so rapidly?

_____

_____

_____

_____

_____

_____

6 Which person in Acts would you most want to be like? Why?

_____

_____

_____

_____

REALIZE
the principle

7 What would it take for you to be like him/her?

_____

_____

_____

_____

Jesus promised his followers they would be empowered by the Holy Spirit to spread the gospel across the world. Acts tells their story, documenting the spread of Christianity throughout the Roman Empire. How were these early believers able to make such a dramatic impact on their world? Fresh from the outpouring of the Spirit at Pentecost, they spoke with holy boldness, taking every opportunity to tell of Christ on the street and in synagogues, homes, prisons, and courtrooms. These men and women were convinced of the truth because

they had seen their risen Lord, and they were filled with the Holy Spirit. God's plan continues today, and he gives us opportunities to spread the Word. The resurrection is real, and the Holy Spirit's power is available. What's stopping us?

8 How had God prepared the world for the rapid spread of the gospel?

_____

_____

_____

9 In what ways has God prepared our world for the spread of the gospel?

_____

_____

_____

_____

RESPOND
to the message

10 In what parts of the world are churches growing most rapidly? Why do you think this is so?

_____

_____

_____

_____

11 What is your Jerusalem? Samaria? Ephesus or Rome?

_____

_____

_____

_____

12 How is your church working to help take the gospel to those areas?

_____

_____

_____

13 In what ways does your church support missions and evangelism?

_____

_____

_____

14 What barriers might be hindering your church's growth?

_____

_____

_____

15 What is your place in God's plan? How can you work for the advancement of his kingdom? (Here are some possibilities: pray, give financial support, help missionaries, reach neighbors, teach Sunday school, greet guests at church, take a church leadership position, etc.)

_____

_____

_____

RESOLVE
to take action

_____

_____

_____

A What were some of the key turning points for the early church? What would it take to turn your church around?

B What social barriers did the gospel break down? What barriers in your church need to be removed?

C What did Peter and Paul have in common? How were they different? How did God use each one uniquely to spread the gospel? How might God use your uniqueness to tell others of Christ?

MORE
for studying
other themes
in this section

REFLECT
on your life

1 Make a list of various sources of power.

2 Which power source do you use the most? Why?

READ
the passage

Read Acts 1:1—2:47 and the following notes:

◻1:3 ◻1:4 ◻1:5 ◻1:6 ◻1:8 ◻1:12,13 ◻2:3,4 ◻2:4 ◻2:14

3 When did the church begin to experience great growth?

4 What happened between the resurrection and the ascension?

5 What happened between the ascension and Pentecost?

_____

_____

_____

6 What does it mean to be "baptized with the Holy Spirit"?

_____

_____

_____

REALIZE
the principle

Jesus said that he would establish and build his church and that "all the powers of hell shall not prevail against it" (Matthew 16:18). In the book of Acts,
Luke records the story of the beginning and early years of Christ's church. Empowered by the Holy Spirit, these courageous men and women turned the
world upside down. The secret to the early church's growth was not clever
strategies or attractive programs or personal enthusiasm—it was the power of
the Holy Spirit. God still wants the church to grow, and the Holy Spirit is still
available for believers. What keeps Christians from experiencing the power of
the Holy Spirit today?

7 What did Jesus promise that the Holy Spirit would do in and through his followers?

_____

_____

_____

8 What did these believers do to receive the Holy Spirit?

_____

_____

_____

9 In what ways was Pentecost a unique event? In what ways can that experience be repeated today?

_____

_____

RESPOND
to the message

10 To whom is the power of the Holy Spirit available?

11 How can a person receive the Holy Spirit?

12 How does a person become empowered and led by the Spirit?

13 What programs and structures in your church facilitate the work and ministry of the Holy Spirit?

14 What keeps people from experiencing God's power?

15 Where are you resisting the prompting and guidance of the Holy Spirit? What can you do to be more open to his work in your life?

_____

_____

_____

_____

_____

_____

RESOLVE
to take action

A What evidence for the resurrection is presented in Acts? What other post-resurrection appearances are presented in the Gospels? How can this evidence strengthen your faith?

MORE
for studying
other themes
in this section

B How did the resurrection affect the disciples? How has Christ's resurrection changed your life?

C Why was it important for the disciples to see Christ ascending into heaven? What does Christ's ascension mean to you?

D What does 1:11 tell us about the return of Christ? What should the promise of Christ's return mean to us?

E Where is the kingdom of God? How does a person become a member of God's kingdom?

F Describe the first church business meeting. How does it compare to meet-ings in your church?

G Outline Peter's powerful sermon. What can you learn from Peter about how to explain the gospel to others?

H For what purposes did the believers meet together? Why were they well liked in the city?

I What attracted nonbelievers to the church? What is attractive about your church?

REFLECT
on your life

1 What were some of your childhood fears?

_____

_____

_____

_____

2 How did you get over those fears?

_____

_____

_____

_____

READ
the passage

Read Acts 3:1—4:31 and the following notes:

❐3:6 ❐3:12 ❐3:13 ❐4:2 ❐4:3 ❐4:7 ❐4:13 ❐4:20 ❐4:29-31

3 What did Peter and John say to the lame man?

_____

_____

_____

4 What was their response to the Council?

_____

_____

_____

5 What happened after the believers prayed?

_____

_____

_____

6 What opposition did the early church experience? How did they respond?

_____

_____

_____

REALIZE
the principle

7 What kinds of opposition have been experienced by Christians you know?

_____

_____

_____

When Jesus was taken prisoner in the garden, the disciples fled in fear at the first sign of opposition. But here, just a short time later, they declared their allegiance to Christ at every opportunity, regardless of the consequences. When they were threatened, they prayed for even more boldness. Today, unfortunately, we often cringe or compromise when challenged or criticized. Instead of bold proclamation, we blend into the culture. How might the church today be more bold in telling others about Christ?

8 Besides standing up and preaching, what are some other ways we can be bold for Christ?

_____

_____

_____

_____

9 How have your friends, neighbors, and co-workers reacted to your Christian faith?

RESPOND
to the message

_____

_____

_____

_____

10 Recall a time when you were bold about your faith and the results surprised you. What happened?

_____

_____

_____

_____

_____

11 When were you afraid to speak up for Christ?

_____

_____

_____

12 What opportunities to share or demonstrate your faith has God given you lately?

_____

_____

_____

_____

13 What can Christians do to become more outspoken in their witness for Christ?

_____

_____

_____

_____

_____

14 Which of the possible actions listed in question 13 would be practical and effective for you at this time?

_____

_____

_____

15 List one or two friends who need to know Christ.

_____

_____

_____

_____

_____

RESOLVE
to take action

16 What bold step could you take to help them understand your faith in Christ?

_____

_____

_____

_____

_____

A By whose authority did the disciples heal and preach? How do we invoke the same authority?

MORE
for studying
other themes
in this section

B In his sermon (3:12-26), what did Peter tell the people to do? Of which sins do you need to repent and confess to God?

C What was God's promise to Abraham? What has God promised you? What does it mean to you that God keeps his promises?

D What evidence of unity in the church do you see in this section? How unified is your church? What can you do to bring unity to your church?

E Why was there no poverty in the early church? What can you do to alleviate suffering among members of your local church?

REFLECT
on your life

1 In what ways do people express opposition to something or someone they think is wrong?

_____

_____

_____

_____

2 How have you been opposed recently?

_____

_____

_____

_____

READ
the passage

Read Acts 4:32—7:60, Stephen's Profile, "The Effects of Stephen's Death" chart, and the following notes:

❑5:17,18 ❑5:21 ❑5:29 ❑5:41 ❑6:14 ❑7:2ff ❑7:8 ❑7:55 ❑7:59
❑7:60

3 What caused the religious leaders to arrest the apostles?

_____

_____

_____

4 How did the apostles respond to this wave of persecution?

_____

_____

_____

_____

5 What did the apostles do to develop leadership in the young church?

_____

_____

_____

_____

6 What evidence is there that the apostles were successful in developing those leaders?

_____

_____

_____

The young church experienced tremendous growth and unity. At first their success seemed limitless. But soon they were tested severely. First Ananias and Sapphira were struck dead for lying about their gift, and then tremendous opposition came from the Jewish religious leaders. Under the guidance of the Holy Spirit and the leadership of the apostles, the church moved aggressively, healing the sick, caring for the needy, and boldly preaching the truth. Finally, however, through false witnesses, Stephen, a young leader in the church and a man full of faith and the Holy Spirit, was arrested and brought before the Sanhedrin. There he confronted the religious leaders with their sin and hypocrisy. Responding with rage, the religious leaders condemned and executed Stephen on the spot. The church today, in existence nearly 2000 years, seems to grow lethargic and powerless during times of prosperity and freedom. We seem afraid to speak the truth, holding tightly to our prestige and position in society. Stephen courageously spoke up and lost his life—what are you willing to risk or lose for Christ? There is a place for confrontation—where do you need to take a stand for Christ?

REALIZE
the principle

7 What might cause religious leaders today to try to squelch Christians who speak the truth?

_____

_____

8 In what ways is Stephen a good model for us to follow?

9 When are you likely to be quiet even though you know you should speak up?

RESPOND
to the message

10 What institutions, organizations, or individuals in your community need to be confronted about their wrong policies or actions?

11 What could you do this week to speak up for truth or to speak out against evil in your community (for example: write letters, make phone calls, march in protest, present your points at public hearings, speak to someone, etc.)?

RESOLVE
to take action

A What did Peter mean when he spoke about obeying God rather than men? When have you obeyed human beings instead of God?

MORE for studying other themes in this section

B What evidence of unity in the early church can you find in this section? What evidence for unity might be found in your church? What do you have that you could share with others?

C Why were Ananias and Sapphira struck dead? What was so bad about what they had done? In what ways do people lie to God today?

D What factors help make a church grow? What are some of the problems that come with growth? How can churches solve those problems?

E In what ways can a local church help spread the gospel around the world? What is your church doing in evangelism? What is your plan for sharing the Good News of Christ?

F If you don't have the public gifts like Peter, John, and others, what can you do to build the church and to spread the Good News?

REFLECT
on your life

1 Try to name at least one Christian leader in each of these categories: Hispanic, Asian, black, Caucasian, poor, former convict, handicapped.

_____

_____

_____

_____

2 Which categories of people are involved in your church?

_____

_____

_____

_____

READ
the passage

Read Acts 8:1—10:48, the "Missionaries of the New Testament and Their Journeys" chart, the profiles of Philip, Paul, and Cornelius, and the following notes:

❏8:5 ❏8:15-17 ❏8:26 ❏8:27 ❏9:2,3 ❏9:3 ❏9:13 ❏10:2 ❏10:45

3 How did the gospel come to each of these people?

Samaritans (8:5-8) _____

Ethiopian (8:26-40) _____

Jewish leader (9:1-20) _____

Roman army officer (10:1-48) _____

4 Why was each of these groups or individuals controversial to the early church?

_____

_____

_____

_____

5 Why was each of these groups or individuals important to the spread of the gospel?

_____

_____

_____

_____

6 How do local churches often react when someone different (in race, dress, looks, etc.) comes into their services?

_____

_____

_____

_____

REALIZE
the principle

7 What different people might be threatening to your church?

_____

_____

_____

_____

As the young church grew and moved out from Jerusalem, it began to include men and women from all walks of life—rich, poor, influential, common, despised Samaritans, an Ethiopian government official, a persecuting Pharisee, and even a Roman centurion. No type of person was beyond God's grace and Christ's love. Of course, these conversions were not without controversy. Some people are threatened by anything or anyone who is different—this was especially true of Jewish believers who had suffered much for their faith in Christ. But often God surprises us with converts we never thought would believe, and he reaches them in ways we would never predict. The Samaritans were reached

as a by-product of persecution; the Ethiopian official was reached through the supernatural transport of God's servant; Paul the persecutor was stopped by a light from heaven; and Cornelius discovered Christ after a visit by an angel and a special vision. Who have you considered to be out of God's reach? Which types of people have you and your church excluded? Remember all the varieties in God's kingdom.

8 How could your church make outsiders feel welcome on Sunday?

_____

_____

_____

_____

_____

RESPOND
to the message

9 What types of people do you tend to assume would never become Christians? Why?

_____

_____

_____

_____

10 What could you do to help bring the gospel to them?

_____

_____

_____

_____

_____

11 What might you do to make your church more open to outsiders?

_____

_____

_____

_____

_____

12 What can you do in your church to make visitors feel welcome, or to make young people feel included and important?

_____

_____

_____

_____

_____

13 Add to your prayer list at least two seemingly unreachable people.

_____

_____

_____

_____

A What happened as a result of the persecution of the early church? How might God use for his glory the opposition and persecution you might be facing?

B How did Simon the sorcerer respond to the apostles' actions and message? What did Peter tell Simon about his offer? In what situations would a rebuke like Peter's be appropriate today?

C How did Ananias help Paul? Why was this difficult for him to do? What kind of difficult task might God ask you to do?

D What was Dorcas's reputation? How can you be like Dorcas?

E Why did Peter find it so difficult to go to Cornelius? What convinced Peter that Cornelius's conversion was genuine? Why did Cornelius want Peter to stay with him for several days? What would it take to convince you to break down certain barriers to the gospel?

MORE
for studying
other themes
in this section

REFLECT
on your life

1 What is the most dramatic answer to prayer of which you have heard?

_____

_____

_____

_____

2 If you were being interviewed for a book about prayer, what personal example would you give in the chapter on answered prayer?

_____

_____

_____

_____

READ
the passage

Read Acts 11:1—12:25 and the following notes:

❑12:1 ❑12:2 ❑12:2-12 ❑12:5 ❑12:13-15

3 Why did Herod Agrippa persecute the church?

_____

_____

_____

_____

4 When do you think the believers began to pray for Peter and James?

_____

_____

_____

5 Why do you suppose the people in the prayer meeting didn't believe that God had answered their prayers?

_____

_____

_____

_____

6 How do you think Peter's miraculous release affected their future prayer meetings?

_____

_____

_____

_____

7 What should this story teach us about our prayers and God's answers?

_____

_____

_____

_____

REALIZE
the principle

As the church continued to grow, beyond Jerusalem and even beyond the Jewish people, so did persecution. The religious leaders stoned Stephen and pursued others. The Roman government then joined the opposition, with Herod Agrippa executing James and imprisoning Peter. So the believers gathered to pray. Then, with a dramatic rescue, God freed Peter from prison. But when Peter came to the door, the assembled pray-ers wouldn't believe he was there and continued praying. God had answered their prayers, but they couldn't believe it. God tells us to pray about everything (Philippians 4:6), expecting him to answer (James 1:6), but often we are surprised when he does. When do you pray, and what do you pray about? Do you expect God to act, or are you surprised?

8 When and where does your church pray together?

_____

_____

_____

_____

9 Describe an answer to prayer that your church has experienced:

_____

_____

_____

_____

_____

RESPOND
to the message

10 What would you like God to do for your church?

_____

_____

_____

_____

_____

11 What would you like God to do for someone you love?

_____

_____

_____

_____

12 What would you like God to do for you?

_____

_____

_____

_____

13 Write a prayer list of ten requests to God. Include your church, others, and yourself. Also write a specific time when you will pray regularly.

_____

_____

_____

_____

_____

_____

_____

_____

_____

_____

RESOLVE
to take action

14 Pray, expecting God to answer your prayers.

_____

_____

A When Peter defended his preaching to the Gentiles, why did he say he objected to eating the animals in his vision? How did the voice answer his objections? What commands in Scripture do you find difficult to obey?

B What convinced the Jerusalem church that God had given the Gentiles the privilege of receiving eternal life? What evidence of the Holy Spirit's power have you seen in others?

C In what ways did Barnabas help Paul grow in the faith? How can you help new Christians grow?

D How did the believers in Antioch react to the news of impending famine in Jerusalem? How has your church responded to the needs of other Christians in other communities? What could you and your church do to help other believers in need?

E How did Herod Agrippa die? Why was he killed?

MORE
for studying
other themes
in this section

REFLECT
on your life

1 What happened this week that encouraged you?

_____

_____

_____

_____

2 How did you encourage someone else?

_____

_____

_____

_____

READ
the passage

Read Acts 13:1—14:28, John Mark's Profile, Barnabas's Profile, and the following notes:

❏13:13 ❏13:14 ❏14:18-20 ❏14:23

3 Why did Paul and Barnabas go on their missionary trip?

_____

_____

_____

_____

4 What caused them to take the gospel message to the Gentiles?

_____

_____

_____

5 What problems did they experience?

_____

_____

_____

6 What does the name _Barnabas_ mean? How did Barnabas live up to his name?

_____

_____

_____

_____

7 Why did Paul need Barnabas's encouragement? Why did John Mark?

_____

_____

_____

_____

8 What might discourage Christians today?

_____

_____

_____

_____

REALIZE
the principle

When Paul, fresh from his conversion to Christ, returned to Jerusalem, the believers were understandably afraid of him and reluctant to welcome him into their fellowship. Barnabas, however, acted as Paul's advocate as he encouraged the church to accept Paul as a fellow believer. Later, Paul and Barnabas became close traveling companions as they were sent out to preach, to take

the Good News of Christ to the ends of the earth. At first we read about "Barnabas and Paul" (13:2, 7). Soon, however, Paul began to receive top billing, yet there were no signs of hard feelings or wounded pride from Barnabas. Graciously he pushed Paul to the forefront and allowed him to lead. Then came the incident with young John Mark, Barnabas's nephew. Paul gave up on Mark after Mark deserted them at Perga (13:13), but Barnabas believed in Mark, stayed with him, and helped him develop into a strong leader in the church. Who has encouraged you in the faith? To whom can you be a "Barnabas"?

9 How do people in your church encourage others?

_____

_____

_____

_____

RESPOND
to the message

10 What potential "Pauls" do you know who might need encouragement?

_____

_____

_____

_____

11 What "John Marks" need to be encouraged in the faith?

_____

_____

_____

RESOLVE
to take action

12 Who will you encourage this week? What could you do to encourage him/her?

_____

_____

_____

_____

_____

_____

A Why did the Jewish leaders in Antioch of Pisidia denounce Paul and Barnabas? When have you experienced similar reactions to outstanding Christians? What did you do?

B Why did the people in Lystra begin to worship Paul and Barnabas? How did the crowds change just a few days later? What does this teach you about praise, adulation, and popularity?

C In what ways were Paul and Barnabas persecuted? How did they respond? How do you react to persecution?

MORE
for studying
other themes
in this section

REFLECT
on your life

1 Describe a church conflict about which you have heard? What started it? How was it settled?

_____

_____

_____

_____

_____

_____

_____

READ
the passage

Read Acts 15:1-35, "The First Church Conference" chart, and the following notes:

☐15:1ff ☐15:1 ☐15:2,3 ☐15:20 ☐15:23-29 ☐15:31

2 What was the purpose for this council at Jerusalem?

_____

_____

_____

_____

_____

3 What process did they use to resolve the conflict?

_____

_____

_____

4 What did the council decide?

_____

_____

_____

_____

The church began in Jerusalem, and all of the early believers were Jews or Jewish proselytes. The influx of Gentile Christians was disturbing and threatening. It's not easy to accept what you had previously avoided and considered unclean. Because the background of most of these new Christians was Greek rather than Jewish, they had very little understanding or appreciation of the Old Testament rituals. This caused a serious dispute in the church that had to be resolved through a special meeting in Jerusalem. There the issues were raised, deliberations made, and a compromise decision reached. The conflict was resolved. Today, hundreds of minute differences and slight shadings of doctrines divide believers. Often, instead of resolving our conflicts, we split churches, start denominations, or give up in disgust. Is your church known for its love . . . or battles?

REALIZE
the principle

5 What divides churches today?

_____

_____

_____

_____

6 What process does your church use to resolve serious conflicts?

_____

_____

_____

_____

_____

_____

7 Think of a recent conflict in your church. How would Paul, Peter, and James have resolved it?

RESPOND
to the message

_____

_____

_____

8 With whom in your church do *you* have a personal conflict?

_____

_____

_____

_____

9 How have you dealt with that conflict so far?

_____

_____

_____

_____

_____

10 What can you do to be a peacemaker and resolve that conflict?

RESOLVE
to take action

_____

_____

_____

_____

_____

_____

A Who was the leader of the church in Jerusalem? What role did the apostles play in the Jerusalem council? Who made the final decision? What does this say about the apostles' attitudes?

MORE
for studying
other themes
in this section

B How was James's decision a compromise? When is compromise appropriate in church disputes? When is it wrong?

C How was the decision of the Jerusalem council to be communicated to the other churches and individual believers? What are the strengths in how this letter was composed? How would you communicate a similar compromise solution to a party in conflict?

D What caused the dispute in the early church? Why was the Jerusalem council so important? Why was their decision so important for the early church? In what ways is the impact of their decision still felt today?

E Why was keeping the law so important to Jewish Christians? What was Paul's reason for resisting the effort to force Gentiles to keep Jewish tradition? What is the difference between helpful guidelines and legalism?

REFLECT
on your life

1 Describe what would be an ideal situation for you to share your faith in Christ. (Where would it happen? How would it be set up? etc.)

_____

_____

_____

_____

_____

READ
the passage

Read Acts 15:36—18:22, Silas's Profile, Aquilla and Priscilla's Profile, and the following notes:

☐16:13,14 ☐16:22-25 ☐17:1 ☐17:2,3 ☐17:6 ☐17:22 ☐17:22ff ☐17:23

☐17:30,31 ☐17:32-34 ☐18:13

2 Why did Paul want to return to Turkey?

_____

_____

_____

3 What caused Paul and Silas to change their travel plans in the middle of their journey?

_____

_____

_____

4 Where did they witness for Christ in Philippi? Who responded to the gospel message?

_____

_____

_____

_____

5 Where did Paul and Silas preach and teach in Thessalonica? Who came to know Christ in that city?

_____

_____

_____

_____

_____

6 Where did Paul preach in Athens? What was the response?

_____

_____

_____

_____

7 In Corinth, what kind of people responded to the gospel?

_____

_____

_____

_____

Because of a disagreement over Mark, Paul and Barnabas decided to separate. Paul chose Silas and, with Timothy, began another missionary journey.
Responding to a plea in a dream, they took the gospel to Philippi, Thessalonica,
Beroea, Athens, Corinth, Ephesus, and other Greek cities. Wherever they
were—on a river bank, in prison, in the synagogue, at a gathering of philosophers—Paul and Silas proclaimed the Good News. They used every forum to
preach, seeing every situation as an opportunity to tell others about Christ.

REALIZE
the principle

Every day, God gives us opportunities to share our faith—with friends, at home, in school, and at work—through how we act and what we say. How have you used those God-given opportunities?

8 What regular opportunities for proclaiming the gospel are in your community?

_____

_____

_____

_____

_____

9 In what ways have Christians taken advantage of those opportunities?

_____

_____

_____

_____

RESPOND
to the message

10 What gifts, talents, and resources do you have that God could use to spread his Word?

_____

_____

_____

_____

_____

11 In what situations or relationships has God placed you where you could share your faith?

_____

_____

_____

_____

12 What might you do to be prepared to take advantage of the opportunities God gives you to tell others about Christ?

_____

_____

_____

_____

_____

RESOLVE
to take action

13 If you have very little contact with non-Christians, what can you do to have more non-Christian acquaintances and friends?

_____

_____

_____

_____

_____

A Why did Paul and Barnabas split up? How did this help the cause of Christ? Describe a time when something seemed bad but turned out to be good.

B How did Paul pass the faith to the next generation? What are you doing to build Christian leaders?

C How did Paul and Silas know where to go? How do you determine when the Holy Spirit is talking to you?

D Why did Paul and Silas act the way they did in prison? What happened as a result? Why did Paul save the jailer's life? How do you respond to adversity?

E What reputation did Paul and Silas have? What is your reputation among non-Christians? What might you do to turn your world upside down?

F What did the Beroeans do after hearing Paul preach? In what ways should they be a good example for us?

G Why did Paul say that the men of Athens were "very religious"? What did they find difficult to accept in Paul's message? What is the difference between being religious and following Christ?

H What was Paul's approach in Athens? What was his approach in the Hall of Tyrannus? When should you vary your ministry approach?

MORE
for studying
other themes
in this section

REFLECT
on your life

1 In what ways would your community change if all the store owners became true Christians?

_____

_____

_____

_____

2 How might the Christian faith hurt sales in some businesses?

_____

_____

_____

_____

READ
the passage

Read Acts 18:23—21:17 and the following notes:

❐19:26 ❐19:27 ❐19:33,34 ❐20:18-21 ❐20:24 ❐20:33 ❐20:34

3 What was the message that Apollos was preaching? How did his message differ from what Paul was preaching?

_____

_____

_____

_____

4 Where did Paul begin his preaching in Ephesus? Why did he change locations?

_____

_____

_____

_____

5 How did the gospel change lives in Ephesus?

_____

_____

_____

6 How did others react to these changes?

_____

_____

_____

7 Describe the relationship of Paul to the Ephesian believers.

_____

_____

_____

_____

On his third missionary journey, Paul traveled to many of the cities he had previously visited, encouraging them and strengthening their faith. In Ephesus, Paul had a powerful ministry, preaching in the synagogue and in a lecture hall. The Holy Spirit worked, and lives were transformed. The whole community was affected—occult books were burned and idolatry was rejected. This caused a violent reaction in the business community—idol manufacturing was big in Ephesus, and Christianity threatened sales. From Ephesus, Paul traveled to Troas, Macedonia, Achaia, and Corinth. After retracing his steps through Macedonia to foil a plot against his life, Paul decided to go to Jerusalem. Then, in an emotional reunion at Miletus, Paul said farewell to the Ephesian elders and continued toward Jerusalem, led by the Holy Spirit. Wherever Paul went, he preached the gospel; wherever the gospel was proclaimed, lives were changed. How is God changing lives where you live? What difference are Christians making in your community?

REALIZE
the principle

8 Why are so many people more concerned about money than about changed lives?

_____

_____

_____

_____

9 What changes would take place in your community if many people became followers of Christ?

_____

_____

_____

_____

10 In what ways might true believers in Christ be a threat to community leaders?

_____

_____

_____

_____

RESPOND
to the message

11 How would you react if your business or livelihood were threatened by faith in Christ?

_____

_____

_____

_____

12 Where might Christ change your values if you took your faith seriously?

_____

_____

_____

_____

13 In what other ways might your faith in Christ change your life (for example: relationships, use of time, possessions, family life, etc.)?

_____

_____

_____

_____

_____

14 Think through your values. What might easily come between you and Christ? Ask God to change your values, putting them in line with his.

_____

_____

_____

_____

_____

_____

RESOLVE
to take action

A How did God use Apollos to strengthen the early church? What gifts has God given you to use for him?

B Why was the preaching of John the Baptist incomplete? How does a person receive the Holy Spirit?

C What false teachers came to Ephesus? What happened when they tried to use Jesus' name to cast out a demon? How did this incident affect the community? What occult practices are evident in your community?

D What was Paul's message to both Jews and Gentiles alike? Why was he willing to face danger and death to deliver this message? What hinders or discourages you from telling others about Christ?

E What warnings did Paul give the Ephesian elders? Describe the farewells in this section. Why were the believers so close? What does this teach us about Christian fellowship?

F Why was Paul determined to go to Jerusalem? Why were people trying to dissuade him from going there? How are you sure of God's leading in your life?

MORE
for studying
other themes
in this section

REFLECT
on your life

1 What words or phrases are red flags for you, bringing out an emotional response where you tend to react without listening?

_____

_____

_____

_____

_____

READ
the passage

Read Acts 21:18—23:22 and the following notes:

❑21:21 ❑21:28,29 ❑22:1,2 ❑22:3 ❑22:21,22

2 Why did Paul agree to have his head shaved and make a vow at the Temple?

_____

_____

_____

3 What aroused the mob against Paul? How did the Romans respond?

_____

_____

_____

4 Why did the commander allow Paul to speak to the crowd?

_____

_____

_____

_____

5 Why did the crowd listen to Paul?

_____

_____

_____

_____

6 What did Paul say that made the crowd angry?

_____

_____

_____

_____

7 How did the Jewish Council react?

_____

_____

_____

_____

When Paul arrived in Rome, he met with the leaders of the Jerusalem church. They suggested that he submit to a Jewish ceremony to help mend relationships with Jewish believers. Instead of peace, however, violence was the result—a mob tried to beat Paul to death. Protected by the Roman commander, Paul could have escaped the crowd, but he asked to speak to them. They listened intently for a while, until he spoke about going to the Gentiles. Then they went berserk. Later Paul defended himself before the Jewish Council, but again he was met with hatred and violence. These people, even their religious leaders, refused to listen and uncover the facts. Instead, they acted emotionally, impulsively, and irrationally, and they missed the truth about the Son of God. People still react with hatred and scorn when they hear or even think they hear a certain word or forbidden phrase. It's part of human nature to listen with our hearts instead of our heads. But if we react without thinking, we may miss the truth.

REALIZE
the principle

8 If you had been in Paul's situation in the Temple, how would you have reacted?

_____

_____

_____

_____

9 Why did Paul want to talk to the people who had just tried to beat him to
death?

_____

_____

_____

_____

10 What are the emotional issues in your community?

_____

_____

_____

_____

11 What are the emotional issues in your church or denomination?

_____

_____

_____

_____

RESPOND
to the message

12 Why do some people refuse to listen to the truth? Of what are they afraid?

_____

_____

_____

_____

_____

13 In what situations and with what kind of people are you likely to close your mind and not listen?

_____

_____

_____

_____

_____

_____

14 Think of a situation where you had a closed mind or of a person to whom you refused to listen. What can you do to be more open-minded and listen carefully before making a judgment?

_____

_____

_____

_____

_____

_____

_____

RESOLVE
to take action

A What did Paul do to try to keep peace in the Jerusalem church? What might you do to be a peacemaker?

B Why did Paul speak in Hebrew to the crowd? How can you speak in language your friends and neighbors would understand? What would be the most effective way for you to tell them about Christ?

C In this section, what opportunities did Paul use to speak for Christ? What opportunities has God given you recently to speak up for him?

D How was it possible for religious people to act the way they did toward Paul? What's the difference between religious office and spiritual leadership?

E How was Paul saved from the plot against his life? What does this story teach you about being used by God?

MORE
for studying
other themes
in this section

REFLECT
on your life

1 What comes to your mind when you hear the phrase, "God's will"?

_____

_____

_____

_____

_____

2 When did you have a clear sense of God's leading?

_____

_____

_____

_____

_____

READ
the passage

Read Acts 23:23—26:32 and the following notes:

❐23:23,24 ❐24:27 ❐25:10,11 ❐25:23 ❐26:28 ❐26:28,29

3 Why did the Roman commander send Paul to Caesarea?

_____

_____

_____

4 Why did Felix keep Paul in prison for two years?

_____

_____

_____

5 Why did Paul appeal to Rome?

_____

_____

_____

6 Compare the reactions to Paul by Felix, Festus, and Agrippa.

_____

_____

_____

_____

_____

7 What proofs for Christianity did Paul present to Agrippa?

_____

_____

_____

_____

_____

Learning of the plot on Paul's life, Claudius Lysias sent him to Governor Felix. Paul impressed Felix with his defense, but Felix kept him imprisoned for two years, hoping to receive a bribe. When Festus took over, the Jewish leaders tried to convince him to send Paul back to Jerusalem to stand trial (they really wanted to kill him). Festus refused, and Paul made his defense again. Then, in a dramatic move, Paul appealed to Caesar. Because of his appeal, Paul defended himself again, this time in front of Herod Agrippa II. In every cirumstance, in prison or court, Paul listened to God and then obeyed. Fearlessly he proclaimed the gospel, sharing the facts about Christ and his personal conversion story. He appealed to Caesar knowing that this would take him to Rome, where he knew God was leading him. Imagine the powerful impact if Christians today would do, say, and go where they knew God was leading them.

REALIZE
the principle

8 Why did Paul want to go to Rome?

_____

_____

_____

9 How does God reveal his will to Christians today? How do we know what he wants us to do?

_____

_____

_____

_____

_____

10 Put yourself in Paul's place. Who would be the Jewish leaders and Roman rulers today?

_____

_____

_____

_____

11 What are you sure that God has called all Christians to do?

_____

_____

_____

_____

RESPOND
to the message

12 When have you followed God's leading to go someplace? How did you know what God wanted you to do?

_____

_____

_____

_____

13 When have you followed God's leading to speak up for him? How did you know what God wanted you to say?

_____

_____

_____

_____

14 When have you been tempted to disobey God by staying where you were or by keeping silent?

_____

_____

_____

_____

15 Where is God leading you in your actions? In your words? Ask God to give you the courage to trust him and to do what he says.

_____

_____

_____

_____

_____

RESOLVE
to take action

A What were the false accusations against Paul? How did Paul defend himself against those accusations? When have you been falsely accused?

B How did Felix respond to Paul's witness for Christ? What did he mean by "convenient time"? When would be a convenient time for you to listen to God's Word?

C In this section, what opportunities did God give Paul to present the gospel? How did Paul know that he should tell about Christ at those times? What opportunities might God give you to witness for him in the near future?

D What evidence does Paul present for the truth of Christianity? What made these proofs so convincing? Why was it so difficult for Felix and then for Agrippa to accept Christ as Savior? What evidence for Christ have you given to others? How did they respond?

MORE
for studying
other themes
in this section

LESSON 13
HE'S GOT THE WHOLE WORLD IN HIS HANDS
ACTS 27:1—28:31

REFLECT
on your life

1 Take a minute to look around you. What evidence do you see of God's protection and provision?

_____

_____

_____

_____

_____

READ
the passage

Read Acts 27:1—28:31, the chart "Paul's Journey to Rome," the map "The Trip Toward Rome," and the following notes:

❒27:9 ❒27:21 ❒28:3 ❒28:17-20 ❒28:30

2 Who was on the ship with Paul?

_____

_____

_____

3 What was Paul's counsel to the ship's officers?

_____

_____

_____

4 How did Paul react to the terrible storm? What advice did he give the others?

_____

_____

_____

_____

5 What happened on Malta?

_____

_____

_____

6 What happened to Paul when he arrived in Rome?

_____

_____

_____

7 In this section of Scripture, how did God protect Paul and provide for his needs?

_____

_____

_____

_____

_____

REALIZE
the principle

Paul, as a Roman citizen, appealed to Rome for justice; he was sent there on a ship with other prisoners. After a few days of rough sailing, Paul advised the ship's officers not to sail farther. But they sailed on—into a terrible storm. Soon the ship ran aground and broke apart. Miraculously, there were no casualties of the shipwreck—they all made it safely to Malta. There Paul was bitten by a poisonous snake, but he was unharmed. Eventually they set sail again and reached Rome. In Rome, Paul was permitted to live wherever he wanted, although he was guarded by a Roman soldier. During this time, believers from all over the city came to Paul, and he was able to teach them. Paul's journey to Rome provides a wonderful picture of God's protection. Paul's work was not finished, so God protected him from the Jews, the soldiers, the sea, and the snake. In Rome, God provided Paul an all-expense-paid forum for his teaching and preaching. Do you believe that God is also watching over you?

8 Describe a situation or incident where God protected someone from danger and serious injury.

_____

_____

_____

_____

_____

9 It has been said that nothing can harm one of God's children unless he allows it. What does that truth mean to you?

_____

_____

_____

RESPOND
to the message

10 How has God protected you recently?

_____

_____

_____

_____

11 How does God provide for your daily needs?

_____

_____

_____

_____

12 Why do we tend to take God's provision and protection for granted?

_____

_____

_____

_____

_____

13 Each day, thank God for all his gifts—food, health, friends, family, safety, freedom, talents, opportunities, etc. What do you want to be sure to remember this week?

_____

_____

_____

_____

_____

_____

_____

RESOLVE
to take action

A Describe the relationship between Paul and Julius, his guard. Why do you think Julius wanted to save Paul's life? Who have you impressed—who is closer to Christ—because of your life-style?

MORE
for studying
other themes
in this section

B How did God work for good the difficult circumstances in Paul's life? In what ways is he working in and through your struggles?

C Why didn't the Jewish leaders in Rome know more about Christians? What image of Christians do people in your community have? Why?

D How did Paul use his Roman imprisonment to spread the gospel? Why was Paul so bold and courageous? How can you be more bold in your witness for Christ?

"For God loved the world so much that he gave his only Son ..."

If one verse changed your life . . . think of what 31,172 more could do.

THE LIFE APPLICATION BIBLE
Applying God's Word to real life

The Life Application Bible can give you real answers for real life. We can give you eight reasons why it has all the answers you've been looking for—right at your fingertips.

1. **Unique Life Application Notes** show you how to act on what you read, how to apply it to needs in your own life.

2. **Megathemes** tell you why the significant themes in each book are still important today.

3. **People Profiles** bring alive over 50 colorful and important Bible characters, their strengths and weaknesses.

4. **The Topical Index** gives you over 15,000 entries that tell you where to find real answers for real-life situations.

5. **Bible Timelines** give you dates, names, and places at a glance.

6. **Cross-references** direct you to scores of important passages.

7. **Outline Notes** give you an overview of content plus ideas for application.

8. **Harmony of the Gospels** uses a unique numbering system to harmonize all four Gospels into one chronological account.

Plus: Book Introductions, Vital Statistics, Maps, and Charts!

Available in *The Living Bible* and the *King James Version.*

AT BOOKSTORES EVERYWHERE. Cloth $34.95 Bonded Leather $49.95

Life Application is a trademark of Tyndale House Publishers, Inc.